Children and Television

BRIAN SIMPSON

continuum
NEW YORK • LONDON

Continuum International Publishing Group
The Tower Building, 11 York Road, London SE1 7NX
15 East 26th Street, New York, NY 10010

© Brian Simpson 2004

British Library Cataloguing-in-Publication Data
A catalogue record for this book is available from the British Library.

ISBN: 0–8264–7268–0 (hardback)
ISBN: 0–8264–7799–2 (paperback)

Typeset by BookEns Ltd, Royston, Herts.
Printed and bound in Great Britain by Biddles Ltd, King's Lynn

Contents

In memory of my father,
Hugh Shields Simpson (1926–2003)

Acknowledgements

The research for this book was undertaken while I was a member of staff at Flinders University of South Australia and was in part supported by the time release funding, for which I am appreciative. I also thank my colleagues at Keele University who provide a wonderfully supportive working environment. Finally, to my wife, Helen, I owe an immense debt for the sacrifices she has made in order for this book to be written.

Introduction

The idea for this book grew from a concern with the manner in which 'television' – particularly 'television violence' – is often cited as a cause of violent crime or behaviour when debates on censorship or control of the media are discussed. This connection is usually made in the context of the behaviour of young people, which raises the question of whether this is another way of blaming young people for broader ills in society. On the other hand, it is rare for even a single reference to 'television' to be included in the index of most texts on juvenile crime. Television, it seems, is presented as an almost omnipresent and increasingly influential force in society, yet outside texts on television itself there is little detailed discussion of how it influences the behaviour of young people.

A parallel concern is the manner in which those same censorship debates focus on the child as a person who has to be protected from television, whether it be from 'unsuitable' programmes, 'bad' programmes or merely too much television. This construction of the child does not seem to match the evolving notion of the child as a 'maturing' individual, with an increasing capacity to exercise some independent thought and choices. It definitely does not match the manner in which children are now conceptualized in juvenile justice systems – as capable of bearing individual responsibility for their actions and even from a relatively young age being treated as an adult in many respects. These different conceptions of the child, which operate across various parts of the legal system, do not seem to equate with the simple idea of childhood apparently found in rules which regulate the relationship between television and the child. The notion of childhood found in such rules appears to be fixed to the romantic notion that children are sensitive and easily distressed. How can such different views of childhood be maintained in different areas of the law?

While childhood for many children is an age of innocence and play, there are also many children who experience violence and fear. There is a tendency to regard such children as having had their childhood 'stolen' or 'taken from them', but that tends to shift the responsibility for their plight away from society as a whole and on to the 'perpetrator', the person who most visibly seems to be responsible for their treatment. In its Report on the 'stolen generation' – those aboriginal children forcibly taken from their families in Australia – the Australian Human Rights and Equal

Opportunity Commission recounted the violence experienced by one
child who was taken and placed with a white foster family:

> The foster family would punish me severely for the slightest thing
> they regarded as unacceptable or unchristian-like behaviour, even if I
> didn't eat my dinner or tea. Sometimes I would be locked in my
> room for hours. Countless times the foster father would rain blows
> upon me with his favourite leather strap. He would continue until I
> wept uncontrollably, pleading for him to stop.[1]

It is difficult not to feel anger with a system that under the guise of
protection, and purporting to act in the child's best interests, exposed this
child to such brutal treatment. When the Report was published the
reaction of many non-indigenous people in Australia was one of shock
and horror, not simply that the removal of such children had occurred but
that it did so in their lifetimes and without any knowledge on their part.
While not all children were abused as the above child was, the simple act
of removal was itself an act of violence against indigenous children which
still haunts many of them. And as the Human Rights and Equal
Opportunity Commission has shown, this violence was committed
pursuant to official state policy.

What has this to do with the regulation of the relationship between
children and television? The example cited above occurred fourteen years
after the introduction of television in Australia. For many adults their
understanding of the world is filtered through television and the fact that
the stolen generation did not receive any attention from the media perhaps
explains why for many Australians the existence of the stolen generation
came as a complete surprise. One need only compare this with the
treatment of the Vietnam War in the 1960s on television – the so-called
first 'television war' – and the role such media coverage played in giving
rise in opposition to that conflict to see how influential television can be in
informing and influencing public opinion. The parallel experience of
children sent to Australia without their consent and often without the
knowledge of their families after the Second World War and continuing
until the 1960s – the 'orphans of the empire' – who also experienced harsh
treatment in the homes to which they were sent is another example of a
childhood rediscovered and revisited with the perspective of more
enlightened times. In a similar manner to the stolen Aboriginal children,
the treatment which the child migrants endured was also as a result of
official policy to send them away.

These examples say something about childhood. Pierce comments
about the experience of the child migrants:

> The cultural history of Australia has long been gloomily fascinated
> with the figure of the lost child, of boys and girls suffering from

want and cruelty, from abandonment and abuse. The child migrants from Britain whose stories are told by Gill, came to a land unhappily, but well fitted to intensify the loneliness and misery of their plight.[2]

This is not the image of an innocent and happy childhood. Yet it seems that stories of such childhood possess a fascination for us, as if we are drawn to the desperation of the plight of such children. In a similar fashion the disappearance of Holly Wells and Jessica Chapman in Soham, in the United Kingdom, turned to national grief when it was discovered that they had been murdered. While such reaction can be explained in terms of such events being an attack on the innocence of childhood, it also has to be considered whether there is a curiosity about how such events represent what childhood is not supposed to be, yet in fact is for many children. We rarely consider when child abuse or harm is reported in the media that many viewers themselves will identify with the victims based on their own experience as a child. At the end of March 2002, there were 27,500 children on the child protection register in the United Kingdom.[3] In the United States 9.8 per cent of all homicide victims were under eighteen between 1976 and 2000 and 10.6 per cent of offenders were also under eighteen in that period.[4] Bullying and intimidation at school is another occurrence in the lives of many children. The reality for many children is that violence and abuse is a part of their lives, or has been. When one considers the codes and standards which apply to television and violent programming in this context they seem distinctly out of touch with the childhood which many children experience, as those rules pursue an approach which attempts to protect children from such a world. It is the world in which many children already live.

One concern with television programming must be the extent to which its content provides for children the resources, the information, the role models and the ideas which may assist them when they experience violence or abuse. If children have a right to receive ideas and information, then this should include information about violence in all its forms. Codes and standards which address issues of violence need to be redrafted to address the needs of children, not simply on the basis that violence is something which children must be protected from, but also as something which many children have a right to know about, including information about how they might address it in their lives. Similar points can be made about sexual content on television. Particularly for older children, information about sexuality and sexual behaviour is an important part of their development. To construct a television code of practice or regulatory system which only understands children as innocent in sexual matters ignores the experience of older children as well as younger children who are victims of sexual abuse. Once again, the codes and standards need to be recast in a way which does not adopt a one-dimensional view of the child, but considers the child in the fullest sense.

But it is not only children who suffer harm or who engage in sexual behaviour at an early age who should be addressed in a rethinking of television regulation. More consideration should be given to the extent to which the idea of childhood which is being constructed in the regulatory framework of television limits children in the manner in which they perceive their own potential. As John Holt observed:

> A sign in a Boston subway says NO ONE EVER RUNS AWAY FROM A HAPPY HOME. But the happiest homes may give to children just that extra confidence, curiosity, and energy that makes them want to test their strength and skill against a larger world. If they are then not allowed to do it – that's when the unhappiness starts.[5]

The idea of childhood which the television codes and classification systems which regulate television reinforce is one which wishes to keep children safe and secure. There is little sense that children need to be challenged, or at least not outside certain parameters. Children's programming, it is said, must be 'educational and informational', although few can agree on what this means. Quality programming seems to be desirable, yet commercial broadcasters bemoan the difficulty of producing such programming in a commercially viable manner. What is deemed 'suitable' for children is essentially that which does not offend parents. And now, family friendly viewing forums have begun to place new pressures on broadcasters to conform to the wishes of advertisers (themselves placed under pressure from various lobby groups) to ensure that 'appropriate' programmes are screened during family viewing times. While this may suit the needs of broadcasters to create large audiences and markets for advertisers, it does little to meet the informational needs of young people. In an age where interactive television and new forms of media will alter profoundly the way in which citizens participate in civic life, it is important that children are included in this process not as 'passive consumers' or 'vulnerable innocents' but to the fullest extent possible as people with independent rights to receive and impart information and ideas. If we continue to treat children merely as the subjects of what adults think is best for them, we risk repeating the harsh treatment meted out to them in the past.

There is no argument here with the role of parents in counselling their children about their television viewing. Nor is it suggested that all programming should challenge and confront. But if the full potential of children is to be realized then serious consideration should be given to the extent to which the narrow conceptualization of the child which underpins television regulation contributes to a narrowing of the perspective of the child and inhibits their creativity and imagination. In this regard it is important to acknowledge that children possess rights with respect to their relationship with the media, and it is to those rights which this book speaks.

CHAPTER 1

Forces that Shape Children and Television Law: Market Versus Regulation

But the argument that the public gets what it deserves emphasizes the undoubted truth that no administrative set of regulations can succeed in raising quality unless there is a wide public interest which will create the atmosphere necessary to success.

(Report of the Royal Commission on Television, Commonwealth of Australia, 1954, p. 37)

This is a book about television and its relationship with children. This will be examined through the law which regulates that relationship, the forces which shape that legal regime and the manner in which those laws influence both debates about television and our ideas about childhood. This book therefore seeks to understand how the 'television industry' constructs childhood through an understanding of the legal and regulatory regime which controls television. It also explores the manner in which the law as an independent body of knowledge is a powerful influence on the way in which we construct and interpret childhood and television.

There is a tendency in popular discourse to speak of the law's response to social problems. This seems to assume that once an area which needs better or further regulation has been identified the role of the law is reduced to providing a solution which removes the problem. This approach does not acknowledge the extent to which the law itself shapes both the problem and the solution. Law, according to this approach, provides the 'choices' as far as different forms of regulation or control are concerned. It is then simply a matter of applying the legal approach which suits best the desired objective. But this understanding of law accords to the legal process a merely reactive role. Law cannot be solely understood in these terms. There is within the discipline of law various discourses about social phenomena which become part of the process which constructs problems and their answers. Thus, in the case of children and their interactions with society, for example, conflicting ideas about childhood and the needs of children interplay to create opposing jurisprudential strands of thought which can lead to different legal outcomes and consequences for the child as elements of the different strands are incorporated into various aspects of the law.

What this means is that the concept of state regulation of the relationship between children and television is highly problematic. Choices exist with respect to the form of that regulation, and while these choices are shaped by different ideas which exist in society with respect to the nature of childhood and the role of television, the law too becomes part of the process which shapes society's views about both children and television. The point here is that this process allows the way in which legal principles relate to children in other areas to also become part of the discussion about children and television. For example, the notion of children's rights to autonomy has evolved in legal thought in the area of medical decisions in recent years, but what application does such thought have in the area of children's television viewing? As part of the law relating to children such principles can have useful application, particularly once it is recognized that the issues which pertain to the relationship between children and television are similar to those which are present in other areas. The drawing of parallels and comparisons in this way is very much a part of legal discourse.

Another problem to do with state regulation of television is that orthodox legal texts on the media tend to focus on the formal rules of regulation as if they are the only regulatory devices that affect this domain. In the case of television (and other forms of media) the state utilizes a vast array of devices to control content and access to television, including parental guidance and industry codes of practice. These forms of regulation transcend any ordinary meaning of law. It is important to conceptualize the idea of law here broadly and see these other forms of regulation as part of the legal process. They too are susceptible to the way the law understands social problems independently of other disciplines.

MARKETS, THE PUBLIC INTEREST AND CHILDHOOD IN BROADCASTING

In his 1999 Spry Memorial Lecture, Gareth Grainger, Deputy Chairman of the Australian Broadcasting Authority, drew on the ideas of Tracey[1] to identify two models of the public interest as it applies to the regulation of broadcasting. The first model imposes a duty on the state to ensure that the 'well-being' and culture of society are sustained through strategic interventions in broadcasting 'to guarantee a range, depth, quality, and independence of programme output which other arrangements would simply not supply.'[2] A second, and opposing, model claims that the state should not intervene to make choices on behalf of its citizens. In this model, 'consumer sovereignty' is supreme.[3] Grainger sums up the models:

Here then are two models between which the audience-as-citizen is being asked to choose: policy guided by the hand of 'public' regulation, employing 'public' values, *serving the public interest*; and policy as the ad hoc result of a myriad individual choices with the collective good and interest in effect being what the public, using economic judgements, say they are. In country after country one can see a collision between a '*cultural*' or *civic model* for the development of broadcasting and the '*economic*' or *circus model* for the larger construction of a culture of communication of which television and radio are one part.[4]

Grainger notes that the legislated objectives of broadcasting regulation in Australia confirm the first of these models. Those objectives, as they appear in the Broadcasting Services Act 1999 (Cth), require the broadcasting regulatory system:

(a) to promote the availability to audiences throughout Australia of a diverse range of radio and television services offering entertainment, education and information; and

(aa) to promote the availability to audiences and users throughout Australia of a diverse range of datacasting services; and

(b) to provide a regulatory environment that will facilitate the development of a broadcasting industry in Australia that is efficient, competitive and responsive to audience needs; and

(c) to encourage diversity in control of the more influential broadcasting services; and

(d) to ensure that Australians have effective control of the more influential broadcasting services; and

(e) to promote the role of broadcasting services in developing and reflecting a sense of Australian identity, character and cultural diversity; and

(f) to promote the provision of high quality and innovative programming by providers of broadcasting services; and

(fa) to promote the provision of high quality and innovative content by providers of datacasting services; and

(g) to encourage providers of commercial and community broad-casting services to be responsive to the need for a fair and accurate coverage of matters of public interest and for an appropriate coverage of matters of local significance; and

(h) to encourage providers of broadcasting services to respect community standards in the provision of programme material; and

(i) to encourage the provision of means for addressing complaints about broadcasting services; and

(j) to ensure that providers of broadcasting services place a high priority on the protection of children from exposure to programme material which may be harmful to them; and

(ja) to ensure that international broadcasting services are not provided contrary to Australia's national interest; and

(k) to provide a means for addressing complaints about certain Internet content; and

(l) to restrict access to certain Internet content that is likely to cause offence to a reasonable adult; and

(m) to protect children from exposure to Internet content that is unsuitable for children; and

(n) to ensure the maintenance and, where possible, the development of diversity, including public, community and indigenous broadcasting, in the Australian broadcasting system in the transition to digital broadcasting.[5]

uch statements of intent with respect to the 'public interest' in roadcasting resonate with other regulatory regimes around the world. n many countries, within the legal frameworks which regulate the elationship between children and television, the public interest weighs eavily. For example, in passing the Children's Television Act 1990 which equires broadcasters to screen educational and informational programmes or children, the United States Congress found that 'as part of their bligation to serve the public interest, television station operators and censees should provide programming that serves the special needs of hildren.'[6] The need for such legislation was said to be based on the failure f market forces to deliver such programming.[7] The United States Congress also invoked the concept of a fiduciary obligation which was wed by broadcasters in return for the use of the public air waves.[8]

This does not mean that the opposing model of broadcasting regulation s identified by Grainger holds no sway. When the Children's Television Act was passed by the Congress, President Bush then withheld his ignature on the basis that the Act conflicted with fundamental freedoms. he explanation of his decision cites primacy of the market and free hoice as the important consideration in the regulation of television. It ead:

> I have decided to withhold my approval from H.R. 1677, the 'Children's Television Act of 1990,' which will result in its becoming law without my signature. This bill is intended to increase the amount and quality of children's television programming and to diminish the commercialization of programming for children.
>
> I wholeheartedly support these goals, but regret that the Congress has chosen inappropriate means of serving them. In an effort to improve children's television, this legislation imposes content-based restrictions on programming. The legislation limits the amount of

advertising that broadcasters may air during children's programming, and the Federal Communications Commission is charged with policing the adequacy of broadcasters' efforts to serve the educational and informational needs of children. The First Amendment, however, does not contemplate that government will dictate the quality or quantity of what Americans should hear—rather, it leaves this to be decided by free media responding to the free choices of individual consumers ...

Finally, the advertising limits imposed by this legislation cannot reasonably be expected to advance their intended purpose. To the extent that children's programming is financed by the revenue from advertising during such programming, restrictions on the amount of advertising will tend to diminish, rather than enhance, the quantity and quality of children's programming.[9]

It is easy to criticize the Presidential refusal to sign the law as the stance of a free market ideologue. Yet this would ignore the serious clash of values which the debate over the Act created. What are in competition here are different views of the public interest. It is the case that in the passing of the Children's Television Act a view of the public interest was in competition with the profit motives of broadcasters. The Presidential reticence places this as a conflict between the public interest in protecting the basic freedoms stated in the United States Constitution's First Amendment and the idea that the state should intervene in matters concerning the nature of programming to be screened on television which may also be justified as being in the public interest. The President's stance may not dispute the public interest in regulating television programming, but he also places the freedom of the market as a legitimate public interest which the state may want to protect as well.

The problem is that there is a tendency in such debates to attempt to reconcile the competing interests by seeking a 'magical' balance them. In the United States part of this balance was to be by way of the Children's Television Act itself through provisions which introduced some requirements to provide special programmes for children. But is such a balance able to be struck? Some doubt the efficacy of such legislation in its aim of imposing a public interest requirement on broadcasters:

Are we now expecting television executives to simultaneously concern themselves with making a profit *and* accepting a moral responsibility for meeting the educational and emotional needs of our children? Has television become both teacher and agent of social reform? I can see the newspaper headline: 'Large purple dinosaur solves problems of family fractionalization and mobility.' I can almost hear the collective sigh of relief: one more social problem can be checked off our lists.[10]

Perhaps such a balance is simply not possible. Or perhaps a concentration on achieving such a balance misses other crucial understandings of the manner in which we construct discussions about children and their relationship with television. We assume that the lack of regard for the 'special needs of children' which the market-place generates can be countered by the airing of 'quality' programmes motivated by a higher concern with the public good. The difficulty is to determine whose view of the public good are we attempting to articulate and what do such programmes look like as a consequence. The answer to this question can only be attempted by subscribing to *a* view of the child. It is the view of childhood that one chooses which will shape the type of programming then produced and whether it will be regarded as being of the appropriate quality'.

There is in fact no 'quality programming' for children outside the adoption of a view of childhood. How can it be otherwise? It would be impossible to evaluate any programming directed at children without an understanding of what childhood means. Or what one thinks it means. Or should mean. And this is the problem: in constructing television for childhood we must of necessity construct a view of the child. It is adults, of course, who construct that meaning. As Hilty writes:

> It is the commonly accepted assumption that children's educational programs are good, and to the average adult children's programs that are educational *do* look good – and perhaps this is the problem. Children's programs represent an adult conception of 'good' education for children. But then what do most adults know and believe about children? Are they really unique and special or are they simply little adults 'revving up their engines' to enter adolescence and adulthood at full throttle? As dramatic as this may seem, this latter view of childhood dominates and shapes adult visions of what is good and appropriate for children's programs. These programs are most often fast-paced and colorful, and all the big ideas are there (e.g. the alphabet, numbers, sight words, multiculturalism, and so on). What could be wrong here? Why is it that when I watch these programs I feel assaulted by the dizzying array of bright lights and colors and even the occasional 'educational' concept?[11]

Debates on children and television are then essentially about how adults understand children and how they want them to be. They are also debates about how adults fear children and what they might become. There is no simple consensus around what childhood means and this is perhaps how it should be. A society which is supposed to be committed to diversity and plurality must not expect otherwise. The problem is that society also needs to be cohesive and it usually falls to the state to achieve that amount of social accord as would allow society to function relatively harmoniously.

The difficulty here is that a cohesive society also requires a functionin market-place as much as it needs harmony within the home. The state h to support the market as much as it has to protect the public interest i other areas. Yet the fear is that, left to the market, broadcasters would n provide children with the type of programming which is important t their intellectual and social development.

It also cannot be assumed that children have no interest in the market a force in society. They are too, or will be, participants in the market place, if not as children then in the future as adults, and clearly hav interests in that regard. So how then does one make sense of the forc that shape the relationship between children and television? It may be matter of power, for it is clear that the discourse which shapes this area an adult one and not one which seeks out the views of children; and it not only an adult discourse but an affluent adult viewpoint. To bring th views of children into discussion about the form of television would in fa be to democratize the process in a manner which even adults do n possess. Is then the process of regulating the relationship between childre and television in this sense about preparation for an adulthood in whic many adults lack power and influence over their own lives? Is the lesson television that many people will have lives on the social margins? Hilt puts the concerns:

> Why are the voices of children absent from our discussions and
> decisions regarding their teaching and learning? During the past forty
> years, youth in America have been introduced to an increasingly
> large number of TV characters whose aims and purposes seem to be
> innocent enough: the preparation of children for academic and social
> success ... Just as we have regularly attempted to find just the 'right'
> educational institution that meets the needs of all children – rich and
> poor alike – we assume that the 'right' television programs will
> redress the inequities faced by poor children and children of color in
> our culture – a paternalistic role, at best, but one that also begs a
> question: How do these programs intersect with the cultures of a
> diverse range of students, many of whom find the hegemony of
> white, middle-class norms and more offensive and detrimental to
> their experience of success and achievement? Where are the voices of
> these children and their parents in discussions of 'disadvantaged'
> children and their 'failure' to benefit from the vast array of children's
> educational programs offered daily on television?[12]

The regulation of television is therefore not a simple matter c implementing community-wide agreement about the role and purpose c the medium. It raises important questions about the legitimacy of the stat in regulating everyday life and its purpose in doing so. Such regulatio requires the adoption of a value system upon which to base th intervention. As Hilty suggests, it is the powerful in society who are most able to impose their views of what constitutes 'good' television programming, the 'appropriate' role for parents in determining the viewing habits of their children, and the extent to which children will be seen as active participants or vulnerable and passive consumers of television. In defining the regulatory objectives the powerful are able to use the process to maintain their power, whether it be rich over poor or adult over child.

When considered from this perspective the regulation of the relationship between children and television is not just a branch of communications law and policy but can in fact also properly be regarded as a part of family law and policy. What this means is that the many debates which occur within that field become relevant for discussions about the regulation of the relationship between children and television. The true meaning of 'parental responsibility' and the capacity for children to make their own judgements are significant issues within family and child law. If the laws which regulate television are now to be properly understood as a facet of this branch of law then those discussions should be playing a greater role too in deciding upon the manner in which the relationship between children and television should be regulated.

FAMILY, MARKETS AND TELEVISION

Lasch describes the modern family as 'the product of egalitarian ideology, consumer capitalism, and therapeutic intervention'.[13] For Lasch the history of the family is one where the state, through such agents as social workers and psychologists, gradually weakened the authority of the father through siding with the mother and children. The trade-off for this compact was increased control by the state of intra-familial relations, including the rearing of children.[14] But the state was not the only institution to create more autonomy for women and children. The rise of consumer capitalism created new demands on the family:

> the culture of consumption promoted the idea that women and children should have equal access, as consumers to an ever-increasing abundance of commodities. At the same time, it reduced the father's role in the family to that of a breadwinner.[15]

Of course, the rise and maintenance of consumer capitalism itself has to be supported by the state. Herein lies the difficulty for those who seek to understand the manner of television regulation in modern society. On the one hand the state seeks to control and guide the manner in which families behave, especially in relation to the child-rearing function. But on the other hand the state must also defend the economic system and ensure its maintenance.

This results in an uneasy tension with respect to the regulation of television broadcasting. The state is both prosecutor of the public interest in good quality programming for children and also defender of what many would see as antithetical to that outcome – the commercial success of broadcasters. This often finds expression in the question as to whether the state or the market-place should regulate television. There is an immediate problem in such a query – for the state must also defend the market-place. So any state regulation of broadcasting creates an immediate conflict as the state also has the role of furthering the role of the market-place as the primary mechanism through which goods and services are distributed. But is this the correct question to ask? I would suggest that such a question misconceives the true nature and purpose of television broadcasting.

Television now exists to serve the needs of advertisers. These are the real customers of television networks. As Minow and Lamay illustrate:

> The Fox Children's Network, for example, boasts to advertisers that 'we deliver more young viewers than anyone.' That is how American television works: the sponsors and advertisers are its real public; the viewers are the 'product' it can 'deliver'; and programs are merely the bait, the means to obtain the product. To lure children, television's main bait is cheaply produced and frequently aired cartoons, many of which look like advertisements and are: the success of these programs is determined not by who watches and likes them but by the revenues generated through the sale of merchandize related to them, from toys to breakfast cereals. As a European broadcasting executive once observed to an American audience, 'Your system trains children to be consumers; ours trains children to be citizens.'[16]

Programming must be geared to create mass audiences to maximize the possibility of their consumption of the goods and services on offer by the advertisers during such broadcasts.[17] But this assumes that viewers accept this role. A cynical, educated and informed viewing audience might be resistant to such messages. If television includes content to educate viewers, then can programming create a reluctant consumer? This is the dilemma for the state. The creation of a citizenry which shuns the virtues of consumer capitalism may threaten the viability of the economy. If people stop spending, then the economy will suffer. This places considerable constraints on the extent to which the state can demand quality programming – such as would inform and educate – in the place of that which is simply geared to creating an audience for advertisers. The creation of mass audiences is usually associated with programming made for 'the lowest common factor' while quality programming implies that which appeals to diversity and niche audiences. In the case of children it usually implies educational programming, or at least programmes which stimulate a child's intellectual development. It is one reason why so much of the debate about programming on television revolves around issues to do with sex and violence. These are universal phenomena which people everywhere can understand and relate to in some way and so broadcasters can be assured of attracting a large audience. But such programmes do not necessarily imply content which is informative about the subject matter or broadens the viewer's understanding of the world.

The stress the state is placed under to balance between the need for quality programming and the needs of the market-place is sometimes sought to be resolved by invoking the notion of the 'public interest'. There is even in some countries the tag 'public interest broadcasting' which is applied to certain programming. The notion of the public interest is a term well known in the law but it also well known within that discipline as a concept which is vague and ambiguous. When used in television law it suggests that there is a definable public interest position discernible from that motivated by the market-place. There is rarely this level of clarity about the concept, as the needs of the market-place overwhelm other considerations. As Ralston Saul notes:

> Advertising production costs are high multiples of those devoted to programming. The money used to produce a twenty-second spot for McDonald's would finance hours of television programming. In terms of straight expenses, the money paid for print news is a fraction of that paid for print advertising. Propaganda is therefore the purpose. Content is the frill of the decoration ... I am loath to add to the negative view of television, but it does quite naturally fit the characteristics of advertising or propaganda. The stream of images and sounds overwhelms meaning. Serious programming exists, but it is not the natural product of the system.[18]

Ralston Saul proceeds to cite the failure of most commercial networks to stop their programming to broadcast a Presidential press conference as an example of the manner in which television does not address the public interest. To this might be added the criticism that much television programming today tends to 'dumb down', focusing on trivia rather than substantive issues, be they of a political or personal nature.[19]

But this may also be viewed as a redrawing of the public interest. Just as it may be deemed patriotic to buy products made in our own country, so too it is now a source of national pride that people are consuming. This source of 'national pride' is not aided by a citizenry which questions the value of increased consumption ahead of other social objectives. Indeed, as Ralston Saul argues, we are no longer citizens but instead have become consumers and customers – even of government services. The role of the state is no longer to act as a buffer to the values of the market-place but to instead play the role of supporter of corporate expansion:

Look at the eagerness with which liberal and social democratic governments are embracing the idea that general schooling should be restructured to act as a direct conduit to the managerial economy. You will find this idea popping up throughout the West. The new Italian centre-left coalition is the latest example. They all say: 'We must be practical. We must produce citizens who can find jobs.' But these changes will not help individuals in the work place. They will, however, prepare the young to accept the structures of corporatism.[20]

Other critics, such as Lasch, appear to simply bemoan the decline in the standard of public discourse. But it would be folly to identify this critique as merely one which rests on a view that standards are dropping and that there is a longing for the 'golden age' of yesteryear. The value of Lasch's critique is that it identifies the social context within which television – and as we look to the future, the new information technologies – operate. Such technologies – as television once did – hold out the promise of raised standards and greater knowledge as we connect to each other and the potentially limitless sources of data and knowledge. But, as he puts it:

As for the claim that the information revolution would raise the level of public intelligence, it is no secret that the public knows less about public affairs than it used to know. Millions of Americans cannot begin to tell you what is in the Bill of Rights, what Congress does, what the Constitution says about the powers of the presidency, how the party system emerged or how it operates. A sizable majority, according to a recent survey, believe that Israel is an Arab nation. Instead of blaming the schools for this disheartening ignorance of public affairs, as is the custom, we should look elsewhere for a fuller explanation, bearing in mind that people readily acquire such knowledge as they can put to good use. Since the public no longer participates in debates on national issues, it has no reason to inform itself about civic affairs. It is the decay of public debate, not the school system (bad as it is), that makes the public ill informed, notwithstanding the wonders of the age of information. When debate becomes a lost art, information, even though it may be readily available, makes no impression.[21]

The common thread that runs through the arguments of Ralston Saul and Lasch is that public participation in civic life is no longer that of active citizen but one of passive consumer. This passive consumption also extends to the manner in which it is acquired and treated. The result is that television programming does not feed the public desire for active debate, for that desire does not exist. Instead, it fuels the fires upon which the warm glow of consumerism burns. As Lasch formulates it:

What democracy needs is vigorous public debate, not information. Of course, it needs information too, but the kind of information it needs can be generated only by debate. We do not know what we need to know until we ask the right questions, and we can identify the right questions only by subjecting our own ideas about the world to the test of public controversy. Information, usually seen as the precondition of debate, is better understood as its by-product. When we get into arguments that focus and fully engage our attention, we become avid seekers of relevant information. Otherwise we take in information passively – if we take it in at all.[22]

Where then is the 'public interest' in the content of television programming?

TELEVISION REGULATION AND THE CREATION OF COMPLACENCY

The context within which regulation of television takes place has to be understood as part of a process whereby the interests of broadcasters and their clients – advertisers – tend to prevail over a public need for informed debate, a need which is not recognized by a large part of the population. For this reason there is little clamouring for more 'quality' in programming and any demand that does exist can be served by niche public broadcasters, who often themselves become trapped by 'corporate' values of budgeting and efficiency which might lead them into such practices as sponsorship or merchandizing. This means that the supposed tension between the competing roles of the state – to advance the public interest in quality programming while also furthering the public interest in the protection of the market-place – is resolved in practice on the basis that the system of regulation must be consistent with the furtherance of corporate capitalism and increased consumption. It is within those parameters that any other socially desirable objectives with respect to broadcasting or programming must occur. It is not a balance between competing notions of the public interest which occurs in television regulation at all, but there is instead an overriding principle that the financiers of broadcasting must ultimately make a profit.

There is a myth that children are a special case and that regulation of television in the name of protecting children can displace concerns with profit. While the parameters may shift a little from time to time, it is difficult to mount a case for such a view. The limits to the regulation of television even in the name of children were recognized in Australia even before the commencement of television broadcasting in 1956. The Royal Commission established to inquire into the structure within which television would operate received many submissions regarding how broadcasting should occur to address the social concerns of the day. Representatives of church, educational, women's and arts associations submitted to the Royal Commission that there should be compulsory breaks in transmission as the shortage of quality programming would necessitate this. But the more central concern of these submissions was that such a break in transmission would be socially desirable.[23] As the Report noted:

> The main arguments advanced for a complete cessation of transmission at certain periods related primarily to children's sessions. It was submitted that a complete break in transmissions was necessary to assist parents in discharging their responsibility of managing their homes and their children. It was submitted that television was so engrossing that no programmes should be transmitted for a period of one or two hours after the children's programmes had ceased, to permit proper attention being given to the evening meal, to enable younger children to be put to bed without the distraction of an absorbing television programme, and to give older children an opportunity to do their homework and read books.[24]

It was also mentioned in one submission that this was the practice of the British Broadcasting Corporation at that time.[25]

In contemporary discussion of children and television such suggestions as the transmission break, however desirable it once may have seemed, would now be regarded as completely unattainable. It is worth considering how such a proposition could be put quite seriously in 1954, yet within a half century came to be regarded as completely unattainable for its proponents, and perhaps seen as silly by its detractors. No doubt where we are today has a lot to do with the ability of the television industry to influence public opinion in these matters. But what that does that mean? How does one change something as amorphous as public opinion? Part of the answer lies in the manner in which the television industry has been able to construct the notion of the public interest in broadcasting.

The response of the Australian Federation of Commercial Broadcasting Stations to the suggestion of breaks in transmission put to the 1954 Australian Royal Commission was framed entirely in terms of the public interest:

> it is important that the position should be flexible so that as additional programme material of suitable quality becomes available, the industry may be able to expand its operations in the public interest, without being impeded by arbitrary restraints.[26]

Precisely what this public interest was is not clear. While concerns with censorship may have been one factor, it is also apparent that the television industry was keen to sell television sets. Clearly, restricted viewing hours might limit the public's desire to purchase television sets.[27] In other words, the connection between public interest and material consumption was made. The United States has a similar history in this regard. Minow and Lamay claim that in the United States there has always been a concern on the part of the broadcasters that their profit margins should be protected, but that this was balanced against the notion that broadcasters had a duty to consider their listeners and to use the airwaves – a public resource – responsibly.[28] This was an even stronger obligation in relation to children, due to the manner in which they were constructed as vulnerable innocents who were easily exploited in the market-place:

> This is especially true where children are concerned, because while adults can take full responsibility for themselves, children typically cannot. They do not have the skills, resources, or knowledge to make the normal market mechanism related to consumer choice meaningful, which means that others – parents, educators, physicians, judges, librarians, and so on – must play a role in making meaningful choices for them. Broadcasters, whose exclusive use of the public airwaves gives them unique access to children in their homes, until recently shared some of this moral and social obligation.[29]

But this public interest concern itself was regarded by the industry as being in conflict with constitutional protections of free speech as contained in the First Amendment of the United States Constitution. When government began to embrace free market ideology in the 1980s, what occurred was in effect the abandonment, not of the notion of the public interest in broadcasting, but of any sense that this would be determined by the regulatory authorities. As part of official state policy public interest concerns would now be addressed by the market-place:

> Significantly, the FCC's decision was based less on economics than on the First Amendment. Too many of the public-interest regulations borne by broadcasters, the agency argued, unduly restricted their right to determine the content of their broadcasts; as a judge of the public interest, the market was more precise, less arbitrary, and far less intrusive. The market itself was imperfect, the commission acknowledge, but its failings were best remedied through market adjustments, not through government regulation of private broadcasters.[30]

But how was this shift in the manner in which the public interest was articulated to occur if children as a consequence were exposed to harm and exploitation? Critics such as Minow and Lamay would have it that the answer is simple: children's interests are being simply subverted to the profit motives of broadcasters. The answer is much more subtle than that. The combination of a television industry able to articulate a meaning of 'public interest' which is consistent with their narrow interests sits alongside regulatory mechanisms which place parents, not regulators or the community at large, as being the main buffer between children and any ill effects of television programming.

How well parents can perform this function is difficult to measure when they too are subject to the culture which television helps to create. Much of what even passes for 'good' programming may only be assumed to be of that standard. Hilty questions the manner in which parents accept the reassurances from industry and regulators alike that 'quality' educational television is possible to produce:

> These programs may completely ignore everything we know about child development and developmentally appropriate teaching and learning – but hey, who cares? The kids seem to love it. They will sit still through hours of this media blitz. And those who don't do this, well, *they* are a problem – short attention span, hyperactive, behaviour-disordered. Complacency in learning may begin in front of the TV. Is it any surprise that children come to school unprepared to take responsibility for their own learning as active participants in the teaching-learning process?[31]

We have to consider the effect this 'indoctrination' into passive learning, as Hilty calls it,[32] has on the child as future citizen. If even 'quality' programming for children does not instil in them a desire to question and critique, then does this mean that television in general creates a complacent and compliant population where the most active contribution they may make to political debate is a text messaged question to a guest politician on a current affairs show? There has been concern for many years about the lack of both quantity and quality of television programmes made specifically for children, based on the fear that the market-place will not produce such programming unless money can be made from it.[33] One needs to add to this a concern with the quantity and quality of programmes which children watch and the manner in which they contribute to, or fail to contribute to, the formation of the child as an active citizen.

Even public broadcasters, often faced with declining funding from government, have to contend with this problem. Part of their response is to produce programmes from which merchandizing opportunities may flow. In this way it is not just commercial television which becomes subjected to market pressures. In 1998, Janet Holmes a'Court, Chair of the Australian Children's Television Foundation, spoke of the 'tail wagging the dog' with respect to the income generating potential of children's programmes and their educational and entertainment value.[34]

She also referred to the trend in Europe to import United States produced cartooning in place of locally made children's programmes. A European report on this 'warned against a growing trend of treating children as consumers first and developing individuals second'.[35]

It is this dilemma as to where to place the child that is at the root of all discussions of children and television. Do we approach the child as the citizen child, the consumer child, the impressionable child or the dangerous child? If television can educate, it can also teach antisocial sentiment. If it can impart ethical principles, it can also corrupt innocent minds. The regulation of television is about many of our fears and many of our fears connect with what we desire for our children. It is little wonder then that a significant role is played by parental guidance in systems of television regulation.

STATE REGULATION 'VERSUS' PARENTAL GUIDANCE

A common characteristic of the formal regulation of television in Australia, the United States, Canada and the United Kingdom is the role of parents in 'guiding' the viewing patterns of their children. The placing of responsibility on parents fits, of course, many agendas with respect to the role of the state both in the family and in the highly charged area of censorship of the media. Ostensibly, recourse to parental choice or guidance deals with the concern that the regulation of television can lead to state intrusion into what broadcasters are allowed to broadcast and what people are allowed to view on television. Freedom of speech and freedom to receive information and ideas through the media are thought to be sacred rights in a democratic society and as a consequence any system of television regulation must be cautious of infringing these rights.

But it is also accepted that television can be an influence on the young and if left uncontrolled may exploit or corrupt them. Once the debate is constructed in this way it is difficult for the state to avoid acting. This concern is not presented, however, as a reluctant state forced to act to protect children from a social evil. What occurs in this area of state regulation of television is that harm to children is constructed in such a manner that it legitimates the state intervening in the family and imposing significant responsibilities on parents to act in ways which are regarded as desirous by the state. This fits with a broader social agenda of conceptualizing children as weak or impressionable and thereby requiring social control of young people. It is thus a system of 'parental control' rather than parental choice. The twist is that while this gives rise to parental control of children it also leads to state control of parents who make 'inappropriate' choices with respect to their children's television viewing which may lead to them being labelled and dealt with as 'bad' parents.

A further point here is that the state's agenda is itself complex, as the state is keen to ensure that children develop the appropriate attitudes not just with respect to their general behaviour in the community, but also that they learn the norms of the market-place. One of the major failings in literature on juvenile justice, for example, is that it often comes to regard the eradication of delinquency as the goal of the system. Clearly, the aim is to ensure that young people become 'productive' members of society, which means in nearly all cases gaining employment (which can also include domestic labour as a spouse) or taking steps towards doing so through schooling. Thus, it must follow that the state has an interest in children being influenced by their television viewing habits into adopting the role of consumer, for consumers must work to earn the money to acquire the consumer goods they seek. It is not only the program content which becomes significant in this process, but how it is watched, when, who with and under what conditions. The television viewing context is much wider than the content of a programme and the messages received by children from this process may be subtle in their form.

PARENTAL GUIDANCE, CORPORATE DIRECTION AND STATE CONTROL

The television industry has redefined the public interest aspect of broadcasting in a way which gives primacy to the role of the market. But the continued influence of a conception of childhood which portrays the child as vulnerable and in need of protection means that the recast notion of the public interest which emphasizes the importance of the market appears to conflict with the idea of children as too unsophisticated to be exposed to those market forces. The challenge for the state thus becomes one of how to nevertheless impose a system of protection in television broadcasting which insulates children from the perceived harmful effects of the medium while not infringing the market rights of television corporations. The outcome in Australia, Canada, the United States and the United Kingdom has been to inject into the process of television regulation a system of parental guidance.

The special role of parents has long been asserted in writing on television and children. The Royal Commission held in Australia in 1954 noted that 'however good the programmes, some parental control is necessary to prevent excessive viewing. That is not a matter which can be controlled by public regulations.'[36] In 1978 an Australian Senate inquiry into children and television described parental control and influence as 'perhaps the most important factor in influencing a child's television viewing habits.'[37] This Committee stressed the role of parents in filtering and interpreting the messages children received from television programmes.[38]

Once television viewing was associated with harm to the child, however, the tenor of debates about the role of parents changed. As Eron and Huesmann wrote in 1987:

> Abuse of children, whether physical or psychological, can have lasting effects on their emotional development ... What is less well appreciated is that the broadcast media are also a source of abuse and can have as deleterious an effect on children's development as direct physical and psychological abuse by parents. A youngster's social development can be affected by continued exposure to certain kinds of media programming. These effects are not merely transient but can have a long lasting, malevolent influence on personality development.[39]

The implications of such an approach to television viewing by children are profound. By comparing 'continued exposure to certain kinds of media programming' with physical and psychological abuse psychologists began to construct new forms of child abuse to which solutions would need to be sought. Suddenly the message is that television not only contributes to aggressive behaviour in children, it *is* aggressive behaviour. For parents it cannot therefore be a simple matter of choice with respect to what their children watch. If certain programmes are harmful, then how could a good parent justify exposing their children to such harm? For Eron and Huesmann the answer to 'television abuse' lay with the parents:

> Parents cannot absolve themselves completely from responsibility for monitoring what their children watch, although it is very difficult for most parents to exercise complete control over their children's viewing habits. A number of aids have been developed to help parents cope with these problems. We have also demonstrated elsewhere that it is possible to reduce the deleterious effect of television violence on children's aggressive behaviour by teaching them that the violence they see is unrealistic, that there are productive ways to solve life's problems, that aggression and violence have serious irreversible consequences, and that too much television is, very simply, bad for children. It is the responsibility of educators, media experts, child-welfare workers, and the researchers themselves to see that such findings are disseminated widely so that parents will know what television is doing to their children and what they can do about it.[40]

The message is not one of parental choice, but a parental warning. Protect your child or let them suffer. In such writings, the problem of children and television is at once constructed and resolved as a scientific problem. The experts are expected to identify the harmful material and good parents will respond appropriately. There is no room for the parent with a different cultural perspective to question what is 'good' programming. This is not presented as a problem of values but a problem of research. The child, of course, is a passive recipient of the whole process, silent and with no role other than as potential victim of televised 'harm'.

Yet this analysis of television and its connection to child abuse ignores other knowledge about the meaning of this type of harm. The problem of defining child abuse has long been regarded as a matter which involves consideration of competing values. Giovannoni and Becerra wrote in terms twenty years ago which are just as applicable today:

> 'Good' child rearing practices are those that produce 'good' adults. Our uncertainty about the ways children are reared and the kinds of adults they become constitutes one kind of problem, one that may be answered through the gradual growth of knowledge about child development. But the value issues cannot be resolved through knowledge alone. Thus, to the complexities of the value conflicts inherent in resolving situations of child abuse and neglect are added the value issues of what we consider to be desirable or undesirable traits, in children and adults. Such value issues are even more pronounced in a society such as ours, with its ethnic, religious, social and economic diversity. Protection of these pluralistic interests and values is integral to the interests of justice and fairness, and failure to consider such value differences can also jeopardize the viability of family life among whole segments of society.[41]

Of course, there will be broad agreement on many basic values in society. This cannot detract, however, from the fact that in many areas there are differences. Such difference is the lifeblood of the society and is itself a precious thing. To construct a policy with respect to television viewing by children which does not consider such different values would be dangerous to the continuance of such diversity.

It is true that to an extent the idea that 'parental choice' should determine what children view on television is an attempt to allow for diversity within the community. The language of parental choice comes from the idea that the state has no legitimate role in dictating to the family what they should watch on television. But my argument is that the notion of parental choice is a smokescreen. The state does bring considerable pressure to bear on parents to control their children's television viewing. It does this because, as is asserted time and again by the scientific experts, television can shape attitudes and behaviour. The state cannot afford to forgo such a tool for social cohesion and social control.

Thus the language in reports by regulatory authorities into children and television is now often couched in terms of parental control. For example, in a report for the British Broadcasting Corporation, Broadcasting

tandards Commission and the Independent Television Commission, the
1thor writes:

> Ongoing changes in home entertainment mean that parents are
> facing new challenges in exercising control over their children's
> media consumption . . .[42]

'he report then goes on to list a number of 'informal control
1echanisms': banning certain programmes and channels and encouraging
thers to be watched; turning off the television or sending children from
1e room 'to avoid undesirable content'; discussing the content; limiting
1e time children watch television; rationing access; and random checks
n viewing.[43] Mention is also made of technological aids such as PINs to
lock programmes and channels.[44] This is not to suggest that parental
ontrol is always exercised, nor that children do not in fact exert some
1dependent control. As the report also found:

> [m]any parents are uncomfortable about imposing external controls
> on television viewing, particularly for older children (around 10 and
> over), as they feel it throws doubt on how well the family unit is
> functioning. They prefer to trust their children: however, although
> children do regulate their own viewing, they do not always comply
> with parental ground rules. Moreover, children may over-estimate
> their emotional maturity and ability to cope, and they may in fact
> gain reassurance and confidence from parents setting boundaries.[45]

'his is not science. Such a statement is based on an idea of childhood
which is generally suspicious of the capacity of children to think for
hemselves. In part this follows from the Communications White Paper
which this report was responding to and which listed the objectives of a
ew regulatory body to include the 'the protection of children'.[46]

This objective was also expressed to be based on the Government's
ther commitments to human rights:

> The common objectives will reflect the Government's commitment
> to Human Rights Act principles and encapsulate our continuing
> determination to protect the vulnerable, especially children.[47]

The point to be made is that in both passages the human right to impart
nd receive information is disconnected from the need to protect children.
'here is no specific articulation of the child's right to receive information,
nd although it could be argued that this is subsumed within a broader
bjective of ensuring that right for all, one suspects that having singled out
hildren as 'vulnerable' it is not envisaged that a commitment to such a
ight for children is seen as a primary objective. Indeed, the new United
Kingdom Communications Bill reiterates its commitment to the
vulnerability of children as a special concern of the regulatory authority

while also expressing as an objective of the regulator 'the desirability c promoting competition in relevant markets'.[48] The view that children ar in need of protection from harmful television content is purportedly base on scientific research indicating the need to protect children from harmfu content. Yet the commitment to increasing competition in the medi ignores an equally large body of evidence that such competition militate against the production of quality programming for children.

The use to which research on parental reluctance to control children' television viewing behaviour is put also has to be considered. In th context of growing community anxiety about parental responsibility, sucl findings further legitimate state intrusion into the family and th imposition of liability on parents for their inappropriate supervision c children's television viewing. Children who watch television unsupervise can be seen to represent a threat to a society which is anxious about th effects of television on the propensity to engage in aggressive behaviour Parental liability laws are becoming more popular as a way of ensuring tha parents act 'appropriately' in the way in which they supervise thei children.[49] Such laws can be critiqued as flawed in that they diver attention away from broader social factors which contribute to offendin; behaviour by young people. In this sense they suggest that parents ar responsible for behaviour which may in fact be caused by factors for whicl the whole community should accept responsibility.[50] Nevertheless, th laws have a popular appeal and the principles upon which they are base can be readily understood to be applicable to the regulation of th relationship between children and television.

Tyler and Segady make a connection between media violence and sucl laws when they refer to the United States Office of Juvenile Justice an Delinquency Prevention's documentation which lists social factors such a 'poverty, disorganized communities, media violence, drugs, and family violence' as the structural causes of delinquency for which parental liabilit laws punish parents.[51] This critique is that to blame juvenile offending or 'irresponsible parents' who fail to prevent their children from viewing violent programmes denies any collective responsibility for the behaviou of young people. Although their critique may use 'media violence' uncritically as a cause of juvenile offending, it does suggest that parenta guidance advice for television viewing is just one short step from becoming the basis of parental responsibility laws for children's televisior viewing.

THE MYTH OF PARENTAL GUIDANCE: STATE CONTROL AND CHILDREN'S LIVES

The ability of parental guidance to be effective as a mechanism fo regulating children's television viewing is open to question as it is built or a compromise between concern for the child and the realities of the market-place. The tension between these two concerns demonstrates the difficult role parental guidance systems create for parents. If television now plays a central role in constructing the individual as consumer – an aim wholly in accord with the broad objectives of those who advertise on television – then parental guidance cannot be seen as being about simple censorship of children's viewing. Parents who steer children away from television or who impart highly critical skills on their children with respect to their consumption of television programming are clearly not being supportive of the need – as articulated by television corporations and their advertiser customers – to grow into avid consumers. Indeed, although one might objectively describe parents who heavily control their child's access to television as 'good' parents, it must be questioned whether such behaviour would be generally regarded as 'normal' parenting. Parents who forbid their children from watching television at all might be more often described as too strict, even bordering on being authoritarian and harsh.

Thus the first criticism of parental guidance as a notion is that it may itself be constructed in a way which is consistent with the aims of the television industry. After all, parents themselves will usually be consumers of television and subjected to the messages contained in the medium which stress the desirability of certain programming in terms of entertainment, education or information. Parental guidance is in this sense a myth. Parents must apply their understanding of appropriateness with respect to what children should watch on the screen based on their own experiences, many of which will themselves be gleaned from television. The ultimate irony, therefore, is that for many parents their main source of information about television will be television itself.

A second criticism of parental control is that at a practical level it means little. The 1978 Australian Senate Committee concluded that although parental guidance was 'important' it was rarely exercised. Their report states:

> The bulk of research available here and overseas on the extent to which parents attempt to control what their children watch on television indicates that very little parental control is exerted.[52]

The Committee referred to one United States study which indicated that in most families children controlled the television in the early evening and parents sought their children's advice as to programme selection.[53] Reference was also made to an Australian survey which suggested that children who watched large amounts of television were less supervised by their parents with respect to their viewing than children who spent less time watching television.[54]

The conclusions of the Senate Committee clearly indicate a concern with the 'proper' role of parents with respect to the viewing habits of their children. They also indicate that there are class differences in this regard. In commenting on those children who watched in excess of 30 (and sometimes up to 80) hours of television per week, the Committee commented:

> Apart from their long hours before the television screen, these children also tend to exhibit certain social characteristics that leave them more vulnerable to the medium's influence than their average or light viewing counterparts. They are usually withdrawn. They do not relate very well with their parents or siblings, do not do very well at school, have few close friends and very little peer group interaction. They tend to come from the lower socio-economic groups and their viewing habits are largely unsupervised by their parents. These children tend to read few books or newspapers. Television becomes virtually their sole companion and their main input of information and entertainment. These children are therefore particularly vulnerable to the influence of television and the ones at greatest risk of being harmed by any negative influences of the medium.
>
> In any assessment of television's impact on the younger members of society, it is obviously with these children that the major concern must lie.[55]

It might be extrapolated from such a statement that 'good' parents both guide and limit their children's television viewing. But equally, 'bad' parents fail to do so. In this way parental guidance as a technique of guiding children's television viewing becomes in effect a form of parental control. The application or non-application of proper parental guidance has become another way in which parents can be judged by others including, one would assume, the caring professions. This outcome might be considered to be a curious one, as the very system of parental guidance appears to be premised on a suspicion of the overall quality of television programming. But the solution, it appears, is to instil in parents the responsibility for controlling their children's viewing, rather than to encourage them to make a concerted effort to change the programming content.

This parental guidance role is further complicated. On the one hand there is the often stated view that improved children's programming must be achieved to ensure that the viewing experience of children is enriching, educational and rewarding. This is often a stated objective of regulators. But on the other hand there sits the view that 'better' programming - however defined - carries with it the potential for increased justification for parents to guide their children towards television rather than away from it. At about the same time the Australian Senate issued its report on children and television Marie Winn, for example, was arguing that improved programming might increase parents' use of television as a babysitter.[56] She cites the broadcasters' defence of their poor quality programmes – that quality programming would simply lead to more criticism of them on the basis that they were preventing children from engaging in other activities:

> It is unlikely that the networks are eschewing good programming for children out of altruism, to avoid tempting kids into watching too much television; junk after all, is generally cheaper and easier to provide than quality entertainment. Nevertheless, the industry's cool indifference to the quality of children's television fare may be far more beneficial for children than the struggle of those who insist that fine children's programs be available at all times. The preponderance of offensive and banal programs may act as a natural check on television viewing since conscientious parents are more likely to limit their children's television intake if only unsavoury programs are available.[57]

The path that has been taken since the late 1970s has been one of emphasizing quality programming for children, the recognition of standards for children's television and the use of classification systems to enable parents to guide their children's viewing. The advent of the V-chip does not significantly alter this approach. Parents must purchase and set this new technology – itself an ironic twist as the good parent may now be one who is prepared to purchase the additional consumer item of the V-chip embedded television set to facilitate their children's consumption of television programming, much of which is broadcast to attract an audience for the marketing of goods. It is an interesting aside that the television industry has not been so inclined to embrace technology which enables viewers to 'zap' advertisements.

In all of these approaches it is implicit that children will watch television, and to the extent that such policies are designed to improve programming they all provide justification for more rather than less viewing. In this way it can be argued that parental guidance is consistent with corporate aims. The battle to limit children's viewing by prohibiting broadcasting during certain hours was lost before it even began. Parents who severely restrict their children's viewing are more likely to be regarded as extreme rather than balanced. The good parent today is one who sits at the side of the child and, reassured by the imposition of television standards, guides their child in how to become a good consumer of the 'good' television world.

It follows that the notion of 'parental guidance' which sits at the centre of formal television regulation in Australia, the United States, Canada and the United Kingdom is a myth. What in fact occurs is the application of 'parental responsibility' principles which are now a feature of many laws to do with children. These laws are more to do with increased state control of children and families than they have to do with the nurturing of parental choice and diversity in family lifestyles. It is a state control which locks children and families into the murky world of the 'public interest' in broadcasting. This world sits uneasily between the concerns of the corporate world, a view of children as innocent and vulnerable (and yet sometimes dangerous) and parents who are expected to act 'appropriately'. It is to the law that many turn for certainty when faced with this complexity.

CHAPTER 2

Legal Discourse and the Regulation of the Relationship between Children and Television

> *...it must be remembered that, in the absence of legal rules or a hierarchy of values, the best interests approach depends upon the value system of the decision-maker. Absent any rule or guideline, that approach simply creates an unexaminable discretion in the repository of the power. Who could then say that the repository of the power is right or wrong ...*
> (*Brennan, J: in* Secretary, Department of Health and Community Services v JWB and SMB (Marion's case) *(1992) 175 CLR 218)*

In an age of global deregulation the relationship between children and television appears to be a special case where continuing state intervention is justified. But what passes for regulation in this field is far from that. The regulation of this relationship has more to do with the construction of a certain version of childhood, the creation of 'appropriate' parenting models and the continuing domination of consumption as the dominant ethos of the times than it has to do with the needs of children. It is true that there is an official concern with the nature, quality and content of children's television, as well as a more general concern with what children might be exposed to in all programming, whether made specifically for children or not. But the various rules and guidelines which result from this official concern are rarely analysed to expose the manner in which they conceal a number of other policy objectives and assumptions about the place of children in society.

THE MEANING OF CHILDREN'S TELEVISION AND THE CHILD

Much debate in the area of children and television centres on a discussion of 'children's television'. This is usually taken to refer to programming designed for children. But such programmes are not necessarily those which children view. This has important implications for policy-makers as it means that attempts to ensure that programmes exist which are 'educational' for children may have little affect on the viewing experience of children if they shun those programmes in favour of others. It may even mean that the way to improving programming for children is to change the nature and content of programmes regarded as general viewing.[1] As we shall see, this definitional problem surrounding children's television can also be manipulated by broadcasters when they are subjected to legal requirements to provide quality programming for children.[2]

The other related problem in this discussion is the meaning to be ascribed to 'the child'. Childhood can be conceptualized in various ways and there is little doubt that the choices made about how childhood is viewed heavily influences the approach taken to the regulation of television for children. For example, children can be regarded as 'little angels' that need to be kept pure and protected from harm, or we can understand children as 'little devils' that will naturally drift towards bad habits unless they are guided in more appropriate directions.[3] These images of childhood also connect with various paradigms of childhood identified by Lee.[4] He lists three paradigms: the property paradigm, protection paradigm and personal paradigm. While his discussion places each paradigm in different historical epochs, it is clear that each persists in various forms today. There are still many parents who discuss their rights as parents in a manner consistent with the property paradigm of childhood which for Lee is a part of pre-industrial societies. This paradigm stresses the parental role as one which is rooted in notions of ownership. While historically this idea of childhood stemmed from the need for the family to put as many hands as possible to work the land as soon as they were fit and able to do so, it also gives rise to an ideological framework which accords to the parent – usually the father – the right to expect the child to behave in the way determined by the parent. While modern societies may have witnessed changes in the underlying need for children to work the land for the benefit of the whole family, the ideological framework centred on this paradigm is still in evidence. Parents still battle over who will raise the children after marital breakdown as if the children are chattels to be allocated. Likewise 'parental control' remains a notion that is often utilized in discussions about the behaviour of young people. References in statutes to parental responsibility[5] also emanate from the same paradigm.

The idea of parental responsibility for the acts of children is subjected to a range of criticisms.[6] A core aspect of such critiques is that such a notion has no regard for the reality of the parent–child relationship. Older children exercise in practice a large degree of autonomy and in addition possess at least some legal autonomy to go with it.[7] To hold parents responsible for the acts of their children contradicts the idea of the autonomy of the child and assumes parents can place limits on their behaviour. When the idea of parental guidance in television viewing is considered one can see the parallel in the inability of parents to control the television viewing habits of their children. Factors such as class, educational background and culture may influence the reality of parental influence. The suspicion is that as with the concept of parental responsibility for the acts of children in other areas, such as truancy and antisocial behaviour, the idea often gives rise to the imposition of middle-class ideas of respectability being imposed on 'failing' working-class parents. What also occurs in this process is the imposition of parental responsibility for the behaviour of children as a means to conceal the social problems created by poverty, inadequate housing, poorly resourced public spaces for children and under-resourced schools with out-of-date curricula.

Parental guidance, when used as a key mechanism for the regulation of children's viewing, also shifts the responsibility for children's exposure to television away from broadcasters and deflects questions about their responsibility towards the community onto parents who are often the least able to implement any real influence over programming content or often their children's television habits. 'Parental guidance' approaches to children's television viewing can be better understood as 'parental blaming'. In this schema, the blame will be placed at the feet of those parents who fail to do what is implicit in the idea of parental guidance – control their children. The paradigm upon which this approach is based thus also connects very well with the view that children are little devils who need to feel the heavy hand of the powerful parent.

The idea that children need to be protected from harm more readily connects with the angelic view of the child. Lee describes the protection paradigm as arising during the time that societies moved to an industrial base necessitating a shift in thinking about the place of children. The protection paradigm therefore constructs the child as an investment for the future rather than having significant present productive value. This paradigm led to a change in the role of parents too. It placed upon them obligations to protect the child from harm in order that he or she would develop in time into a socially useful adult. Protection from harm also implied ensuring that children attended school – to acquire skills for their future role – and that they did not work excessive hours as would interfere with their education. It also implied duties on the part of parents to provide more generally the circumstances for their physical, intellectual and emotional development. It is often associated with the legal principle which requires that in matters affecting children, their 'best interests' or 'welfare' should be the paramount consideration. An interesting by-product of the adoption of this paradigm was a decline in the value of the child when accidentally killed. In claims for wrongful death of a child such a loss had represented substantial economic harm for the family concerned. But as children became investments for the future the loss of a child became a net saving for a family. This resulted in the lowering of amounts awarded to parents of children so killed.[8] Such judicial decisions confirmed the parent as provider rather than controller of children. Today, bodies such as the Australian Institute of Family Studies publish annual updates on the cost of raising a child, and legislation around the world emphasizes parental obligations to support children.[9] All of this reinforces the message that the role of adults is to nurture the child and guide their development.

While the need for such reports and legislative provision seems self evident, this is only so because of the dominance of the protection paradigm at this point in history. When one works 'within' a paradigm the norms and values which underpin it present not as choices but as self-evident 'truths'. Thus few people question the obligation of parents to support their children or that it is primarily the role of parents to protect their children from harm. But from time to time different paradigms do clash. For example, a parent who is required to pay child support for children residing with the other parent may complain that they are doing so without receiving the benefit of having the children in their care. Such a complaint utilizes aspects of the property paradigm while the legal requirement to pay child support clearly has its foundations in the protection paradigm.

The potential for a contest between different conceptualizations of childhood is even more marked when one considers the personal paradigm. This paradigm is characterized by notions of personal autonomy and the independent rights of the child. It is a paradigm associated with post-industrial societies.[10] This understanding of childhood relies on a sense that the social problems of the nineteenth and early twentieth centuries which gave rise to the protection paradigm are less relevant in an age of information technology and greater social awareness. In this age children should be given more independence to explore and create their own self-reliance free of the concerns of the past. The independent rights of children are asserted from within this paradigm, together with the notion that children have a greater capacity to decide matters for themselves. These ideas of the child are reinforced in various legal documents and decisions, most notably in various provisions of the United Nations Convention on the Rights of the Child and landmark court decisions.[11] This paradigm also has appeal to those who regard the protectionist approach as paternalistic. While the personal paradigm stresses the independence of the child and the need to let children speak on their own behalf where possible, the protection paradigm has been identified as having led to children being dealt with harshly in the past for their own good. Nevertheless, it is fair to say that the protection paradigm in general remains the dominant paradigm today.

LEGAL UNDERSTANDINGS OF THE CHILD AND THE COMPLEXITY OF CHILDHOOD

While it is probably true that some parents continue to assert ownership rights over their children in the face of a more dominant protection paradigm, the idea that children may claim rights independent of their parents is anathema to many. The premise of the personal paradigm is that the world is a place which does not present the same dangers to children as it once did and now requires children to be allowed to develop greater independence of thought and action to meet the challenges of a new world order. But at the same time this view is confronted with a growing fear on the part of many parents that the world is a less safe place for their children and that new forms of media challenge the traditional view of childhood as a time of security and innocence. That is, the fear expressed by many adults is not just of those who seek to abuse children, but also from those who seek to grant to children autonomous rights. In a sense, to the protective parent the abuser and the advocate for children's autonomy share one thing in common – both may represent attempts to take from children their childhood innocence.

The fear of the loss of childhood innocence takes many forms. Children are less likely to walk to school today than ten years ago – anxious parents prefer to drive them for fear of them being harmed by strangers even though children are becoming more obese and less inclined to exercise. Systems which filter 'harmful' material on television and the internet are promoted as 'parental control' devices, despite the fact that once set they require no ongoing parental involvement and thus deprive children of the opportunity to develop their own ability to make judgements either independently or through discussion with adults. The free movement of children on the streets is becoming more curtailed by the increasing use of curfews and anti-loitering ordinances as adults are driven by a fear of young people in public spaces as well as a fear that their own children might be harmed by others in such spaces.[12]

There is then a growing complexity, confusion and contradiction about childhood, what is best for children and how we should respond to their needs. This may seem obvious but this is a point that is often left out of discussions about how the law responds to social problems. More typically, a problem is identified and then there is a call for the law to respond. Law is judged on the adequacy of the response, rather than on the complexity and confusion of the social problem.

But law is not simply a reactive device. It has to translate the social problem into legal discourse. In doing so it has to work with the complex and often contradictory conceptions of childhood discussed above. King and Piper, employing the thought of Teubner, explain this process as one which requires law to simplify and reduce the various complexities it faces in order to perform its task.[13] This analysis also considers law to be an autonomous system with its own norms, able to produce its own account of social reality.[14] This is particularly apt in relation to children and television. There is a plethora of social science studies on the effects of television on children. But these studies do not address the adequacy of *law* to accommodate the concepts with which those studies work and then to place them within laws which regulate television. King and Piper speak of the degree to which there can be 'welfare in law'.[15] The point is transferable to the present discussion and we can ask to what extent concerns about the effects of television can be placed in law and regulation.

DUALISMS IN THE CONSTRUCTION OF TELEVISION LAW

As King and Piper argue, the two great − and opposing - strands of thought in child welfare: welfare, with its emphasis on underlying causes and social responsibility, and justice, with its concern with procedural fairness and individual responsibility, lead to the notion of 'balance' in attempts to reconcile those strands:

> The problems that arise from these attempts by law to respond to current demands for just but sensitive decision-making have tended to be portrayed again in terms of clashes of ideology. According to this view, if the courts' decisions do little in practice to protect children and promote their welfare, the cause is to be found in the imbalance between the two different ideological objectives of welfare and justice which the law pursues. All will be put right if the right balance can be found. Justice and welfare have therefore become concepts with a dual function. They are used to explain the complexity and confusion of court decision-making in the main areas concerning children: juvenile justice, child protection and matrimonial disputes, but they also serve as rallying points in those campaigns which seek to promote one or other as the preferred way of dealing with children's issues in the courts.[16]

In matters to do with laws which regulate television one can see similar debates occurring. On the one hand there is the view, as in child welfare, that too much regulation and control of what children watch will impinge on the rights of the family, that is parents, to decide what their children should view. On the other is the concern that the laws should be strengthened to impose stricter controls on television content in order to protect children from harmful images. The resolution of these not always reconcilable aims lies in the extent to which it is possible to create the right 'balance'. It is, as King and Piper state generally in the area of children and the law, about the construction of a dualism within the law around which decisions about children and television are made.

There are a number of examples of this in television regulation systems. The *European Broadcasting Union's Guidelines for Programmes When Dealing With the Portrayal of Violence* attempts to 'balance' between the need to protect viewers from harm while not compromising the facts:

> One person's shock is another person's news or art. Thus a decision in this field means striking a balance between the current social consensus on what is acceptable and the broadcaster's duty to reflect reality as he or she sees it.[17]

A voluntary code issued by the Canadian Radio-Telecommunications Commission in 1993 suggested a similar balance:

> While broadcasters shall not exaggerate or exploit situations of aggression, conflict or confrontation, equal care shall be taken not to sanitize the reality of the human condition.[18]

While these codes do not mention children, it is usually with them in mind that such 'balances' are to be struck. The Canadian Code above highlights concern for children amongst its background comments to the Code.[19]

In the United Kingdom a similar dualism was constructed around the Code of Practice issued by the British Broadcasting Standards Council in 1994. It stated the two principles upon which the Code was based:

> The first principle is that of the contract implied between the viewer and the broadcaster. The Code, like the wider-ranging Codes and Guidelines produced by the broadcasters themselves, sets out the terms upon which the broadcaster seeks admission to the homes of the audience and the terms of which admission is generally considered to be granted. The offence to which broadcasts some-times give rise is usually the product of a breach of those terms, a flouting of the expectations which the terms have set ...

> The Council's second principle may be seen as a balance to the first, namely that this respect for the audience provides the justification for the right to experiment and to challenge conventions. This must be safeguarded if broadcasting is to remain the forum for fresh works of the imagination and the continuing exploration of contemporary realities.[20]

In effect the Council is stating what it perceives to be the foundation upon which broadcasting is built. Upon analysis it can be seen that this foundation is a sham. The principles employ legal concepts to attract legitimacy. The proposition is that the broadcaster and the viewer enter into a contract and in those matters which create offence it can be understood as a simple breach of contract. There is, of course, no such contract. Broadcasters enter the homes of viewers because they possess vast resources to either dictate or manufacture programme choice, occasionally moderated by viewer feedback. For commercial broadcasters it is the contract with the advertiser and sponsor which matters. The dualism which has been constructed between reducing offence and harm (however defined) and protecting creativity is a false one. There is no balance. Clearly, much offence is caused by programmes which challenge conventions, and that is often their purpose – to shock. How does one strike a balance between those who value such programmes and those who are seriously offended? One cannot find a 'balance' in such instances, as it involves two fundamentally opposed value positions to do with the role and content of broadcasting.

The other dualism which is created in discussions of children and television is, as discussed earlier, that of state control versus parental guidance. It is important to restate the central argument of that discussion – that the notion of parental guidance as a solution to determining how regulation of television for children should occur is a smokescreen which obscures at the same time the inadequacy of the law to address the complexity of childhood and television while also, to paraphrase King and Piper, serving as a rallying point for those who seek to promote a particular form of regulation in this context. It is a false dualism, for the state does regulate television regardless of the perceived role for parental guidance. Parents operate within the parameters proscribed by the state and do not exercise a large degree of discretion over their children's viewing. To do otherwise carries the risk for them of being classified as inappropriate parents.

TELEVISION SCIENCE IN LAW

King and Piper discuss the degree to which child welfare is reconstructed by law and how that process of reconstruction obscures understandings of the problems which are being sought to be addressed. My argument is that a similar analysis can be applied to the manner in which the law incorporates 'television science' – all the social scientific research on the effects of television on children in particular – into legal discourse.

The problem is in deciding whether the reality which law constructs through this process is appropriate when addressing the needs of children. As King and Piper state in response to the question of whether other sciences have a better understanding of social reality:

> Our argument is not that science is superior in any absolute terms but rather that, while law's truths may be effective within law's own normative domain, their idiosyncratic nature and dependence upon normative operations may make them highly inappropriate as a

basis for reality construction in the types of issues that concern the well-being of children. If law as an epistemic discourse has such severe limitations as we suggest, those characteristics which restrict law's appropriateness to deal with such issues need to be recognized.[21]

As they illustrate, notions such as 'justice' and 'welfare' do not mean the same thing in child welfare science as they do in the law. The law is an independent institution which frames its own criteria for determining the welfare of the child, for example. Notions of 'welfare' and 'justice' are conceptualized in quite different terms within the law when compared with the social sciences.[22] Law tends to individualize 'justice' for example, social policy tends to see 'justice' in terms of 'social justice'. There is then the problem of mutual understanding between the two systems of thought and more importantly the limits to which law can incorporate the knowledge of other disciplines within its framework:

> there are limits to 'welfare in law' because there are limits to law's effective action set by the intrinsic nature of law and by law's own concept of its role. Law's *raison d'être* is as a body which conceptualizes the world into rights and duties on which it can adjudicate and which swings into action when an individual, personal or corporate, wishes to activate a right or impose a duty. The law's actions are largely reactive. They are determined by the nature of rights and duties embodied in law which, in civil law jurisdictions and increasingly in common law jurisdictions, is made by external agencies, notably the legislature. Therefore if the law does not provide a parent with the right to *satisfactory* accommodation for rearing children then the law cannot provide it . . .[23]

The application of these ideas about law to the suggested harmful effects of television and the ability of law to embrace such concerns appears particularly apt. Television violence is often associated with inappropriate behaviour in children and youth, sexual imagery and content is thought to be potentially damaging to children's development and the general effects of television on children are heavily debated. It is assumed that a legal response is a simple extension of these concerns. But it is not considered whether the adequacy of the law's responses has more to do with the nature of law in this process than it has to do with simple differences of viewpoint amongst social scientists.

There is an even more fundamental point. Law appears to be instinctively suspicious of other disciplines. As King and Piper show, it is a self-referential system which does not depend on other discourses to perpetuate itself. Thus law can choose how to process the information it receives from other scientific discourse and produce a new discourse which may or may not draw upon that other knowledge, and where it does choose other knowledge it may do so in ways which create in effect new meanings. On this point they refer to the work of Teubner:

> Interference of the law and other social discourses does not mean that they merge into a multidimensional super-discourse, nor does it imply that information is 'exchanged' among them. Rather, information is constituted anew in each discourse and interference adds nothing but the simultaneity of two communicative events.[24]

The problem the law has with social science is that law seeks to rely on science to support the conclusions it reaches about certain events:[25]

> For law, scientific procedures exist as methods which assist in the reinforcement of congruent expectations. When controversy exists, it is constructed by law as a dichotomy between a right answer and a wrong answer, the choice between one category or another. It is not surprising, therefore, to find legal commentators attempting to classify the value for law of different sciences according to the 'objectivity' of their knowledge, that is their falsifiability according to Popper's criteria.
>
> Sciences which rely upon unfalsifiable statements, namely the social and behavioural sciences, through their insistence upon notions of consequences and causality in those very areas of social life where law is seeking to offer congruence and predictability, present a direct challenge to law's non-empirical, normatively-directed version of reality. Law, as a discourse, is not interested in consequences, but in maintaining expectations that certain consequences will occur (for example, that society will be free from corruption or that general deterrence will result from heavy prison sentences for certain crimes) regardless of and often in contradiction of any empirical evidence that may exist.[26]

For law then the problem with social science is that it can appear to be inexact and unreliable for its purposes. King and Piper argue that this has more to do with the nature of the discipline than the validity of the nature produced. As they explain:

> The procedures for validating child welfare knowledge are concerned almost exclusively with empirical evidence. They include, as well as experimental methods of the natural sciences and quantitative social scientific techniques such as social surveys and experimental designs, those more controversial processes such as psychoanalysis and individual case studies. These procedures are concerned with causes and consequences and with identifying these, as far as possible, through empirical procedures. Obviously, the

interpretive element is likely to be greater in child welfare, as in all social sciences, than in the natural sciences, but it would be wrong to use this to disqualify child welfare from the scientific community since interpretative concepts are also an essential feature of physical sciences.[27]

The nature of child welfare science, as King and Piper term the social and behavioural sciences dealing with children, will lead to conflicting conclusions from time to time. As they put it, '[h]ow does the social worker choose between the different theories of child development or between research results which draw attention to very different factors for predicting child abuse?'[28] The inexact nature of child welfare science flows directly from the nature of the phenomenon which it studies - human behaviour[29] - and, as King and Piper argue, the context in which it operates:

> The problem for child welfare which distinguishes it from the physical sciences is ... to be found in the context in which its knowledge is applied rather than in the knowledge itself. In order to make its way in the world it has been forced to coexist in close proximity with other non-scientific discourses, such as law and politics, because, apart from the psychoanalyst's consulting room and the observation psychologist's studio, it has no decision-making forum, no social institution where its procedures control the construction of reality.[30]

Law, of course, does have such forums. And within its own discourse its view will prevail 'by force of law'. It can in that sense create its own reality about children, childhood, and the effects of television. Law can allow 'balances' to be struck which make no sense to those in discourses outside legal discourse. And it can do this by selecting those aspects of social science discourse which fit the reality it wishes to construct.

An example of this is contained in the Report of the Australian Parliamentary Committee inquiring into video material. This committee was particularly concerned with the effect of the availability of sexually explicit or 'X-rated' video material on the community. In relation to the harmful effects of such video material the authors of the dissenting report asserted[31]:

> What became clear to us was the flexible use of data, both statistical and of a research nature, by protagonists of both the harmful and 'unproven-harm' points of view. The interchangeable use of material, often taken out of context, made us particularly wary of accepting the conclusions of the research. It is widely recognized by researchers that much work in the social, behavioural sciences is invalidated because researchers build into their hypotheses and

research models, the biases which lead to their research work supporting their expectations. We have been alert to the warning sounded by Edward C. Nelson, a clinical psychologist, who, in an extract he provided to the Committee from a book he co-edited, said:

> ... there is considerable evidence to show that people tend to interpret evidence so as to maintain their initial beliefs – a finding which challenges the simple assumption that data relevant to such beliefs are processed impartially. This research indicates that judgements about the value and meaning of scientific evidence are biased by the consistency of that evidence with the reader's attitudes, beliefs and expectations. Through such biased assimilation, individuals tend to reject empirical evidence that disputes their initial views and to accept and derive satisfaction from evidence that appears consistent with their beliefs. (Maurice Yaffe and Edward C. Nelson, eds, *The Influence of Pornography on Behaviour*, Academic Press, London, 1982, p. xi)

It was in this context that the dissenting report analysed the various studies placed before it. The process was not one of 'scientific' evaluation – indeed, how could such an evaluation be made given the inherent bias in research? - of each study but a quest for the truth laced with a suspicion of those who conduct such research. The conclusion they reached reflects this juristic approach to the evaluation of the social science research on the harmful effects of video material:

> The interpretation of available crime data does not support the view that there is a cause and effect relationship between the use of 'pornography' and sex crimes. Although it would seem plausible to many that there is a relationship given the purported 'seediness' of pornography, we could not say, given the evidence, that there is a definite causal connection. It is interesting to note that the Fraser Committee was 'not prepared to state, *solely on the basis of the evidence and research it has seen*, [original emphasis] that pornography is a significant causal factor in the commission of some forms of violent crime, in the sexual abuse of children, or the disintegration of communities and society.'[32]

This is not cited to question the validity or otherwise of the stated conclusions *per se*. Rather, it is to the process of reasoning that attention is drawn. The minority on the Committee employed an approach which examined the evidence as a court might, assessing credibility and questioning its reliance not in terms of the particular research but under a suspicion that researchers in general may be biased. It also sought a causal connection in an area which by its nature carries such doubts. King and Piper may retort:

> To define child welfare as nothing more than a collection of subjective, often contradictory, opinions stemming from class and cultural values, fails to distinguish procedure from performance. Child welfare decisions may at times be ineffective and its interpretations may have ideological undertones, but this does not affect the scientific nature of the discourse or the knowledge produced within the discourse. Its communications are very different in kind from those in which lawyers or politicians are engaged.[33]

Of further note is the manner in which the minority on this Committee utilized the conclusions of a particular clinical psychologist who provided a critique of the research methods of others which clearly fitted the approach they adopted. This co-option of one behavioural science view of the research clearly gave an appearance of legitimacy to the arguments contained in the dissenting report about the reliability of the evidence presented to the Committee. But on what basis was this particular view of research chosen and included as throwing light on the questions facing the Committee? King and Piper take the view that this is done on the basis of the extent to which the 'other' views of the world fit with the discourse of law:

> It is not enough to state that law and child welfare science are different autopoietic systems each using their own procedures for constructing reality, for within the domain of child welfare science knowledge there exist a diversity of sub-discourses which themselves produce different versions of reality, albeit using 'scientific' procedures. From these different versions law acknowledges and actively promotes those which are compatible with its own autopoitic nature. These are given the status of *psychology-within-law* or *psychiatry-within-law*. Law produces, therefore, not only versions of children, childhood, parents and parenthood as epistemic subjects, but also versions of child psychology and child psychiatry. Law's version is reinforced by those self-selecting experts whose daily concerns and theoretical orientations (or absence of theoretical orientation) both draws them into law and then traps them within the legal discourse.[34]

ALTERNATIVE LEGAL DISCOURSES: FROM VULNERABLE CHILD TO CHILD CITIZEN

What all of this means is that how one creates a framework for the regulation of television for children will greatly depend on how one views the child, the proper role of childhood and the extent to which the law can incorporate those various views of childhood into legal discourse. Yet many reports on children and television begin not with an articulation of the 'child' but with a desire to harness television for the 'public interest' in relation to children and their viewing. In other words, the nature of childhood is assumed rather than stated and thus the objectives in relation to children and television remain vague and uncertain as a consequence. Instead of asking whether the role of television regulation is to reinforce respect for parents, protect children from harm or teach children independent thought, there is a tendency to support all of these aims without recognizing that they emanate from different paradigms and so often conflict with each other. We cannot ignore the existence of abuse of children within their own families. It may be a simple matter to assert all of these objectives at a general level, but instilling respect for abusive parents who might also harm their children and stifle independent views on how they should live illustrates the potential for contradictions with respect to the aims of a broadcasting policy built around 'parental guidance' and family viewing, for example.

This tendency to suppress discussion of the relevance of the various paradigms of childhood in debates about television further confuses any discussion about programme content. It seems impossible to judge the quality of such content without having some clarity with respect to the meaning of childhood. If the role of television is to conceal the realities of social life from children and keep them blissfully happy in their ignorance then the conclusions one draws from the content of programming will be quite different from what one might say if the objective is regarded to be the encouragement of children to be informed and engaged with social issues. Again, it is easy to draw conclusions which most will agree with though for perhaps quite different reasons. For example, a recent parliamentary inquiry in Victoria, Australia, into the impact of television and multimedia on children and families began its report with the assertion:

> Most people would agree that television as a medium is neither wholly good nor bad for children. Television cannot be easily characterized nor its content simply categorized. Programming can be stimulating, creative and of high quality or it can be dull and badly produced; it can display positive social interactions among people, or it can portray violence and antisocial behaviour. Children are often cognitively active when watching television. There is now a solid base of data showing that even very young children watch television actively. They attend when the content is comprehensible and interesting; they do something else when it is incomprehensible or uninteresting. They learn from television. When programmes are

planned and designed to teach, children can learn academic skills, information and social values. Even when programmes are not designed to teach, children learn from them and sometimes what they learn is antisocial aggression or negative stereotypes.[35]

The difficulty with this statement is that what is to be regarded as 'stimulating, creative and of high quality' will differ with different views of childhood held by different people. For those who desire children to be exposed to challenging ideas about problems such as child abuse, youth suicide or the use of drugs, programming which incorporates such issues into the storyline will be feted. But others who wish to preserve children as 'innocent angels' will likely regard such programmes as damaging to the child. That such views of programmes are heavily value laden is apparent from the inquiry's reference to how children learn from television. Planned and well designed programmes according to this parliamentary committee teach 'academic skills, information and social values'. But one may ask, just whose social values will such programmes promote? And how does one define a negative stereotype? Indeed, how does one define positive traits without at the same time defining negative ones?

Official reports on television appear to avoid such questions. It is easy to claim that television is many things to many people, that it is good and bad at the same time and leave it at that. To analyse the role that different conceptions of childhood have on social and political debate about television is both confronting and challenging as it opens up the true extent to which our societies embrace cultural diversity and difference. The idea of childhood is really about ideas to do with the type of people we hope our children grow up to become. That is, ideas about children and their role in society ultimately come to be ideas about the type of citizenry we expect society to have. If we truly embrace diversity then we should not expect, nor even necessarily encourage, parents to all possess the same hopes and expectations for their children.

The problem is that such notions can be perceived as being socially divisive. Parents who seek programming which confronts their children with the 'realities' of life may be seen as bad parents by those who consider such programmes as harmful. How can one construct a regulatory framework for television which embraces such different values? It is easier to assert that television can be 'good or bad' without defining too clearly which programmes fall into which categories. Who then will disagree? Such statements reflect a compromise for political reasons rather than provide any insight into the problem. They also suggest that such matters as the quality and content of television programmes and their effect on children are matters for scientific inquiry rather than ideological analysis.

In contemporary debates about children and television the protection paradigm continues to represent the 'commonsense' view of children's interests. But as Barker and Petley observe, this has more to do with the views of adults than any inherent truth about how children should be seen:

> Campaigns about the media have an inevitable accompaniment: the incantation of phrases about the 'need to protect children'. This is the flip-side of the worries about 'dangerous classes', of course, since they are often spoken of as 'childlike'. Only rarely does this come right to the surface ...
>
> Usually, though, just to repeat the phrases about children is enough – who but a fool or villain would not want to protect them? It somehow is never enough to reply that real, live children are complex beings who survive many worse things than a scary story or two. The reason for this is that this whole discourse is not about real, live children but about a *conception of childhood*.[36]

They then quote Dorfman and Mattelart who suggest that what we see at work here is an attempt to perpetuate a fantasy about the nature of childhood:

> [A]dults create for themselves a childhood embodying their own angelic aspirations, which offer consolation, hope and a guarantee of a 'better', but unchanging future. This 'new reality', this autonomous realm of magic, is artfully isolated from the reality of the everyday. Adult values are projected onto the child, as if childhood was a special domain where these values could be protected uncritically ... Thus the *imagination of childhood is conceived as the past and future utopia of the adult*.[37]

Barker and Petley conclude that the conception of childhood which is invoked here 'is so empty as to be manipulable; it can be turned to political uses, charged with the emotions that we do really feel for our children.'[38] While their main concern is to explain the manner in which debates about violence on television have been conducted to create a moral panic, it can also be seen from their discussion how the notion of the innocent child can be called upon from a range of perspectives for various purposes. The idea of the 'innocent child' is a notion very similar in its application to the legal principle that matters affecting children should be done according to their 'best interests'. Just as there would be few who would wish to harm the innocent child, so too there would be few who would desire actions to be undertaken contrary to the best interests of children. Yet in both cases what determines whether or not action is taken to protect the child or is in the best interests of the child is vague, unclear and often can conceal other less praiseworthy action.

The idea of the child's best interests, for so long regarded as an integral part of family and child welfare law, has been seriously challenged in recent years as a fiction which underpins idiosyncratic views of decision-makers in matters affecting children.[39] This challenge has even been articulated by a judge of the High Court of Australia, who said of the best interests criteria in matters associated with the welfare of children:

> It is arguable that, in a field where the law has not developed, where ethical principles remain controversial and where each case turns on its own facts, the law should not pretend to too great a precision. Better, it might be said, that authority and power be conferred on a suitable repository – whether it be parents or guardians, doctors or the court – to decide these difficult questions according to the repository's view as to the best interests of the child in the particular circumstances of the case. In that way, it can be said, the blunt instrument of legal power will be sharpened according to the exigencies of the occasion. The absence of a community consensus on ethical principles may be thought to support this approach. But it must be remembered that, in the absence of legal rules or a hierarchy of values, the best interests approach depends upon the value system of the decision-maker. Absent any rule or guideline, that approach simply creates an unexaminable discretion in the repository of the power.[40]

That case involved the sterilization of an intellectually disabled child. The majority of the court held that such a sterilization would be permissible provided court approval was granted, the court being guided by the 'best interests' formula when making its decision. Justice Brennan dissented, holding that such a procedure would never be justified for simply therapeutic reasons. His dissent must rank as one of the strongest judicial critiques of the 'best interests' principle written to date. His argument was that if one is to protect the autonomous rights of any powerless group then one cannot compromise their rights by trading them off against the interests of others. In effect this is to weaken the rights of the powerless, possibly to the point of non-existence. His judgment connects well with the personal paradigm of childhood which places more emphasis on the independent rights of the child to bodily integrity than the protective powers of the parent to decide their child's welfare according to their view of the child's best interests – a process which too easily allows for the interests of the parents to override any real consideration of the child's position. Justice Brennan was clearly suspicious of an approach that would have the child's future needs determined by well meaning, but not necessarily objective, adults in a manner that simply opened the process to considerations far removed from the welfare of the child.[41]

These concerns are no less relevant in the field of the regulation of television as it affects children. It is implicit in many debates about the need for such regulation that the child is a vulnerable being in need of protection from certain images and content, while at the same time he or she is a being who is maturing towards adulthood and so requires programming which assists in that developmental process. These views of the child are often in competition with each other, as some programmes may scare the child yet provide information which assists their understanding of the world. In addition, some commentators argue that children need to be protected from violence on television even though they may be drawn to such programming. There are deep psychological reasons behind why children may wish to view such material, such as peer pressure, the vicarious experience of violence and even morbid curiosity.[42] But whatever the reason, the prevailing view amongst such commentators is that children need to be protected from such material.

The community has within it a number of different beliefs and perceptions of television. It is criticized for promoting passive viewing, that it is too visual, suppresses imagination, reduces concentration spans and entices children away from other more valuable learning experiences.[43] These are all views that can be criticized as being false.[44] Television has been described as a 'plug-in drug'[45] and has been blamed for the criminal activity of the young.[46] At the same time it has been promoted as an important source of information and learning experiences, particularly for disadvantaged children, as Huston and Wright maintain:

> Publicly broadcast television is the most democratic and equitably available medium we have in modern society. Virtually every family with children has a working television set. For many families, turning on the home television is less costly than travelling to a free public library. Videocassette recorders are found in more homes than is cable subscription, and the use of selected children's videotapes in place of broadcast viewing would be a healthy trend, for in order to be on a child's bookshelf, a videotape has to have been rented, purchased or taped off the air by a deliberate parental action. By contrast, access to cable stations, computers, or the Internet requires continued investment. The continuing media revolution is raising important questions about equal opportunity for children from rich and poor families, particularly given the fact that income inequality among families with children has increased considerably since the 1970s. For the 20-plus per cent of the children in the United States who live in families with incomes below the poverty threshold, and for the many more living in near poverty, constructive television offers a resource to reduce educational and institutional inequality. We as a society ought to be working much harder to use it effectively to teach all children things they will need to know in an electronic age.[47]

This point underscores the importance of what is at stake here. Children can benefit from television and should have a right to seek programming which prepares them for adulthood. But who will assert that right on their behalf? The concern is that adults – broadcasters, regulators, politicians and parents – will compromise that right to allow their claims to prevail. For this reason it is important that the child's need for better programming be reconceptualized as an independent right of the child, capable of being claimed by the child or in his or her name. It is this which will protect the child from the harshness of market forces, not vague notions of the 'public interest' based on a protectionist approach to children and reliant on others for its interpretation.

This idea that television can be made better for children lies beneath many campaigns for the improvement of programming for children. But these campaigns often fail to properly articulate their vision of the nature of childhood. It is assumed that 'better' television for children is a known quantity, presumably on the basis that it is somehow instinctively known what childhood should be too. One champion of 'better' television for children, former United States Federal Communications Commission chairman, Newton Minow, has described television as a 'vast wasteland' and has called for a reinterpretation of the 'public interest' concept as it applies to television broadcasters. His argument is that the notion of public interest in communications law was left vague in order to encourage investment in broadcasting while retaining some capacity to reject licence applications so as to ration the available channels.[48] The result is that there has been little accountability for broadcasters due to the absence of a clear definition of public interest in the law.[49] Improved accountability to the public interest would lead to better programming for children according to this argument.

What Minow fails to see is that there is no singular 'public interest'. There are many views of the public interest, not just from those with consumer and commercial interests in television, but also within those who purport to represent children. As I have argued in this and the preceding chapter, while the idea of the innocent or vulnerable child has pervaded much of the writing on television regulation for many years, there is a rapidly evolving idea of the child which stresses the independent capacity of the child. This idea of the child is being articulated more often within legal discourse as it stems from the ideologies of human rights and equal rights. It is an idea which does not rely on the 'scientific discovery' of what may harm children as the critical factor in determining what protection children require, but instead stands on a value position which regards personal autonomy as paramount in a democratic society because it is through the ability to assert one's right to self determination that the interests of an individual are most effectively advanced.

Thus those who wish to preserve the innocence of childhood will bemoan commercial broadcasters' attempts to market to children as leading to the destruction of childhood. But those who advocate for the independent rights of children will regard such broadcasting as market-place information which children, as much as adults, have a right to view. Likewise, while some complain about the screening of the violent images of the World Trade Center being attacked as being harmful to children, others will argue that children too need to understand the world we live in. Minow reveals his particular conception of childhood when he discusses the manner in which television has, as he would see it, blurred the boundaries between the 'adult world' and childhood:

> In the Middle Ages, before most people could read, there was no clear distinction between childhood and adulthood, such as there was fell at about age seven, when a child's knowledge of the world was deemed to be roughly equal to that of most adults. The invention of the printing press changed people's perceptions of childhood by greatly extending the reach of adult literacy and, simultaneously, the range of knowledge separating children from adults. In fact, widespread adult literacy gave rise to the very concept of childhood, and to the corresponding idea that children are possessed of special rights and protections owing to their innocence and ignorance.
>
> Television changed all that. Unlike the theatre and cinema, it comes directly into the home, and unlike printed stories, its tales are not cautionary ones or moral lessons but commercial products whose purposes are hidden from small children. Unlike any print medium, television's stories are accessible to any child, no matter how young, physically and emotionally dependent, or illiterate. In fact, television establishes a new standard of visual literacy, which requires none of the intellectual or reasoning skills necessary to understanding print, but merely eyes to see.[50]

Thus Minow cites authors such as Postman who has argued that television has caused childhood to 'disappear'[51] and claims that the effect of television has been to 'breach the boundaries of childhood'[52]. The point of course is that Minow is witnessing not the destruction of childhood by television, but the loss of a particular view of what it means to be a child. It may be true that television is opening up to children 'a new world' – the question is whether that world only belongs to adults. Minow would have it that there is a clear distinction between the 'adult' world and the child's world:

> Between 1950 and 1960 television dropped the veil from the adult world, making available to children many of the experiences and knowledge theretofore available only to adults. In doing so, television also served to undermine the authority of the adult world – government, schools, church, parents – to lay down the rules of

social behavior. Through television, even the smallest children could see men blown apart on a battlefield a world away; they could witness real and fictional murders, riots, wars, and natural disasters. They could watch cartoon characters shoved through keyholes, thrown off cliffs, run over by trucks, ripped through with buckshot. Anything that adults could see, they could see too. What might once have been judged inappropriate for a thirteen-year-old, television made available to toddlers not able to speak. And for most children, whose frame of reference is smaller than an adult's, the statistical and physical aberrations appearing on television became the norm.[53]

Is this division between the two 'worlds' so clear? Children too are the victims of violence in the home, have been subjected to forced removal from their families in the case of indigenous children,[54] the victims of child migration schemes between the United Kingdom and Australia often resulting in their physical and sexual abuse,[55] are the targets of prejudice when they belong to immigrant groups or minorities, and witness poverty and deprivation in many communities. What Minow seems to be mourning is a peculiarly middle-class view of childhood, safe and secure in its innocence of the all the world's ills. This is simply not the world for many children. Their world is perhaps even more stark and unsafe than the world that is often portrayed on television. For those children the problem may be that television depicts violence and brutality at times, but that it sanitizes it and does not therefore impart the knowledge and skills to assist children to deal with the reality of it in their own lives.[56]

Regulation of the relationship between children and television then is not simply about the role of television in society but is ultimately about competing conceptions of childhood. It is therefore about what we want our children to be. The problem is that this is not always recognized by policy-makers for, as mentioned above, what childhood is about is often assumed rather than properly articulated. This absence of thought and the degree to which this creates difficulties for state regulation of television is apparent when we examine the various schemes which exist to regulate television and the way in which it interacts with children in various parts of the world.

CHAPTER 3

Regulating the Relationship between Children and Television

The point is that we cannot decide, once and for all, whether it is parents, teachers, counsellors, psychologists, family courts, judges or whatever, who know what is best for children. In important matters, nobody can know better than the child himself.
(John Holt, Escape from Childhood *(Pelican, 1974), pp. 175–6)*

The regulation of television as it affects children tends to be achieved in a number of ways: the imposition of standards and programming requirements, the use of ratings or classification schemes and support for the production of children's programmes. In this chapter I will focus on the systems of programme standards and programming requirements as well as classification schemes which operate in four countries: Australia, the United States, Canada and the United Kingdom. Although the support of children's programmes – through such structures as foundations set up to finance productions of 'children's drama' – is part of an overall approach to the nature and quality of children's programming it does not raise immediate regulatory issues, and so I have decided to leave it outside the current discussion.

The regulation of television is now heavily influenced by the philosophy of 'self-regulation', with imposed requirements or codes only where it is thought industry regulation will not necessarily protect the interests of certain groups. This makes the idea of 'self-regulation' problematic. Regulatory authorities retain the power to veto industry formed codes of practice or impose their own conditions on broadcast licensees to protect certain interests, such as those of children. It can be claimed that commercial broadcasters in the countries discussed here have internalized the need to protect children – as their own codes attest to – and this appeases those in the community who adopt a conception of the child as in need of such protection. It does not, however, address the extent to which children have independent rights or needs in broadcasting. In addition, there is a clear tension between the views of children which fit the needs of broadcasters wishing to create markets for their sponsors and of those in the community who seek to deny to children the status of consumer. In the former case the broadcaster would much prefer that children be seen as competent to make choices in the market-place. This requires some acceptance that children – though this would not so readily apply to very young children – have independent minds which can make decisions about their own interests. Those who are more protective of the child, on the other hand, are wary of exposing children to the perils of the market-place, fearful of the child being manipulated by advertising ploys. Thus to the extent that commercial television's codes of practices and other regulatory requirements do express the need to protect the vulnerable child, given the imperative of commercial broadcasters to generate profit, it is open to question just how far that protectionist objective will be taken by such interests.

A distinction must also be drawn between commercial television and state-owned television stations in those countries which have the latter. Although the regulation of both types of broadcasters follows similar principles, there are occasional differences to note. Historically, state-owned television did not have the motive of creating markets for sponsors through the chase for ratings. In this case, they could see children in slightly broader terms than a 'market'. While this aspect of state-run television still has some currency, demands that even state-owned television account for their public investment through evidence of popularity in ratings, together with merchandizing opportunities arising from programming, has somewhat blurred the distinction between commercial and state-owned television.

AUSTRALIA

(a) Commercial Television

The Broadcasting Services Act 1992 establishes a regulatory regime for commercial broadcasters which is governed by a combination of industry codes of practice with state oversight of those codes together with imposed standards in the case of children and Australian content. It is the Australian Broadcasting Authority which has the responsibility for overseeing this regulation. While the underpinning philosophy of the legislation is industry 'self-regulation', in the area of children's television programming state devised regulation is imposed by way of the Children's Television Standards.

(i) Children's Television Standards

Section 122 of the Broadcasting Services Act requires the Australian Broadcasting Authority to 'determine standards that are to be observed by commercial television broadcasting licensees' that relate to programmes for children. Section 129(2) of the Act further allows the Authority to require that a programme to be classified under the Children's Television Standards is approved prior to broadcast. This is the only exception to the rule that the Authority cannot require pre-approval of programmes.[1]

This legislation empowers the Australian Broadcasting Authority to set standards for 'programmes for children', but this is not necessarily the same as programmes that appeal to children or programmes that children watch. The Children's Television Standards indicate how the Authority has interpreted the power to determine standards in this area. The Standards define children to be those people who are younger than fourteen years of age.[2] The main effect of the Children's Television Standards is to require a television broadcaster to screen a certain amount of children's programmes per year. At present the requirement is to broadcast 390 hours of such programmes per year, 130 hours of which are to be 'P' classification programmes – that is, programmes specifically designed for pre-school children – and 260 hours of 'C' classification programmes – that is, programmes designed specifically for primary school children.[3] It is a further requirement that C classified programmes be broadcast for at least 30 minutes on weekdays, some time between 7 a.m. and 8 a.m. and between 4 p.m. and 8.30 p.m., to a total of 130 hours, with another 130 hours of such programmes to be broadcast in those time periods or between the hours of 7.30 a.m. and 8.30 p.m. on weekends or public holidays.[4] P classified programmes must be broadcast for at least 30 minutes between the hours of 7 a.m. and 4.30 p.m. Monday to Friday.[5]

Previous standards included a compulsory C time of 4 p.m. to 5 p.m. This meant that all commercial broadcasters screened C classified programmes at the same time each weekday. Broadcasters preferred this approach as it meant that there was not competition as all broadcasters had to run C programmes at the same time.[6] As such programmes do not attract any significant advertising revenue they represent a financial burden to the networks. In 1991 the Australian Broadcasting Tribunal (the forerunner to the Australian Broadcasting Authority) decided to free up the C time period so that it was not a fixed one-hour time slot each weekday. This was an attempt, as explained by the Tribunal, 'to encourage quality programmes through competition with popular programmes in prime time and at weekends and to provide the child viewer with more C programmes', provided broadcasters did not continue to screen their C programming at the same as each other.[7]

In practice little has changed and the broadcasters followed precisely what the Tribunal had feared. The 4 p.m. to 4.30 p.m. time slot on weekdays tends to be the period when commercial broadcasters screen C programmes, creating a de facto time period when there is none of the competition envisaged by the Tribunal.

It is important to note that the Children's Television Standards are not designed as a simple classification system of what is 'suitable' for children to view. Rather, the broad objective of the Standards is to improve the quality of children's programming on the basis that 'children should have access to a variety of quality television programmes made specifically for them, including Australian drama and non-drama programmes'.[8] In this sense the Standards are about raising the quality of programming for children through an attempt to redress the market forces which are thought to militate against the production of higher 'quality' programming.

The difficult task is to define 'quality' in this context. The Children's Television Standards do provide criteria for a C or P classification by defining a 'children's programme' as one which:

(a)   is made for children or groups of children within the preschool or the primary school age range;

(b)   is entertaining;

(c)   is well produced using sufficient resources to ensure a high standard of script, cast, direction, editing, shooting, sound and other production elements;

(d)   enhances a child's understanding and experience; and

(e)   is appropriate for Australian children.[9]

How these criteria are to be interpreted presents many difficulties. In 1991 the then Australian Broadcasting Tribunal attempted to explain the terms used. The explanations relied heavily on the concept of 'childhood' without properly articulating what that notion meant. For example, the Tribunal, when discussing the requirement that to qualify for a C classification a C programme must be made specifically for children or groups of children within the primary school age range, commented:

A programme does not necessarily have to include children. But whether it includes children or not, the programme needs to deal with issues of interest to children and from a child's perspective. Many well intentioned programmes have failed because of an adult orientation, overly complex language and concepts, or tedious interviews with adult 'experts'.[10]

This requires some understanding of a 'child's perspective' as opposed to an adult orientation. So here again we are thrown back to our discussion of conceptions of the child. Are we to take the perspective of the sweet innocent child, or the child who has been exposed to the world in all its depravity? The Tribunal also drew a distinction between programmes which are aimed at a family audience rather than those which are made specifically for children.[11] The test which is posited to determine this distinction was whether the action and script are 'child driven'. If the children are removed, asked the Tribunal, is there still a story? If yes, then the programme is likely to be targeting a family audience rather than being 'child specific'.[12] This test remains in the guidelines issued by the Australian Broadcasting Authority to assist in the assessment of children's programmes.[13] It may be a worthy objective to seek programmes which are for children alone, but there will be many in the community who would regard 'family viewing' as the very type of programmes that children should be viewing. And in any event, it is still a vexed question as to whether programmes made for children alone, as opposed to a family audience, might mean programming that children might be attracted to but which adults may regard as inappropriate. Clearly, this is not the intention of the Standards, but there seems no reason why as a matter of logic this could not be the case.

The degree to which the administration of these criteria relies on subjective judgements about children is further exemplified in the current guidelines on the assessment of C and P programmes. The Australian Broadcasting Authority has stated:

> There may be some confusion about programmes that children like and programmes that are made specifically for them. They are not mutually exclusive, but just because children enjoy certain types of programmes it does not mean that they are made specifically for them. On the other hand, a good children's programme will be made specifically for the age group and will be enjoyed by the age group.[14]

Once again this requires some understanding of what is appropriate for an age group. The Authority does not attempt to unravel what that might mean in its discussion. Clearly, this criteria and its interpretation raise child development issues. While a member of the Authority makes the ultimate decision to classify, it is based on the recommendation of officers of the Children's Television Section and, where considered necessary, also on the advice of independent consultants.[15] This is an approach well used in matters affecting children – to act on the advice of child welfare or child development experts. But this process makes two assumptions. The first is that it assumes that there is a clear consensus on such matters within the disciplines being consulted. Often there is not. The second assumption that is made is that the question of what is suitable for children is a scientific question at all.

What is missing from the process is any recognition that ideas about childhood will change over time and therefore what is a suitable programme for the C or P classification will also alter. This whole process also depends on the personnel involved in the decision-making process, as what might be considered to be a 'good' programme will be subject to the particular conceptions of childhood of those who classify. It is not a simple matter of applying criteria based on an objective truth about children's programming. The regulatory regime fails to write into the rocess any consideration of this aspect of the decision-making, relying istead on standards which present as unclear and highly subjective.

Similar problems arise with respect to other criteria in the Children's 'elevision Standards. In relation to the requirement that C and P rogrammes must be 'entertaining', the Australian Broadcasting Tribunal 1 1991 wrote that 'a poor children's programme is often full of clichés, ne dimensional characters, is flat and badly written, and tries to be worthy" rather than entertaining.'[16] This statement is repeated in the irrent assessment procedures.[17] On the other hand, the Australian roadcasting Authority regards a good children's drama programme to be ne which includes 'a good story, humour, unpredictability, appropriate ace and presentation in a contemporary visual style.'[18]

While there is little doubt that the proponents of such a formulation ould not expect uniformity in programming, there is a certain notherhood' aspect to the explanation of this criteria. It would seem ifficult to make any sense at all of this criteria, nor its explanation above, ithout having in one's mind a particular conception of childhood and iereby a view of the 'child audience'. After all, what is an 'appropriate' ace for a children's programme and how does one determine npredictability in this regard? The answer must be that it has to be ssessed from the perspective of the child. This is borne out in discussion f the requirement in Children's Television Standard 2(c) that children's rogrammes must be 'well produced using sufficient resources to ensure a igh standard of script, cast, direction, editing, shooting, sound and other roduction elements.' The Australian Broadcasting Authority has issued uidance on this requirement:

In terms of production, this criterion requires professional casting, performance and direction and maintenance of the child, rather than an adult, perspective.

In terms of direction it means using all the craft, skill and technique expected by a sophisticated children's audience experienced in the traditions of film and television.

Scripts which are too thin, derivative, too long to engage and sustain a child audience, too focused on adults or adult issues, or which contain gratuitous violence or unsafe practices for children would be unlikely to meet this criterion. Also programmes containing stiff and awkward performances by major characters which result in a poor realization of the characters would be unlikely to meet the criterion.[19]

'he explanation given by the Authority of this criterion thus relies very ieavily on a distinction between the adult world and the world of hildren. But even within this explanation there are contradictions. On the one hand there is a sense of children lacking the concentration powe of adults to be able to sustain themselves through certain types o programming, while on the other hand there is resort to the 'sophisticatec children's audience' when discussing the direction qualities required There is here evidence of conflicting images of the child and childhood a work.

What has to be asked is whether the Children's Television Standard are really about meeting the needs of children at all. Perhaps they can be better understood as a process through which a particular idea o childhood is constructed. This is evident in the above guideline when one considers the reference to 'adult issues' and the note that programe 'which contain gratuitous violence or unsafe practices for children' woule not meet the criterion. Such notions cannot be properly articulatec without first having clarity about what one understands about the meaning of childhood. In these guidelines such an understanding is assumed, anc the assumption clearly is that 'the child' is an immature and vulnerable being.

This is not to say that there is no consideration of what childhood i about in the discussion of the Standards by the Australian Broadcasting Authority. The requirement in Children's Television Standard 2(d) tha children's programmes should enhance a child's understanding anc experience has led the Authority to state that compliance with the criterion necessitates an appreciation of the developmental stages of the child:

> Children's programme producers should understand the emotional, intellectual, social, and other characteristics relevant to specific age groups of children and create programmes that address the specific needs and interests of those children.

> Producers should take care to ensure that developmental issues are appropriate to the age group. For example, the concept of births, death, historical time, games with rules, lying or punishment undergo several distinct changes between the ages of 6 to 12 years. Also, proverbs are not usually understood until 12 to 14 years, riddles are not appropriate until mid-primary years, and quiz questions should be appropriate to the target age group.[20]

Of course, childhood is a developmental period. But this understanding of childhood is itself subject to contests about the pace at which children develop. The view of children put forward in Australian Broadcasting Authority documents coexists with laws which place criminal responsibility on children at ten,[21] regard children competent to make decisions about their health care and medical treatment before they turn sixteen in certain cases,[22] and able to express their wishes at any age in family court

matters where the child's best interests are being determined.[23] It is true
that such provisions can be understood as part of a developmental view of
childhood also, for example, the weight to be given to the child's wishes in
the Family Court of Australia will be dependent on the 'child's maturity or
level of understanding'.[24] But the idea that any child may express a wish in
such cases comes from an alternative discourse which regards with
suspicion any attempt to discover the child's best interests without paying
any attention to the views of the person most affected. In this sense, it is a
progression towards acknowledging the child as an autonomous being
irrespective of age. For sure, the ability of the child to claim independent
rights may well depend on their level of maturity, but there is a distinction
between being regarded as autonomous from the outset and only
acquiring that status after one reaches a certain stage of development.

The arguments of King and Piper discussed in the preceding chapter are
particularly salient here. The contradictions in the laws, or as in this case,
the regulatory framework, surrounding children can be understood as the
result of a process whereby the social policy objectives of the community
must then be translated into a legal form. At this point there will be
problems of expression, conflict with other objectives and discourses
within the law and inevitable political compromise. Thus, while few
would disagree with the aim of 'quality programming for children', the
legal problem is how that is to be expressed in rule form. This is not a
problem of political will, nor simply a problem with the language and
form of the law. It goes to the heart of legal culture – that there is not one
legal discourse. There is a legal discourse which speaks to protection and
nurture of the weak and vulnerable. But there is also another legal
discourse which supports the independence and autonomy of children as a
means to protect them from tyranny. In the latter discourse there is the
further problem of the articulation of 'children's rights', a concept which
in itself contains many tensions.[25]

One could look to the Children's Television Standards and critique
them on the basis that they are full of well meaning but nevertheless vague
criteria. In this sense they may achieve the political objective of pleasing
everyone in their broad terms but actually achieving little in terms of their
inability to properly define the type of programming which qualifies under
their requirements. The problem of course is that the administration of the
standards is ultimately about the type of children we wish to produce in
society and therefore is also about competing conceptions of childhood.
This leads to the difficult and vexed issue of the degree to which the state
should interfere in the family and the raising of children. The irony of the
Children's Television Standards is that they are expressed as if there is a
natural consensus in society about both the meaning and purpose of
childhood and the role of the state in the family. There is no such
consensus.

The consequence of this lack of agreement is that the law must avoi
rather than address these conflicting views about children for the sake o
social cohesion. Thus the terms of the Standards can at one level be seen t
be ambiguous to achieve this objective. At the same time, a view o
childhood which is implicitly reinforced by the very existence of th
Standards is that that there is a need to protect immature and innocer
children from 'bad' programming. This is of course then compromised i
practice by the minimal requirements imposed on broadcasters. Th
obligation is to broadcast only seven and a half hours of children
programmes per week, and most of this is done in common time perioc
at least tacitly agreed to by all broadcasters, thus reducing the commerci
risks involved. It is also the case that such programmes are aimed at onl
younger children in Australia, thus completely avoiding the problem o
addressing the problem of what childhood means for older childrer
Finally, the Standards are not legislated in the formal sense but operate a
administrative requirements. This avoids at the political level any detaile
debate about these issues. It is in many ways 'left to the experts
Nevertheless, the overall impression created by the Standards is tha
children require protection from what would be a lack of programmin
for their needs if they did not exist.

Standard 10 continues to reinforce the view of childhood implicit i
the Standards – that children must be protected - through the manner i
which it states how programmes will be deemed unsuitable for childre
during the C and P periods, that is during programmes directe
specifically to pre-school and primary school age children:

> No programme, advertisement or other material broadcast during a
> C period or P period may:
>
> a. demean any person or group on the basis of ethnicity, nationality,
>   race, gender, sexual preference, religion, or mental or physical
>   disability;
> b. present images or events in a way which is unduly frightening or
>   unduly distressing to children;
> c. present images or events which depict unsafe uses of a product or
>   unsafe situations which may encourage children to engage in
>   activities dangerous to them;
> d. advertise products or services which have been officially declared
>   unsafe or dangerous by a Commonwealth authority or by an
>   authority having jurisdiction within the licensee's service area.[26]

The promotion of programmes based on anti-discriminatory practic
appears unobjectionable but even here there is the problem of how on
educates children about the reality of discrimination. Is the message her
that this is not an issue to be broached at all with young childrer

Vagueness also appears in this Standard too. The presentation of images and events cannot be 'unduly frightening or unduly distressing' to children. The emphasis here is on the word 'unduly', suggesting that some fright or distress is acceptable. But when does it become undue? At this point it is clear that the issue passes from the legal arena to the child sciences. And that is hardly regulation at all. The Standards also state requirements with respect to Australian content in children's drama. A broadcaster must televise 32 hours each year of first release and eight hours of repeat Australian children's drama.[27] Advertising to children is also covered by the Standards and is discussed in Chapter 6 below.

(ii) Codes of Practice

As part of the system of self-regulation of broadcasting, section 123 of the Broadcasting Services Act 1992 requires commercial broadcasters to develop codes of practice in consultation with the Australian Broadcasting Authority. The Act requires these codes to address such matters as the prevention of the broadcasting of unsuitable programmes as determined by community standards, the protection of children from harmful programming and the classification of programmes based on community standards, the protection of children from exposure to programme material which may be harmful to them, and the classification of programmes based on community standards.[28] The codes must also take account of community attitudes with respect to depictions of physical and psychological violence; sexual conduct and nudity; the use of offensive language; drugs, alcohol and tobacco; vilification of any group based on race, gender, sexual preference, age, religion or disability; and any other area of concern to the community.[29] A further legislative requirement in relation to the content of the codes is that the system of classifying films for broadcast is to be the same as the system used by the Office of Film and Literature Classification.[30] The codes must also provide that films classified as 'M' (recommended for viewing for persons over fifteen) be broadcast between 8.30 p.m. and 5 a.m. and between the hours of noon and 3 p.m. on schooldays,[31] and that films classified as 'MA' (suitable for viewing only by persons over fifteen) be broadcast between 9 p.m. and 5 a.m.[32] This latter provision came about in direct response to 'community concern' about the type of films being shown in the 'M' period and prior to the use of the 'MA' classification for television.

The codes of practice must then be registered by the Australian Broadcasting Authority if it is satisfied that the Code contains 'appropriate community safeguards' with respect to its content, has the approval of a majority of broadcasters covered by it and there has been an opportunity for public input.[33] There are also provisions which allow the Authority to review the codes and determine its own standard where a Code is failing 'to provide appropriate community safeguards' with respect to a matter in section 123(2).[34] The codes can also be amended by Parliament.[35] Thus, while there is a high degree of industry input into the construction of codes of practice, the legislation places some limitations on the extent to which a Code is the product of the industry. Nevertheless, this is a different process to the previous system where the Australian Broadcasting Tribunal had much greater powers to determine and impose television standards.

Commercial Television Australia is the industry body which represents 'free to air' commercial television in Australia. It has developed a Code of Practice which is registered with the Australian Broadcasting Authority under the above provisions. The content of this Code grants children little autonomy with respect to television viewing from its outset. One of the objectives of the Code is to 'ensure that viewers are assisted in making informed choices about their own and their children's television viewing.'[36] 'Children', it seems, are not synonymous with 'viewers'. It is with respect to the classification of programmes that the Code has most relevance for the relationship between television and children. The classification system for all programmes – not just films as is required by the Act – is in effect the system of film classification applied by the Office of Film and Literature Classification.[37] The Code divides the day into classification zones and requires that 'only material which is suitable for a particular classification zone is broadcast in that zone'.[38] While the classification system is not expressed as being only concerned with the regulation of television for the benefit of children, it is implicit in the system that this is much of its purpose. However, to the extent that the system of classification performs more general functions it is still the case that the idea of the child plays a central role in the allocation of a particular classification to a programme.

The Code creates a hierarchy of classifications: G, PG (Parental Guidance), M (Mature), MA (Mature Audience), AV (Adult Violent) and material not suitable for television. Each classification has a corresponding time zone during which only material classified at that level or lower may be screened. The G time zone is from 6 a.m. to 8.30 a.m. and then 4 p.m. to 7.30 p.m. weekdays and 6 a.m. to 7.30 p.m. on weekends.[39] The PG time zone is from 5 a.m. to 6 a.m., 8.30 a.m. to 12 noon, 3 p.m. to 4 p.m. and 7.30 p.m. to 8.30 p.m. on weekdays that are also schooldays (during school holidays the zone extends to include 8.30 a.m. to 4 p.m. during the day) and 5 a.m. to 6 a.m. and 7.30 p.m. to 8.30 p.m. on weekends.[40] The M time zone is 12 midnight to 5 a.m., 12 noon to 3 p.m. and 8.30 p.m. to 12 midnight on weekdays that are also schooldays, and 8.30 p.m. to 5 a.m. on weekdays during school holidays and weekends.[41] The MA time zone is 9 p.m. to 5 a.m. on all days.[42] The AV time zone is 9.30 p.m. to 5 a.m. on all days.[43]

The classification system can be viewed as an example of the way in which the law co-opts child welfare science into its discourse but in the process modifies and changes the meaning of that terminology as it becomes a part of legal discourse. The classification system appears to be premised on the notion that as children mature they are able to understand more difficult concepts and can be exposed to images on television that might be harmful if they were shown to younger children. It is thus the idea of the 'maturing child' borrowed from child development theories which is built into the classification process. But once the 'maturing child' becomes part of the classification system – that is, part of legal discourse – the near impossible task of determining objectively whether particular programmes are suitable or not suitable for children, and if so at what age level, becomes not a matter for child welfare sciences but the legal and regulatory process. That process readily becomes one where reliance is placed on the classifiers' idiosyncratic views as to how programmes should be classified.

The resultant scheme has the appearance of an ordered system with clearly stated criteria ready to be applied to programmes presented for classification. But it operates as a smokescreen which disguises the value positions of those undertaking the task of classification. If there is a consensus as to what a G or PG or M programme looks like, then it has more to do with the extent to which certain value positions about what is appropriately screened on television at particular times of the day have been internalized by large sections of the community than it has to do with the strict application of the administrative criteria contained in the Code of Practice. The degree to which the Code obscures the process in this way rather than clarifies it can also be seen upon close examination of the classification criteria. The 'G' classification criteria, for example, state that programmes classified under this heading are 'not necessarily intended for children' but the programmes so classified 'must not contain any matter likely to be unsuitable for children to watch without supervision.'[44] The Code continues to set out more detailed criteria under which a programme may be classified G:

2.11.1 Violence: Visual depiction of physical and psychological violence must be very restrained. The use of weapons, threatening language, sounds or special effects must have a very low sense of threat or menace, must be strictly limited to the story line or programme context, must be infrequent and must not show violent behaviour to be acceptable or desirable.

2.11.2 Sex and Nudity: Visual depiction of, and verbal references to, sexual behaviour must be brief, infrequent, contain little or no detail and be strictly limited to the story line or programme context. Restrained, brief and infrequent visual depiction of nudity only when absolutely necessary to the story line or programme context.

2.11.3 Language: Mild expletives or language which may be considered socially offensive or discriminatory may only be used in exceptional circumstances when absolutely justified by the story line or programme context.

2.11.4 Drugs: Visual depiction of, or verbal reference to illegal drugs must be absolutely justified by the story line or programme context, contain very little detail and be handled with care. The programme must not promote or encourage drug use in any way. The use of legal drugs must also be handled with care.

2.11.5 Suicide: Only limited and careful verbal reference to suicide is acceptable, when absolutely justified by the story line or programme context, and provided that it is not presented as romantic, heroic, alluring or normal.

2.11.6 Social or Domestic Conflict: Themes dealing with social or domestic conflict must have a very low sense of threat or menace to children.

2.11.7 Imitable and Dangerous Behaviour: Imitable and dangerous behaviour should only be shown when absolutely justified by the story line or programme context, and then only in ways which do not encourage dangerous imitation.

2.11.8 Other: Where music, special effects and camera work are used to create an atmosphere of tension or fear, care must be taken to minimize distress to children.

Many of the criteria for a G classification thus require judgements about what constitutes 'distress to children', what may cause them a 'very low sense of threat or menace' or what behaviour they may imitate. In all of the above criteria the sense is that the manner in which a programme deals with the listed areas is to be at the 'lower end' of the scale, 'strictly limited to the story line', 'absolutely justified by the story line or programme context' or 'handled with care'. These words suggest a need to protect children from harmful images, yet they might also support an argument that they justify exposing children to certain realities of life, for such programming may find justification in its reality as opposed to gratuitous scenes depicting violence or drugs, for example. The point is that although the classification criteria might suggest to some that this is an administrative process in which categories are objectively applied to programmes, there are clearly matters of judgement which can only be made by reference to views of children which will be subjective and often contested. The most significant judgement to be made is what is unsuitable for 'children', yet it seems that more stress is placed on the word 'unsuitable' than how children are to be understood. For while the criteria attempt to unpack the notions of what is suitable and unsuitable, at no turn is there any attempt to define the child.

The other classification criteria contain similar ambiguities. The PG classification is centred on programming which 'may contain careful presentations of adult themes or concepts but must be mild in impact and remain suitable for children to watch with supervision.'[45] The Mature classification is for material recommended for viewing for persons over fifteen,[46] while the Mature Audience classification is 'suitable' for viewing only by persons over fifteen.[47] The distinction between the M and MA classification seems to be a fine one, the major distinction appearing to be a 'higher level of intensity' with respect to sexual depictions, coarse language, adult themes or drug use. Another distinction is that programmes classified M carry with them the consumer advice that they are 'recommended for mature audiences' while programmes classified MA or AV carry the consumer advice 'suitable only for adult audiences'.[48]

The classification system clearly relies on notions of the 'child', the state of being 'mature' and the 'adult' – none of which can have any uniformity of meaning. For the child though, the distinction drawn between what is 'suitable' for children and what is 'appropriate' for a mature audience at the least suggests that the 'maturing child' is not a concept readily embraced by this classification system. It is of course true that the system states fifteen to be the age at which children might be included in an adult audience and that the idea of parental guidance for younger children supports a view that the system does embrace some scope for the gradual inclusion of the child in the audience which will be exposed to more 'adult' concepts and themes. To the extent that a fifteen-year-old is still a child, does this suggest that at least some children are being recognized as having a degree of maturity sufficient to allow them to view 'adult' programmes?

The answer to this question is not clear. In setting the age of fifteen as the cut-off point above which people may be included in the most mature audience for television programmes, it must be asked whether this challenges the view of the child as immature and not competent. It has to be considered whether the general view of the child which permeates the classification criteria is one which regards the child as someone needing protection and so as a consequence the setting of the mature audience threshold at fifteen has instead the effect of limiting the suitability of programming which might comply with the upper-level classifications. It would seem odd that a classifier at one moment is to work with a view of the child as vulnerable and impressionable but then will readily discard that view of the child for one which accords to a fifteen-year-old the competence to handle complex and confronting programming. The twist then is that one consequence of the classification system is that in the M, MA and AV criteria the use of fifteen as the age threshold combined with a culture of the vulnerable and impressionable child may well combine to limit the type of programming which adults are able to access on television. The idea of the child can thus be used in ways which extend far beyond the regulation of what is screened to children, and in practice operate as a control on the programming in effect deemed to be suitable for adults.

(b) Australian Broadcasting Corporation

The state-owned Australian Broadcasting Corporation (ABC) has its own legislation and is not subject to regulation by the Australian Broadcasting Authority.[49] It has nevertheless developed a Code of Practice which is notified to that Authority.[50] The ABC Code of Practice makes little explicit reference to children. There is a 'specific programme code' for children's programmes which simply states:

> While the real world should not be concealed from children, special care will be taken to ensure programmes children are likely to watch unsupervised will not cause alarm or distress.[51]

In relation to news items there are some references to children:

> 4.8 News Flashes. Care will be exercised in the selection of sounds and images used in news flashes and consideration given to the likely composition of the audience.

> 4.9 News Updates and News Promotions. Television news updates and news promotions should not appear at inappropriate times, especially during programmes directed at young children. They should include very little violent material and none at all in the late afternoon and early evening.[52]

The ABC Code of Practice also applies the classification system of the Office of Film and Literature Classification to its programming and thus the ABC Code of Practice replicates the Commercial Television Code of Practice in this regard. The ABC Code also refers to matters of content, such as sex, violence and language. In doing so there is no specific reference to the age of the audience although the overarching principle of the ABC Code is 'context':

> The guiding principle in the application of the following general programme codes is context. What is unacceptable in one context may be appropriate and acceptable in another. However, the use of language and images for no other purpose but to offend is not acceptable.

The code is not intended to ban certain types of language or images from bona fide dramatic or literary treatments, nor is it intended to exclude such references from legitimate reportage, debate or documentaries. Where appropriate, audiences will be given advance notice of the content of the programme.[53]

There is little doubt that the ABC programmers would operate with a similar approach to children as exists in the commercial television context: that much is apparent from the statements in the ABC Code of Practice which do refer to children. The ABC is also required to have regard to the standards – which must include the Children's Television Standards – determined by the Australian Broadcasting Authority.[54] The views of childhood which are implicit in those standards are thus likely to be internalized within the ABC. Indeed, 'children's programming' for pre-schoolers which is produced by the ABC has won many accolades and would be fairly judged to be consistent with the professed aims of the Children's Television Standards discussed above. However, it must be recognized that the special position of the ABC as a broadcaster with a Charter to be innovative and independent[55] might explain the lesser emphasis on age-specific criteria in its Code of Practice when compared with the commercial television equivalents.

(c) Other Television Services

Codes of practice also exist for the publicly-owned multicultural Special Broadcasting Service (SBS), Pay-TV, and Community television stations. In the case of the SBS Code of Practice there is recognition of the special brief the channel holds to reflect the multicultural diversity of Australia. Unlike other codes, it states as part of its function its role:

to counter attitudes of prejudice against any person or group on the basis of their race, ethnicity, nationality, gender, *age*, sexual preference, religion, physical or mental disability, occupational status, or political beliefs. While remaining consistent with its mandate to portray diversity, SBS will avoid broadcasting program-ming which clearly condones, tolerates or encourages discrimination on these grounds. (my emphasis)[56]

This is one of the rare mentions in a code of practice of age discrimination as a special concern of a broadcaster.[57] This at the least suggests the possibility of highlighting age discrimination against children and young people and approaching their needs from a concern with their independent rights rather than vulnerabilities. In other areas such as violence and news reporting the SBS Code follows the pattern of other codes – to exercise care in reporting certain events or screening violence 'given the likely composition of the audience'[58] – the usual obscure reference to the child audience. On the use of violence the Code attempts to strike the usual balance between the need to protect children and allow for the depiction of reality:

> 3.2 Violence and Suicide. SBS acknowledges that violence is part of everyday life which must be dealt with responsibly. SBS recognizes that for many people, particularly children, the portrayal of physical and psychological violence has a unique potential to distress and disturb. Accordingly, it is SBS policy to keep violence in its programmes to a minimum and in no circumstances to present it gratuitously.[59]

The television codes for SBS and Pay-TV also apply the uniform classification system of the Office of Film and Literature Classification. In the case of Pay-TV there is recognition of the contractual relationship between the subscriber and the broadcaster which gives rise to its role as a 'niche' broadcaster.[60] While the effect of the classification system is that Pay-TV operators are unlikely to utilize a different conception of the child than commercial television, the shift in the nature of the service, such as 24-hour cartoon channels, means that there can be other effects on children and the idea of childhood through the availability of subscription television, particularly with respect to seeing the child as a 'consumer'.

The Community Television Code of Practice has one reference to children:

> 2.4 Community broadcasting licensees will establish programming practices which protect children from harmful programme material.[61]

This suggests a fundamental dilemma for community television. The aim of community broadcasting is to increase access to the air waves, as is reflected in their Code of Practice:

> The purpose of this code is to encourage programming that reflects the principles of community broadcasting; to break down prejudice and discrimination; and to prevent the broadcast of material which is contrary to community standards.[62]

The dilemma lies within this objective. If such broadcasting is to break down entrenched views about certain groups within the community, then how can it advance the idea of childhood as one which carries with it rights and autonomy if community standards are still grounded within a framework which adheres to the idea of childhood as one within which children have little capacity for independent action and require protection from harm rather than exposure to social life? This is the criticism which can be levelled more generally at the codes which operate in Australia. The child is presented as a one-dimensional figure, vulnerable and easily harmed. There is little evidence in those codes that the child is capable of determining some matters alone. Even when the older child is mentioned, as in the M and MA classification, the suspicion is that this operates more as a brake on what adults will be able to view than a liberation of the child from the shackles of the particular view of childhood evident elsewhere in the codes.

UNITED STATES

The Australian approach of devising children's television standards may be contrasted with that of the United States, where a legislative basis has been given to the aim of achieving quality programming for children. In the United States the Children's Television Act 1990[63] requires the Federal Communications Commission (FCC) when reviewing broadcast license renewal applications to 'consider the extent to which the licensee ... has served the educational and informational needs of children through the licensee's overall programming, including programming specifically designed to serve such needs.'[64] This has, of course, raised the question of how 'educational' and 'informative' programming is to be defined under the Act.[65] It is possible to engage in the usual legalistic analysis of those words: but that discussion makes little sense without some consideration of the broader context within which this law operates, in particular the manner in which it conceptualizes the child.

The very existence of the Children's Television Act, with its aim of catering for the special needs of children, is some evidence that children have been identified as a special group in the United States. But what is not clear, as is the case with the Australian Children's Television Standards, is how effective such law can be in delivering improved children's programming, for, in spite of the existence of such legislation, the quality of programming for children is often criticized. One analysis might not fault the law, but instead blame the difficulty in achieving quality programmes for children on a lack of commitment to 'public interest' obligations on the part of broadcasters. Others may cite a lack of precision in the law as to what that commitment actually entails as being the problem. Such a critique of the law is presented by Kunkel:

> While the Children's Television Act was heralded as a landmark that would establish accountability for broadcasters' public-interest obligations to children, the language of the law did not specify what was actually required.[66]

The difficulty is in determining how one would be able to specify such requirements in the law. It does not seem to be a simple matter of stating with greater clarity the public interest requirements under the Act, as it is the public interest requirement which is heavily contested by different interest groups in broadcasting. Once the public interest concern is translated into a legal need to broadcast a particular type of programming – educational and informational – the focus shifts to the meaning of those words in the statute. The problem with defining 'educational and informational' under this Act is then not one of precise language, but lies with the determination that people with different perspectives bring to the debate, convinced that their meaning is correct. This can be appreciated through an understanding of the history of the legislation.

The Federal Communications Commission (FCC) explains how it will enforce the Children's Television Act through rules which it issues. As Kunkel points out, prior to the passing of the Children's Television Act, the FCC had taken the view that self-regulation would be sufficient to provide quality programmes for children and that no further directives were required. In time this approach came to be regarded as a failure in that 'good' programmes for children were thought to have all but disappeared by the 1980s. In a response to public opinion Congress passed the Children's Television Act in 1990.[67]

But this was the beginning rather than the end of debates about quality programming for children in the United States. The Act does not specify what 'educational' and 'informative' programming is and it fell to the FCC to clarify the concepts. At first the FCC resisted to do so due to the ideological bent of the members of the Commission who favoured free market approaches over government regulation.[68] Thus the FCC adopted a definition which was broad and general – educational programming was defined as that which 'furthers positive development of the child in any respect, including the child's cognitive/intellectual or emotional/social needs.'[69] Also, the definition of a child was taken to be those under sixteen years of age.[70] Thus the United States approach at this point differed markedly from the Australian aim of targeting programming for younger children.

Inevitably, the imprecision of the definition applied by the FCC led to concern with the nature of the programming said to comply with the Act. One study found that many of the programmes claimed by broadcasters to comply with the Act were in fact programmes made for general audiences or programmes such as cartoons with little to suggest they were educational.[71] This was a direct result of the vagueness of the rules. Kunkel cites one example:

> Under Alfred Sikes, who resigned as chairman of the FCC the day before President Clinton took office, commission officials had argued that 'the law is so vague that stations were well within their rights to say that shows like *Leave it to Beaver* were educational.'[72]

The new FCC chairman appointed by President Clinton, Reed Hundt, is credited with initiating the process which saw the FCC attempt to better define the requirements of the Children's Television Act and move towards a three hour per week quota of children's educational programming.[73] This began with a Notice of Proposed Rule Making in April 1995.[74]

But this shift in approach was to be no radical departure from the past. The vague criteria for educational programming previously adopted had created a situation whereby broadcasters could allow their commercial interests to prevail over the 'public interest' in children's programming. This might have suggested the need for more direct intervention on the part of the state. The FCC proposal, however, was still grounded in the importance of the market-place as the controlling force for quality in programming. Primarily, the responsibility for ensuring that children's interests would be met fell to the 'market' according to the FCC:

> In developing these proposed changes, the Commission has followed three principles. The first principle is that judgments of the quality of the licensee's programming, educational or otherwise, are best made by the audience, not by the federal government. To enable audiences to make these judgments, the Commission must ensure that key members of the market – e.g. Parents – receive the information they need to participate in a meaningful fashion. Therefore we propose to require broadcasters to identify educational programming in materials provided to publishers of television schedules, and to improve the quality of, and public access to, the information broadcasters make available regarding their efforts in providing children's programming. By improving the information available to parents and local communities, we can enable them to be better informed consumers, influencing the market through their choices . . .[75]

As Kunkel asks, just who are the consumers or audience of television? In response to the claim that the legislation has not delivered 'quality programming' for children, Kunkel expresses little surprise:

> The most simple explanation for the lack of educational programming for children is that most television in the United States is driven by fundamental commercial interests. The economics of the industry are such that (with the exception of public broadcasting) two key factors dominate decisions about what content will be aired. First, the material must appeal to the widest possible audience, an axiom popularly known as the Law of Large Numbers. Additionally, there is a bias toward presenting programs that will attract viewers with the greatest potential buying power, also known as the Law of Right People. Both of these factors reflect the principle that television broadcasters derive their revenues from advertisers, who are in fact the true 'clients' of the industry.[76]

The point we must return to further explain the dearth of educational programming is the lack of clarity as to what precisely constitutes such programming. While Kunkel makes valid points about the profit motives of broadcasters, he still fails to understand that 'quality' children's television is not a given and that such a concept can only be understood by reference to the particular conceptualization of the child to which one subscribes. This is a point in fact well understood and exploited by broadcasters themselves. Apart from the *Leave it to Beaver* example cited above, in seeking to claim their adherence to the Children's Television Act, broadcasters have submitted that cartoons fulfil the requirements of educational programming when their content in that regard might be questionable.[77] To some extent this has been addressed by the rules announced in 1996 which require educational programming to have a clear educational objective, have a target age group, be regularly scheduled and broadcast between 7 a.m. and 10 p.m. In addition there are improved reporting procedures to the FCC in which broadcasters must state how they have been complying with the Act. These changes are seen as positive by certain community based groups who seek improved quality in children's programming.[78] Nevertheless, the definitional problems remain and the flexibility with respect to the time period during which the required programming must be screened suggests a large amount of discretion continues to reside with the broadcaster.

Clearly, ongoing faith in the market-place constrains the extent to which clarity can be brought to the educational and informational objectives of children's programming. A more important constraint, however, which operates with respect to the role of the market is the manner in which concern with profit interacts with a view of the child as special, vulnerable and innocent to produce a particular type of programming for children, possibly cheap to produce, which does not challenge deeply held views about childhood yet confirms their marginal place in the broader society. If children were viewed as active participants in civic life, there is little doubt that children's programming would reflect that. But children's programming constructs the child as 'special' and in need of nurture on adults' terms. This may well suit the needs of the corporate world which may prefer to see 'educational and informational' programmes which inform children about innocuous subject matter than programmes which teach children to question the values of the market-place. A glance at the reports supplied by broadcasters to the FCC pursuant to their obligations under the Children's Television Act would appear to confirm this occurs. Included on the list of 'core' educational television programmes for one reporting period in one locality were such programmes as *Disney's Lloyd in Space*, *The New Adventures of Winnie the Pooh*, *Bob the Builder*, *Skate*, *This Week in Baseball*, and *Where on Earth is Carmen Sandiego?*[79] All of these

rogrammes have related merchandize or are associated with activities
hich have products connected with them.

-chip classification

1 the mid-1990s V-chip technology – which blocks programmes
1rough the use of embedded codes in broadcast signals – began to be
resented as the key to ensuring parents could screen from their
hildren programming which they did not wish them to see. It thus
ained popular support as it allowed for 'parental guidance' even when
arents could not be, or did not want to be, present while their children
iewed television. It also seemed to represent a technological solution to
problem which appeared fraught with moral judgements – just what
1ould a parent allow their child to see on television? Technology, it
emed, would provide the answer.

Legislation to require the use of V-chip technology in television
roadcasts and reception was passed by the United States Congress in
996. The sections of the Telecommunications Act 1996[80] which provide
or this technology to be utilized are headed 'violence', which indicates the
olitical context within which this law was passed. It was much to do with
erceived connections between juvenile crime rates and the influence of
levision. The law in effect was responding as much to a fear of children
nd not, as is often suggested, simply a need to protect children. If
nything was being protected it was the *idea* of childhood as a time of
nnocence. Violence, however, was not the only concern. The number of
eenage pregnancies in society has also fuelled concerns about the sexual
ehaviour of young people and the role television plays in influencing
exual mores. Some of this stated concern is no doubt to do with the cost
o the state of welfare payments for single parents. The Act articulated a
emarkable number of assumptions and assertions with respect to the
elationship between television and children. It begins:

SEC. 551. PARENTAL CHOICE IN TELEVISION
PROGRAMMING.

(a) FINDINGS – The Congress makes the following findings:

(1) Television influences children's perception of the values and
behavior that are common and acceptable in society.

(2) Television station operators, cable television system operators,
and video programmers should follow practices in connection with
video programming that take into consideration that television
broadcast and cable programming has established a uniquely
pervasive presence in the lives of American children.

(3) The average American child is exposed to 25 hours of television

each week and some children are exposed to as much as 11 hours of television a day.

(4) Studies have shown that children exposed to violent video programming at a young age have a higher tendency for violent and aggressive behavior later in life than children not so exposed, and that children exposed to violent video programming are prone to assume that acts of violence are acceptable behavior.

(5) Children in the United States are, on average, exposed to an estimated 8,000 murders and 100,000 acts of violence on television by the time the child completes elementary school.

(6) Studies indicate that children are affected by the pervasiveness and casual treatment of sexual material on television, eroding the ability of parents to develop responsible attitudes and behavior in their children.

(7) Parents express grave concern over violent and sexual video programming and strongly support technology that would give them greater control to block video programming in the home that they consider harmful to their children.

(8) There is a compelling governmental interest in empowering parents to limit the negative influences of video programming that is harmful to children.

(9) Providing parents with timely information about the nature of upcoming video programming and with the technological tools that allow them easily to block violent, sexual, or other programming that they believe harmful to their children is a non-intrusive and narrowly tailored means of achieving that compelling governmental interest.[81]

Although headed 'parental choice', it is to the last sentence of the section that this law leads – the 'compelling governmental interest' in ensuring that parents are provided with the means, not to choose, but to 'block violent, sexual or other programming that they believe to be harmful to their children'. Given the 'findings' by Congress with respect to the effects that television has on children, it would be difficult for a parent not to choose to block much of this material without appearing to be an irresponsible parent. It is also important to note the reference in the Act to this technology being a 'non-intrusive' means to achieve the 'compelling governmental interest' in blocking violent and sexual content in broadcasts. This addresses the legal requirement for the restriction on First Amendment guarantees of free speech. It is not expressed here as restriction of the child's rights, of course, as they are hardly recognized at all. But we have to consider the purpose for which freedom of speech operates. Without the V-chip it would be necessary to block such programmes at source and that would raise clear First Amendment issues

or the free speech of broadcasters. By passing the blocking power to
arents, the broadcasters may speak although their audience is more
imited. Yet what if they wished to speak in their programming to
hildren? The legislation does not consider that at all. Once the
rogramming is constructed as 'dangerous' it appears justified to block
uch programming in a manner which purports to be 'non-intrusive'. The
question has to be asked though, as to how non-intrusive is this method?
t is true that the broadcasters rate the programme, but pursuant to a state
pproved rating system. It is true that parents decide which rating level to
block, but only after their need to be 'responsible' parents is reinforced in
various ways, including promotion of the technology itself. These
ttitudes to parenting and the place of children in society, especially with
espect to their perceived lack of need to receive information
ndependently of others, are internalized by all involved and allow for
he control of children's television viewing in a highly intrusive manner
or the child.

As this indicates, the rating system is central to the operation of V-chip
echnology. A rating code enables the signal to be encoded with a rating
hat the V-chip can identify and then block. A television rating code was
hus legally required to be set up by the new Act, as was a requirement that
elevision sets be fitted with the required technology.[82] The rating system
which was adopted was based on the rating system for films and used by
he Motion Picture Association of America. The rating classifications now
n place are as follows:

TV-Y (All Children – This program is designed to be appropriate
for all children.) Whether animated or live-action, the themes and
elements in this program are specifically designed for a very young
audience, including children from ages 2–6. This program is not
expected to frighten younger children.

TV-Y7 (Directed to Older Children – This program is designed for
children age 7 and above.) It may be more appropriate for children
who have acquired the developmental skills needed to distinguish
between make-believe and reality. Themes and elements in this
program may include mild fantasy or comedic violence, or may
frighten children under the age of 7. Therefore, parents may wish to
consider the suitability of this program for their very young children.
Note: For those programs where fantasy violence may be more
intense or more combative than other programs in this category,
such programs will be designated TV-Y7-FV. For programs
designed for the entire audience, the general categories are:

TV-G (General Audience – Most parents would find this program
suitable for all ages.) Although this rating does not signify a program

designed specifically for children, most parents may let younger children watch this program unattended. It contains little or no violence, no strong language and little or no sexual dialogue or situations.

TV-PG (Parental Guidance Suggested – This program contains material that parents may find unsuitable for younger children.) Many parents may want to watch it with their younger children. The theme itself may call for parental guidance and/or the program contains one or more of the following: moderate violence (V), some sexual situations (S), infrequent coarse language (L), or some suggestive dialogue (D).

TV-14 (Parents Strongly Cautioned – This program contains some material that many parents would find unsuitable for children under 14 years of age.) Parents are strongly urged to exercise greater care in monitoring this program and are cautioned against letting children under the age of 14 watch unattended. This program contains one or more of the following: intense violence (V), intense sexual situations (S), strong coarse language (L), or intensely suggestive dialogue (D).

TV-MA (Mature Audience Only – This program is specifically designed to be viewed by adults and therefore may be unsuitable for children under 17.) This program contains one or more of the following: graphic violence (V), explicit sexual activity (S), or crude indecent language (L).[83]

This classification system has many similarities with the Australian version for programming generally, although it does divide 'children' into a few more groups, from very young to older. The initial ratings did not provide any content advice, relying solely on age based classifications. This was criticized by parents in research studies as being unhelpful.[84] The problem with any classification system is to determine whether the relevant criteria for a particular rating have been satisfied. But as Cantor points out, a programme rated at a higher age level for sexual content would not carry with it the advice that there is also violence in the programme but at a lower age level than the other content.[85] The content advice given only relates to the reason for the higher rating as that is the only rating required to operate the V-chip blocking device set for a particular level. The broadcasting industry also claim to give more than one rating is too complicated.[86]

The industry's viewpoint that a mix of ratings becomes complicated may dishearten those who present themselves as 'parent's advocates', but there may be some validity in the stance of broadcasters. The complication, though, may be more to do with the fundamental assumptions that the rating system is based upon. As will be discussed in the next chapter, there is no simple definition of 'violence', particularly in the fantasy world of television. As Cantor critically notes in relation to the form of the rating system:

> The industry's insistence on using euphemisms, rather than describing content clearly and accurately, was a major complicating factor. Refusing to accept the three levels of sex, violence, and coarse language that most advocacy groups had recommended, the industry insisted upon adding D for situations in which sex is talked about but not shown. In addition, they balked at using the word 'violence' to refer to the mayhem that goes on in many children's shows, such as *Power Rangers* or *The X-Men*. Instead, they use the letters 'FV' to refer to fantasy violence – whether the violence is indeed of the impossible variety or whether it is quite realistic but simply performed by animated characters. In the case of D and FV, the change was insisted upon by the industry to reduce the possible loss of advertising revenue that they expected the word 'sex' on the one hand, or 'violence' on the other would cause.[87]

While she is critical of the industry stance, the notion that 'fantasy violence' is a legitimate label is difficult to dispute in the absence of any clarity of definition in the first place. Such use of the classifications also indicates the significant cultural meaning attached to the ratings and so the various interests which attempt to influence how and when they are applied. Advertisers may wish to be associated with 'positive' ratings, although as Cantor claims, age based ratings also produce a 'forbidden-fruit effect' whereby children will want to view programmes rated above their age range.[88] This is akin to film producers wishing to avoid a 'G' (general classification) rating for fear of making the film less attractive to the lucrative teenage market. Classification systems thus provide producers with the knowledge they need to acquire a higher age rating – some additional coarse language, or a fleeting nude scene may be sufficient to increase the rating and make the film more marketable and attractive to, usually, older children.

The classification or rating system devised to allow for blocking technology to 'assist' parents in filtering the television viewing of their children thus becomes caught in the market interests of the broadcasters. There is, however, another aspect to this with implications for the conception of childhood at work in television law. The idea that parents should employ technology to prevent children from viewing certain programmes ultimately relies on a view of children as little angels and little devils – angels that are likely to be harmed by sex, violence or language, devils who may be tempted by classifications which suggest to them the possibility of lurid viewing. The broadcasters also identify children as a market to which their sponsors may wish to market their goods. The idea of childhood broadcasters may then work towards is one which conceptualizes children as being sophisticated enough to discern the 'attraction' in a programme with a 'higher' rating as distinct from programmes with lower ratings. Thus, while one understanding of the thought behind V-chip technology is that the child requires parental supervision and it is to parents that the advice is pitched, another view is that children may well utilize the advice contained in rating systems and decide what they will watch – V-chip permitting. This can also be exploited by broadcasters and advertisers. It is these opposing views of the capacity of children which ultimately sits beneath the ratings system. It is not simply a battle over the appropriate labels to apply.

CANADA

The Canadian Radio-television and Telecommunications Commission (CRTC) is the regulatory body established in Canada which oversees television broadcasting. Under the Broadcasting Act 1991 broadcasting policy is stated to include the objective that it 'serve the needs and interests, and reflect the circumstances and aspirations, of Canadian men, women and children, including equal rights, the linguistic duality and multicultural and multiracial nature of Canadian society and the special place of aboriginal peoples within that society.'[89] The Act provides that the CRTC has the responsibility for regulating broadcasters in Canada in accordance with the broadcasting policy set out in the Act.[90] The CRTC has issued policies in relation to such areas as TV violence,[91] gender portrayal[92] and a broad policy framework for Canadian television.[93] This latter policy contains specific provisions on children's programming. It states under the heading 'children's programming':

> 65. The Commission maintains its current policy of not requiring conventional licensees to broadcast minimum quantities of pro-gramming directed to children and youth. For television stations that are part of the largest multi-station ownership groups, programs directed to children or youth in the priority categories will qualify as priority programs[94] when scheduled in the peak viewing period of 7 p.m.–11 p.m.

> 66. The Commission's decision to expand the definition of peak time will provide an appropriate viewing time for family and childrens' programs.

> 67. The Commission has examined the availability of children's programming offered by the broadcasting system as a whole, including the CBC, educational services and specialty and pay services. The majority of conventional English- and French-

language television broadcasters offer children's programming on a regular basis, and the system as a whole provides a wide variety of Canadian and foreign programming directed to children and youth. In addition, children's programs have an extended life cycle, as 'evergreen' programming enjoyed by many generations. The recognition of the excellence of Canadian children's programs, and its exportability ensure its availability without a regulatory requirement.[95]

It is unclear as to the extent to which the Canadian policy distinguishes family programmes from children's programmes, particularly in the light of the reference to those programmes often having inter-generational appeal. It is also of note that the time period within which such programmes might be broadcast extends to 11 p.m., which appears to be late in the evening when compared with other countries' discussions of times relevant for children's programming. In this context 'programs directed to children or youth' seems to be an extremely vague concept.

The only other express reference to children in the policy is in relation to the care required of broadcasters when programming for the evening period:

> 42. The Commission recognizes that, while the largest audiences for television programs are available after 8 p.m., the audience between 7 p.m. and 8 p.m. is very significant, both because of its size and the fact that it tends to be made up of large numbers of children, youth and adults.

> 43. The Commission expects that broadcasters will address the needs and expectations of their audiences when planning programming for the evening period. The Commission is convinced that greater flexibility in scheduling will expand opportunities for broadcasters to provide high-quality and diverse Canadian programming.[96]

This policy statement could support programming that, when broadcast to an audience which includes children, addresses their 'needs and expectations' in a manner which conceptualizes the child as desirous of programmes that challenge stereotypes of young people and seeks to educate, inform and entertain them. The other interpretation, of course, is that it is the 'needs and expectations' of the parents watching that will be addressed by broadcasters and that they will not provide programming that parents deem to be unsuitable for children. It is more likely that the latter is the direction in which programming will proceed given the assumptions about children which tend to prevail in the context of broadcasting. This can be seen from an examination of the other regulatory mechanisms in Canada.

The other body in Canada with special responsibility in the area of television standards is the Canadian Broadcast Standards Council. It has the role of policing the self-regulation of Canada's private broadcasters.[97] This regulatory function includes the application of codes on ethics,[98] violence[99] and sex role portrayal.[100] The Code of Ethics contains special references to the place of children with respect to 'children's programs':

1. Recognizing that programs designed specifically for children reach impressionable minds and influence social attitudes and aptitudes, it shall be the responsibility of broadcasters to provide the closest possible supervision in the selection and control of material, characterizations and plot.

2. Nothing in the foregoing shall mean that the vigour and vitality common to children's imaginations and love of adventure should be removed. It does mean that such programs should be based upon sound social concepts and presented with a superior degree of craftsmanship, and that these programs should reflect the moral and ethical standards of contemporary Canadian society and encourage pro-social behaviour and attitudes. Broadcasters should encourage parents to select from the richness of broadcasting fare the best programs to be brought to the attention of their children.

3. Broadcasters shall refer to the Voluntary Code Regarding Violence in Television Programming for special provisions relating to the depiction of violence in children's programming.[101]

Children are impressionable, have imaginations and need encouragement to be pro-social and parents have the role of supervisor of their children's viewing. These are the messages from the Code. But where is the child citizen, the future adult or even the maturing child? Such conceptions of the child appear to be invisible in this schema. While the 'richness of broadcasting fare' could embrace a great diversity of material, can it be truly expected, for example, that such broadcasting would challenge deeply held assumptions about the nature of childhood?

In the area of scheduling the Code establishes a 9 p.m. threshold after which one might expect to find an 'adult audience', thus allowing for 'adult viewing'. However, this is complicated with the acceptance that 'older children' may be viewing after 9 p.m., in which case viewer advisories are required to presumably allow parents to make judgements as to whether their children will be permitted to watch. Thus, under the heading 'scheduling' the Code provides that:

(a) Programming which contains sexually explicit material or coarse or offensive language intended for adult audiences shall not be telecast before the late viewing period, defined as 9 p.m. to 6 a.m.

Broadcasters shall refer to the Voluntary Code Regarding Violence in Television Programming for provisions relating to the scheduling of programming containing depictions of violence.

(b) Recognizing that there are older children watching television after 9 p.m., broadcasters shall adhere to the provisions of Clause 11 below (viewer advisories), enabling viewers to make an informed decision as to the suitability of the programming for themselves and their family members.

. . .

(d) Broadcasters shall take special precautions to advise viewers of the content of programming intended for adult audiences, which is telecast before 9 p.m. in accordance with Clause 10(c).

(e) Promotional material which contains sexually explicit material or coarse or offensive language intended for adult audiences shall not be telecast before 9 p.m.

(f) Advertisements which contain sexually explicit material or coarse or offensive language intended for adult audiences, such as those for theatrically presented feature films, shall not be telecast before 9 p.m.[102]

The Code then proceeds to suggest a number of viewer advisories that may be used to inform viewers as to the content of programmes about to be broadcast.[103] What is again observed in this Code is the vague test of 'intended for adult audiences'. This is vague, not because of the intention of the producers, but vague due to the difficulty of ascertaining what an 'adult audience' is to mean. This is given a clear 'legal' meaning in the sense that it can be described as 'not for children'. But such a definition obviously relies on the internalizing of a particular view of the child as having no autonomy in the field of television viewing. This is the almost subliminal message of the Code – that children are passive players in broadcasting who require others to decide matters for them.

The CRTC issued its *Policy on Violence in Television Programming* in 1996.[104] This policy required a classification system be developed to allow the V-chip technology to operate in Canada. As in the United States, the use of this technology is presented as being about parental choice. The website of 'V-Chip Canada' declares:

Television has all kinds of great programming for children that educates, enlightens and entertains young minds.

But not all television programs are suitable for younger viewers. This is why Canadian broadcasters, cable companies and program producers have worked together to develop useful tools to help parents manage their family's viewing choices.

Parents are concerned about the impact of TV on their children. Broadcasters and cable companies also want to ensure that children are not exposed to violence and other content intended for older viewers. This is why Canadian television program rating systems were developed through the Action Group on Violence on Television (AGVOT) three years ago. These program ratings have been displayed by the use of icons on the top left corner of the television screen at the beginning of programs.

As of March 2001, these ratings will also work with V-chip-equipped television sets, to give Canadian parents, guardians and caregivers even more control in screening out shows they do not wish their children to watch.[105]

As occurs in the United States, the emphasis here is on the notion of 'parental control' of children's viewing. There is no discussion of what constitutes 'violent programming', nor is there any consideration of the positive features of children being exposed to a broad range of ideas on television. Instead, the emphasis is on the harmful effects of certain programs and how parents can protect – or control – their children.

The AGVOT[106] classification system which is used for English language programming (the Régie classifies films in Quebec and is used for French language television classification[107]) has the following ratings: E: Exempt; C: Children; C8+: Children eight years and older; G: General programming, suitable for all audiences; PG: Parental guidance; 14+: Viewers 14 years and older; 18+: Adult programming. Each classification is explained in the system thus:

C: CHILDREN

Programming intended for children with this designation must adhere to the provisions of the Children's section of the Canadian Association of Broadcasters (CAB) Voluntary Code on Violence in Television Programming.

As this programming is intended for younger children under the age of 8 years, it will pay careful attention to themes which could threaten their sense of security and well-being. As programming for children requires particular caution in the depiction of violence, there will be no realistic scenes of violence. Depictions of aggressive behaviour will be infrequent and limited to portrayals that are clearly imaginary and unrealistic in nature.

Violence Guidelines
– might contain occasional comedic, unrealistic depictions.

Other Content Guidelines
Language – no offensive language.

Sex/Nudity – none.

C8+: CHILDREN OVER 8 YEARS

This classification is applied to children's programming that is generally considered acceptable for youngsters 8 years and over to view on their own. It is suggested that a parent/guardian co-view programming assigned this classification with younger children under the age of 8.

Programming with this designation adheres to the provisions of the Children's section of the CAB Voluntary Code on Violence. These include not portraying violence as the preferred, acceptable, or only way to resolve conflict; or encouraging children to imitate dangerous acts which they may see on the screen.

Programming within this classification might deal with themes which could be unsuitable for younger children. References to any such controversial themes shall be discreet and sensitive to the 8–12 year age range of this viewing group.

Violence Guidelines

– any realistic depictions will be infrequent, discreet, of low intensity, and shall portray the consequences of violence
– violence portrayed must be within the context of the storyline or character development
– might include mild physical violence, comedic violence, comic horror, special effects; fantasy, supernatural, or animated violence.

Other Content Guidelines

Language
– no profanity
– might have infrequent use of language which may be considered by some to be socially offensive or discriminatory, and then only if employed within the context of storyline or character development.
Sex/Nudity – none.

G: GENERAL

Considered acceptable for all age groups. Appropriate viewing for the entire family.

This is programming intended for a broad, general audience. While not designed specifically for children, it is understood that younger viewers may be part of the audience. Therefore programming within this classification shall contain very little violence, either physical, verbal or emotional.

It will be sensitive to themes which could threaten a younger child's sense of security, and will depict no realistic scenes of violence which minimize or gloss over the effects of violent acts.

Violence Guidelines

– minimal, infrequent
– may contain comedic, unrealistic depictions
– contains no frightening special effects not required by storyline.

Other Content Guidelines

Language
– may contain inoffensive slang
– no profanity.
Sex/Nudity – none.

PG: PARENTAL GUIDANCE

This programming, while intended for a general audience, may not be suitable for younger children (under the age of 8). Parents/ guardians should be aware that there might be content elements which some could consider inappropriate for unsupervised viewing by children in the 8–13 age range.

Programming within this classification might address controversial themes or issues. Cognizant that pre-teens and early teens could be part of this viewing group, particular care must be taken not to encourage imitational behaviour, and consequences of violent actions shall not be minimized.

Violence Guidelines

– any depiction of conflict and/or aggression will be limited and moderate; it might include physical, fantasy, or supernatural violence
– any such depictions should not be pervasive, and must be justified within the context of theme, storyline or character development.

Other Content Guidelines

Language
– might contain infrequent and mild profanity
– might contain mildly suggestive language.
Sex/Nudity
– could possibly contain brief scenes of nudity
– might have limited and discreet sexual references or content when appropriate to the storyline or theme.

14+: OVER 14 YEARS

Programming with this classification contains themes or content elements which might not be suitable for viewers under the age of 14. Parents are strongly cautioned to exercise discretion in permitting viewing by pre-teens and early teens without parent/ guardian supervision, as programming with this classification could deal with mature themes and societal issues in a realistic fashion.

Violence Guidelines

− while violence could be one of the dominant elements of the storyline, it must be integral to the development of plot or character
− might contain intense scenes of violence.

Other Content Guidelines

Language − could possibly include strong or frequent use of profanity.
Sex/Nudity − might include scenes of nudity and/or sexual activity within the context of narrative or theme.

18+: ADULTS

Intended for viewers 18 years and older.

This classification applies to programming which could contain any or all of the following content elements which would make the program unsuitable for viewers under the age of 18.

Violence Guidelines

− might contain depictions of violence, which while integral to the development of plot, character or themes, are intended for adult viewing, and thus are not suitable for audiences under 18 years of age.

Other Content Guidelines

Language − might contain graphic language.
Sex/Nudity − might contain explicit portrayals of sex and/or nudity.[108]

The ratings are fraught with problems of definition and meaning. For example, the C classification − for children under 8 − prohibits 'realistic scenes of violence' but 'portrayals that are clearly imaginary and unrealistic' may be used infrequently. Yet the G classification − for all children − permits 'no realistic scenes of violence which minimize or gloss over the effects of violent acts'. Does this mean that children under eight may be exposed to realistic portrayals under one classification but not another? The C8+ classification proscribes portrayals of violence 'as the preferred, acceptable, or only way to resolve conflict'. Does this limit a programme from suggesting to a child that acting in self-defence may sometimes be acceptable? Violence for children in the C and C8+ classification should not threaten a child's 'sense of security'. But how does television programming meet those cases of children who do not experience security in their own lives? Can programmes include characters that the abused child, for example, might identify with? Another interesting feature of the Canadian system is the 18+ category. While Australia operates with a fifteen year old threshold for 'adult' audiences, and the United States applies a seventeen year old threshold, in Canada the age threshold is the highest for this upper category. This can be seen as restricting children's access to certain programming for a longer period when compared with other countries. But it can also operate to allow for greater diversity in overall programming because in this classification system the older audience may be deemed more able to deal with material which may not be thought appropriate if children under eighteen and over fifteen were included.

Overall, the Canadian policy which underpins this classification system is certainly protectionist towards children and explains the place of children in the scheme as follows:

> The main objective of the Commission's approach has been to protect children from the harmful effects of television violence, while preserving freedom of expression for creators and choice for adult viewers. To accomplish this, the Commission has adopted a cooperative strategy, with a reliance on industry self-regulation. The Commission's approach has also been guided by the principle that all elements of the broadcasting system should appropriately contribute to the attainment of the objectives so that Canadian children will be protected from harmful programming regardless of its source.[109]

The relationship between children and television is clearly stated. They are the potential victims of its harmful effects and their interests are constructed as a possible source of conflict with the interests of both programme creators and adult viewers. This is the concern: that it is not simply the presentation of children as being in need of protection that contributes to a particular construction of the child, but also that children are placed outside the world of creative flair and 'adult' information. The child viewer is not represented as a person to whom the programme producer might wish to reach out to and inform. Instead, the child is constructed simply as a person that may threaten the producer with censorship.

UNITED KINGDOM

The United Kingdom system of television regulation shares similar concerns with those of Australia, the United States and Canada. Section 108 of the Broadcasting Act 1996 (UK) requires the Broadcasting Standards Commission to prepare codes of guidance on violence, sexual conduct and standards of taste and decency in broadcasting. Broadcasters and other regulatory bodies (such as the Independent Television Commission which licences commercial television) must reflect in their codes the 'general effect' of the Broadcasting Standards Commission codes.[110]

One of the main forms of regulation of television with respect to its relationship with children is through the application of the 'Watershed'. This is explained in the Broadcasting Standards Commission's Code on Standards:

> The television Watershed, which starts at 9.00 p.m. and lasts until 5.30 a.m., is well established as a scheduling marker to distinguish clearly between programmes intended mainly for family viewing and those intended for adults. Some 90% of adults are aware of the Watershed and its significance. The Watershed should not be an abrupt change from family viewing to adult programming. It is not a waterfall, but a signal to parents that they need to exercise increasing control over their children's viewing after this time. Parents should also be aware that even programming leading up to the Watershed might not be suitable for all children. The child audience covers a wide age range from very young children to adolescents, and even some 'children's' programmes or news programmes may be unsuitable for younger child audiences. Broadcasters should provide sufficient information to assist parents and others to take the degree of responsibility they feel appropriate for the children in their care.[111]

While there are similarities between the Watershed and classification zones which operate in other countries, it is also apparent from this explanation that the United Kingdom approach is cognizant of the difficulty of precision in matters to do with the suitability of programmes for children. The distinction between 'family viewing' and 'adult viewing' is acknowledged to be blurred and there is no sense that after 9 p.m. children will not be viewing at all. The child audience is also identified as varied and diverse, an awareness not always explicit in other systems, although the Australian fifteen year old threshold for adult audiences may be similar in effect. The lack of use of clear zones is also reflected in the caution that '[b]roadcasters should further bear in mind that children tend to stay up later than usual on Friday and Saturday nights and during school holidays and that programmes which start before 9.00 p.m. and run through the Watershed may continue to be viewed by a family audience.'[112]

There is thus a great deal of reliance on the judgement placed on the broadcaster to consider the likely audience composition: but there are also important value statements expressed through the Code. First, much reliance is placed on the responsibility of parents to guide their children's viewing, with the role of the broadcaster reduced to providing sufficient information about programme content so as to allow parents to make an informed choice.[113] Second, it is implied in the Code that children will be in bed earlier on school nights than non-school nights. Such a statement may be seen to emanate from a peculiarly middle-class assumption about the importance of school, sleep and staying-up. Third, the Code makes reference to the diverse nature of the child audience, 'from very young children to adolescents'. While this pays some attention to the complexity of childhood as a concept it does not take this further and explore the difficulty this creates for any system of regulation which revolves around notions of the child.

The other major concerns expressed in the Code with respect to children are to do with violence, sexual conduct and swearing. Violence and sexual conduct will be discussed in more detail in Chapters 4 and 5. The overall approach is one of concern with the harmful effects on children of such imagery or dialogue. In relation to swearing the Code states:

> The paramount concern of most adults is for children, especially children under 10. In research conducted by the Commission, most respondents (89%) said that all programmes shown before the Watershed should contain language suitable for a family audience. Respondents were also concerned about the use of bad language by those whom children take as role models, for example footballers or pop stars.[114]

The resolution of this issue is left to '[c]ommon sense and a study of the relevant research' which 'should indicate where the areas of difficulty lie'.[115] Once again, the regulatory framework invokes social science research married with that most wonderfully rare commodity according to lawyers – common sense – to provide the answer to how to create appropriate standards of programming. The result is likely to be a vagueness that allows in practice for much latitude.

The general approach in the United Kingdom is thus one which grants a large amount of discretion to broadcasters, peppered with due concern for the child audience. Although the guidelines may be vague at one level, the message is clear. Children are to be protected from harm, distress or upset. 'Appropriate programming' for children is premised on the innocence of childhood. The Independent Television Commission confirms the approach of the Broadcasting Standards Commission. It has a lengthy policy with respect to family viewing and the Watershed:

Material unsuitable for children must not be transmitted at times when large numbers of children may be expected to be watching.

However the ITC accepts that, even though some children are always likely to be present in the audience, the likelihood varies according to the time, subject matter and channel. The majority of homes do not contain children and viewers have a right to expect a range of subject matter.

The necessary compromise is embodied in the ITC's Family Viewing Policy which assumes a progressive decline throughout the evening in the proportion of children viewing, matched by a progression towards material more suitable for adults.

Within the progression, 9 p.m. is normally fixed as the time up to which licensees are responsible for ensuring that nothing is shown that is unsuitable for children. The earlier in the evening a programme is shown, the greater the care required.

Not all daytime or early evening programming will be suitable for very young children. Licensees should provide sufficient information, in terms of regular scheduling patterns and on-air advice, to assist parents to make viewing choices.

After the watershed, and until 5.30 a.m., material more suitable for an adult audience may be shown. However, care should be taken in the period immediately after the watershed. There should be a gradual transition and it may be that a programme will be acceptable at 10.30 p.m. for example that would not be suitable at 9 p.m. Decisions will also depend on the nature of the channel and the audience it attracts. Material which is particularly adult in tone should be scheduled appropriately and clearly signposted.

Particular care should be taken over programmes of special appeal to children which may start before the watershed but run beyond that time; and with programming during school holidays, when children will be part of the audience throughout the day and may also go to bed later. Dates of school holidays vary across the UK.

There is evidence that children find violence which resembles real life more upsetting than violence in a fantasy context but any sequence which might unsettle younger children needs special care. Particular distress can be caused where such violence occurs in a domestic setting and scenes of serious domestic conflict whether or not accompanied by physical violence or threat, can cause fear and insecurity. News bulletins should take account of the Family Viewing Policy (see 1.7(ii)).[116]

This Code relies heavily on the 'progression' during programming periods from family viewing times to adult viewing times. The language of the Code also reflects the idea of 'balance' as it places the concern with children as a competing interest between those homes with children and those without children who expect a range of subject matter on the television screen. The use of the idea of the family is also worthy of remark, as it is implicit here that a 'family' in this context means adults with children, while the 'majority of homes' who do not contain children do not appear to be categorized as families. Instead, they presumably are always 'adult viewers'. This is an important use of the idea of family as it implies that when children enter a home the status of the adults alters to that of protectors of their children.

The Independent Television Commission Code also refers to the European directive in relation to television and harm to children:

1.3(i) Warnings in Relation to Programmes Likely to Harm Children

European Council's Television Without Frontiers Directive 1997 (Article 22.1) requires that broadcasters take 'appropriate measures to ensure that television broadcasts ... do not include any programmes which might seriously impair the physical, mental or moral development of minors, in particular programmes that involve pornography or gratuitous violence'. The legislation also requires broadcasters to include either acoustic warnings before, or visual symbols throughout, to alert viewers to other programmes, broadcast in unencoded form, that are likely to impair the physical, mental or moral development of minors. Such programmes, even broadcast late at night, must therefore, at a minimum, be preceded by verbal warnings to this effect.

Warnings should be included, for example, where programmes include the strongest acceptable sexual material, violence or themes (such as child abuse or the use of drugs) treated in a way likely to be harmful to children.[117]

Although a formal classification system does not exist in the United Kingdom the effect of the direction to warn viewers of particular types of content operates to impose a de facto classification system requirement. This then carries with it the fundamental problem with any classification system – how to determine the appropriate classification?

Classification systems as they exist invariably focus on possible harm to children; this then must involve evolving a view of the child around which to form such judgements. Under the European directive the test is whether the programme is 'likely to impair the physical, mental, or moral development of minors'. This is very close to legal tests which operate under child protection legislation which have been subjected to many critical comments in legal thought. In particular, the subjective nature of udgments under child protection laws are often identified with the vague mbit of such laws. Of course they can be made to operate 'effectively' if ane consistently resorts to a particular conception of childhood. At the nd of the day, 'harm to minors' will usually lead to programmers ssuming the vulnerability of the child and creating programmes which do aot challenge that view of the child.

The British Broadcasting Corporation also produces its code of aractice, known as *Producer's Guidelines*. These guidelines, as required by aw, also 'reflect the general effect' of the Broadcasting Standards Commission codes of practice.[118] As with the other codes which operate n the United Kingdom, the Watershed is a central part of the *Producer's Guidelines* too. The *Guidelines* set out the principles on the Watershed vhich include the following:

The BBC has a well-established policy of making 9 p.m. the pivotal point of the evening's television, a Watershed before which, except in exceptional circumstances, all programmes on our domestic channels should be suitable for a general audience including children. The earlier in the evening a programme is placed, the more suitable it is likely to be for children to watch on their own.

However, the BBC expects parents to share the responsibility for assessing whether or not individual programmes should be seen by younger viewers.

The Watershed reminds broadcasters that particular care should be taken over inclusion of explicit scenes of sex and violence, and the use of strong language.

However, seventy per cent of homes do not contain children and many viewers expect a full range of subject matter throughout the day. On the other hand, many children may still be watching after 9 p.m., particularly at holiday times or weekends or if a programme of special appeal to young people has been scheduled. This is particularly true at Christmas, when family audiences may be watching after the Watershed. Producers should be aware that dates of school holidays differ across the United Kingdom.

Particular care should be taken in the period immediately after the Watershed. There should be a gradual transition towards more adult material and sudden changes in tone should be avoided but, where unavoidable, they must be clearly signposted. Adult material should never be positioned close to the Watershed simply to attract audiences in a sensationalist way. Material which is particularly adult in tone should be scheduled at an appropriate time, where necessary sometime after the Watershed. The post Watershed period runs from 9.00 p.m. until 5.30 a.m. the following morning.

. . .

Scheduling can be vital to public acceptance of challenging material. Whether or not scenes of violence, sex, great distress or strong language cause offence to an audience can depend not just on editorial or dramatic context, but on sensitive scheduling decisions. A good rule of thumb is to avoid taking the audience by surprise. Announcements and warnings can play an important part in this ...[119]

The idea that 'challenging material' should be scheduled with sensitivity suggests here that this is the material that some, if not all, children should be protected from viewing. The objection to this statement is not that this is always a wrong approach to children's viewing: rather, it is that the guidelines on scheduling pay little attention to the extent to which children too may claim a right to watch such material in their own interests. The interests of children are submerged to that of their parents and the responsibilities placed on them to control their children's exposure to television. There is, however, some acknowledgement that children will participate in television in a different capacity in these guidelines. A significant section is devoted to children and programmes in the context of children who may be actors, interviewees, participants, the subjects of a programme or programme makers.[120] This is an important variation from other codes as it clearly conceptualizes the child as an active participant in television and not merely part of the audience. The detail of this section of the *Guidelines*, however, indicates that the general concern with children in this context is still their welfare. For example, in relation to the interviewing of children the *Guidelines* state:

Interviews with children need particular care. Children can be easily led in questioning and are often open to suggestion. Young children in particular may have difficulty in distinguishing between reality and fantasy and teenagers do not always have the skills to distinguish truth from hearsay and gossip. Programme makers should be careful about prompting children and should allow them to speak for themselves. Children should not be talked down to or patronized. Where teenagers have been involved in criminal or anti-social behaviour, programme makers should be aware they sometimes exaggerate for effect. Criminal or anti-social behaviour should not go unchallenged.

On extremely sensitive subjects, such as abuse or family break-down, programme makers should consider consulting a professional with experience of interviewing and counselling children about the best way of approaching interviews and minimizing distress.[121]

The notion that young children 'may have difficulty in distinguishing between reality and fantasy' is of course the historical reason for the legal provisions which would not allow for the conviction of an accused person on the uncorroborated evidence of a child witness. This is not a view which currently holds sway in the criminal law,[122] particularly as it may be regarded as making convictions in child abuse cases especially difficult. The old law on the evidence of a child was subjected to intense criticism on the basis that it conceptualized the child as unable to give truthful evidence because of the notion of the 'impressionable child'. Such rules did not protect the child, as they made the perpetrators of abuse more able to avoid liability. The irony then of the *Producer's Guidelines* is that under the guise of seeking to protect the welfare of the child they perpetuate that view of children which has been discredited as a basis for assessing children's evidence in criminal cases. Likewise, the guidance that criminal or antisocial behaviour should not go unchallenged pays little heed to the body of work which would argue that the acts of young people are often criminalized because of the powerlessness they possess as young people. How does a young person effectively challenge this 'authoritative' view of crime, if the guidelines expect the authoritative view to be reasserted in the face of that critique?

Finally, this example also indicates recourse to the child welfare experts as a means of resolving the question of what is appropriate to programme. In the complexity of decision-making about how to handle children and their relationship with television, the law will tend to 'leave it to the experts' rather than attempt to evolve legal criteria usually fraught with irreconcilable tensions. The issue is whether these difficulties in formulating workable legal criteria are due to a lack of scientific advice, hence making reliance on the experts necessary and desirable, or whether it is because they are questions which go to the view of the child one adopts. In the latter case, it may be that this has more to do with ideological standpoints than it has to do with science. It is also then about the type of adults we wish to produce in society. This is a moral question, not a scientific one.

MAKING SENSE OF REGULATION

The broad approach to the regulation of children and television in the four countries discussed in this chapter can be seen as similar. This should not surprise as the countries all subscribe to similar views of childhood and perceive the problem of the relationship between children and television as giving rise to identical issues to do with sex, violence, parental responsibility and the interests of broadcasters. It is true that the content of the regulatory processes and rules in each country do differ and that these do give rise to subtle differences which may well have importance in particular cases. But this can be a distraction from a more substantive analysis of children, the state and television. King and Piper remark on this phenomenon in relation to child welfare law generally:

In the law, much that is common between jurisdictions is lost beneath a mass of rules and procedures which occupy the minds of professional participants and convince them that their problems are specific to country, city or even the particular court in which they practice.

These legal concerns, in all their complexity, tend increasingly to submerge policy objectives beneath a mass of statutes, procedures, rules and cases to be learnt and absorbed by students and practitioners alike. Not only do they obscure normative processes at work within the law, but they also make comparisons between policies and practices in different jurisdictions ever more difficult. The result is a paradox. While the problems posed by children and young people are almost identical in all Western industrialized countries and the general responses of these countries are broadly similar, the laws, legal procedures and practices putting these responses into effect and governing their administration are very different. Moreover, these differences are increasing as the legal response becomes ever more sophisticated and complex.[123]

It is important that we do not become submerged in the morass of detail which, while of some legal significance, may deflect our attention from the way in which across many countries children are systematically subject to paternalistic laws on the regulation of television which, under the guise of protection, exclude them from full participation in decisions which relate to what they can watch on television, restrict what is deemed suitable for them to view and, most importantly, constructs them as unable to claim for themselves autonomous rights.

CHAPTER 4

Images that Harm? Children and Violence in Television

Bart: 'Lisa, if I ever stop loving violence, I want you to shoot me.'
Lisa: 'Will do.'
    (The Simpsons Episode 3F16, 'The Day the Violence Died')

Lisa: 'So it's true: some cartoons **do** encourage violence.'
    (Same episode)

A concern with the effects of 'violent' images on television is as old as the medium itself. But over a half century of thought on this problem has not clarified whether 'television violence' does lead to behaviour which might be termed 'aggressive'. The formulation of programme standards and other regulatory responses to 'media violence' appears to have more to do with what people believe to be the case than any proved causal link. In a United States poll in the early 1990s it was reported that 80 per cent of Americans believed that 'violence on TV shows is harmful to society'.[1] Such beliefs often have much to do with communities seeking to understand horrific crimes such as mass killings. Many reports into media violence have occurred as a response to specific incidents or a perception of increased violent crime, as Atkinson and Gourdeau observe:

> a sharp increase in real violence has the effect of fuelling latent public apprehension about the correlation between such violence and violence depicted in the media. The resulting political pressure leads government authorities to set up public inquiries or implement rules or codes which are, in part, intended to reassure the public.[2]

Thus concern with media violence might be understood as a society unable to explain certain events and the state responding through seeking to make that public feel secure. It may well be that 'scapegoating' the media for broader social ills is the result of this process and not the gaining of any substantive insights into the connection between television and violent acts.

Another constant, it seems, has been the manner in which debates about violence on television have been constructed in that time. What does not change, at least in popular discourse, is the tendency to quantify the amount of 'violent' images screened on television as well as the number of studies which conclude that there is a causal link between television violence and aggressive behaviour. Thus the final report of the Royal Commission set up to inquire into television prior to its introduction in Australia mentions a 1953 United States survey conducted by the Parent-Teacher's Association in Chicago which had calculated that in the week from Christmas to New Year's Eve children's programmes had depicted '295 violent crimes including 93 murders, 78 shootings, 9 kidnappings, 9 robberies, 44 gun fights, 2 knifings, 33 sluggings, 2 whippings, 2 poisonings and 2 bombings.'[3] A campaigner for improved programming for children in 1993 claimed that 'the average South Australian child will have witnessed 18,000 acts of murder before it leaves school – supplemented by 87,000 acts of violence.'[4] This apparent need to place a number on the amount of violence on television continues today. In 2000 a submission to an Australian State Parliamentary Committee's inquiry into the effect of television and multimedia on children and families heard evidence that 'the average American child will have watched 8000 murders on television by the time he or she is twelve years old'.[5] This latter figure, as we have seen, is stated in the United States Telecommunications Act 1996. One has to question the source of these figures. Apart from the difficulty in counting, it seems strange, for instance, that a South Australian child will watch two and half times more acts of murder on television than an American child, but 13,000 less acts of violence. Clearly, these statistics suffer from problems in definition and guesswork.

The above State Parliamentary Committee also reported on the effects of television and multimedia on children and families.[6] In its discussion of television violence the Committee noted that while a number of United States reports – including those prepared for the National Commission on the Causes and Prevention of Violence in 1972[7] and those undertaken by the National Institute of Mental Health[8] and the Commission on Violence and Youth[9] – came to the view that 'the effects of media violence on the behaviour of children, youth and adults who view such programming are harmful',[10] it had heard views that there was 'division between commentators as to whether the evidence on television violence is clear or inconclusive'.[11] Nevertheless, the weight of 3000 studies, said the Committee, 'indicate[d] a positive association between television violence and aggressive behaviour'.[12] Although it had to be acknowledged, that television was only one factor in determining aggressive behaviour.[13]

While the chapter of the above Report which examines television violence appears to be a careful exposition of various research projects undertaken into the phenomenon, what is most remarkable is that there is a complete absence of critical analysis of the concept of violence used in the research cited. Nor is there any explanation of what the Committee understood by that term. The Report uses the term 'violence' in myriad ways: 'high level of violence',[14] 'violent acts',[15] 'television violence',[16] 'violent scenes',[17] but does not question what those terms actually mean. It seems implicit in the discussion that 'violence' is a 'commonsense' term and relates to scenes which contain guns, blood, depict pain and so on. It appears to be on this basis that the Committee referred to research into the content of television programming which had concluded that 'high levels of violence in television entertainment' existed.[18] But what was being measured by this research?

VIOLENCE AS IDEOLOGY

The problem with such studies as cited in the Victorian Committee's report is that they fail to understand the ideological context within which 'violence' is understood and constructed. As Hodge and Tripp explain:

> The key term here is 'aggression'. The problem with aggression is that it is essentially a social act which can only take place in a social context, subject to judgements by various social agents, including the so called aggressor. 'Aggression' is an ideologically loaded term. It implies violence which is physical, and probably unjustified (though not when used of an 'aggressive' marketing policy). However, not all actions labelled 'aggression' are the same in kind, differing only in degree. Not all aggression is undesirable, though this is the strong impression given by many researchers, and even more by people who use that research. Some aggression – the capacity to defend oneself for instance – is essential to survival. A government programme aimed at eliminating aggression from the entire populace would be viewed with deep suspicion, as the equivalent of a universal lobotomy. When researchers take this kind of factor into account ... they find that television violence that is represented as 'legitimate' leads to greater expression of aggressive feelings. This would be worrying if all aggression is regarded as bad. It would be encouraging if legitimate aggression is seen as valid; but if the very concept of 'legitimacy' was seen as immensely problematic, then nothing follows automatically from [such a] study.[19]

From this viewpoint the problem is not 'violence' but how the concept is interpreted and constructed. Hodge and Tripp argue that children are participants in this process of interpretation:

> Children typically have the capacity to be active and powerful decoders of television, and programmes watched by them are potentially rich in meaning and cultural value; though not all programmes and ways of viewing are of equal benefit for all children.[20]

Television programmes have to be given meaning. The notion that there exists 'television violence' as an objective and measurable phenomenon is seriously flawed. It could be contended that what constitutes 'violent programming' is simply a matter of common sense. But where does one place media discussion of war and terrorism in this debate? Is constant media speculation about terrorist threats 'violent programming'? Such programming may be justified on the grounds of public interest. But its impact on attitudes and behaviour could be greater than screen images of a dramatized killing or robbery as part of a police series. Likewise, racist or sexist statements made as part of a televised studio discussion could be processed by viewers as being relevant to their lives and acted upon in ways which could be considered as violent to certain groups in the community. Yet such programming is rarely, if ever, categorized as 'violent' by television researchers and lobbyists.

What is also being argued here is that children may well decode television programmes as being worthy of their attention or as irrelevant and boring. It cannot be assumed that 'good' children's programmes will have appeal to children, but neither can it be assumed that children will be automatically attracted to 'bad' programmes. The idea that children need to be guided towards quality programmes and away from programmes which 'tempt' them through the attractive – but negative – imagery owes more to the idea that children are little devils that must be made into good citizens than any scientific understanding of children.[21] Hodge and Tripp remind us that the role of the child in interpreting the television images which they view cannot be forgotten.

But there is also a wider point that arises from Hodge and Tripp's analysis. Narrow conceptions of what is appropriate for children to view will inevitably give rise to narrow programming. Diversity and breadth in the types of ideas, experiences and images which the child will witness on television will be lacking if it is thought that certain programming is invariably harmful. It is at this point that the idea of violence can be seen as a screen for wider anxieties in adult society. Violence as an aspect of conflict suggests difference and discomfort. Broader social trends appear to suggest that many adults are seeking more and more to avoid contact with persons who challenge their values and lifestyles. In particular, this can be seen in our cities which have pushed out the poor and homeless to the fringes while the middle class and affluent occupy the centre.

In this regard it seems to be no small coincidence that 'television violence' is linked with criminal behaviour. In doing so the imagery which is designated as harmful is associated with those that do harm. In the process, discussions about the causes of crime are shifted away from consideration of social factors such as poverty, unemployment and poor housing to the 'inappropriate choices' of the underclass in their television viewing habits. Concern with the level of violence on television is thus read as a legitimate attempt to save children from falling into a life of vice and crime. Violence is constructed as 'bad', people who copy it are described as 'evil'[22] and censorship and regulation of such programming is as a consequence necessary for the protection of society.

Hodge and Tripp on the other hand argue for a much more positive idea of violence on television:

> Media violence is qualitatively different from real violence: it is a natural signifier of conflict and difference, and without representations of conflict, art of the past and present would be seriously impoverished.[23]

This is not to suggest that they advocate an approach to television violence which supports no regulation. As they state:

> The issue of violent content cannot be considered apart from the modality value of media representations of violence. The strong move by lobbyists, especially overt in the USA but also effective in Britain and Australia, to limit the depictions of violence on television is therefore based on a radical misconception of how the media work. This said, it remains true that high-modality violence is likely to be disturbing to young children, who will neither enjoy nor learn well from such programmes. Furthermore, the ideological meaning of some kinds of violence – as in some kinds of pornography or racism – must be sufficiently offensive to be banned on those grounds: not because of violence as such but because of the worldview they are proclaiming and legitimating.[24]

Hodge and Tripp thus stand for a radically different understanding of violence than that which tends to prevail in many debates about television regulation. Instead of adopting without question the need to protect children from the harmful effects of screen violence, they portray children as active consumers of television. It is true that this approach has been criticized as being based on too narrow a conception of child development and of romanticizing the relationship between children and television.[25] But it does serve to remind us that there can be no simple cause and effect relationship between television violence and children. Children have to interpret the meaning of the programmes which they watch and this can be negotiated with family members, peers and teachers.[26] It follows from such an analysis that violence cannot be immediately classified as 'bad' or 'negative' – it will depend on how it is interpreted. Likewise, I would add that what even constitutes violent programming must be negotiable in the mind of the viewer. Calmly spoken words which express bigotry may be more violent than a dramatic depiction of a car chase in terms of the behaviour they may encourage.

Explanations of the claimed link between media violence and aggressive behaviour can be understood as an ideological struggle. This is supported by the work of Atkinson and Gourdeau. They make the point that when one examines various inquiries into media violence in the 1970s and 1980s in different parts of the world it is possible to identify quite different conclusions with respect to the connection between media violence and criminal behaviour. As they note:

> It is interesting to compare the LaMarsh Report,[27] conducted in the 1970s, with the Wyatt Report[28] and that of the Australian Broadcasting Tribunal,[29] both of which date from the 1980s. The LaMarsh Report clearly reflects the commonly-held assumptions of sociology and communications specialists in the 1970s. The authors of the report conclude that violence in the media is dangerous because it encourages real violence, and categorically reject the argument that violence can be cathartic. They also dismiss out of hand methodological arguments refuting analyses of the effects of media violence. While the LaMarsh Report attributed violence in the media to economic issues, the profit motive – in short, to capitalism – by the end of the 1980s, studies into media violence no longer focused on the motivating factors ...
>
> The Wyatt Committee and the Australian Broadcasting Tribunal, which were established to consider the issue of audiovisual violence, are much more cautious in their conclusions and recommendations. Both conclude that there is no consensus as to the actual effects of audiovisual violence and emphasize the difficulty in coming up with a satisfactory definition of violence. Whereas the Wyatt Report appeals to 'common sense', the Australian Broadcasting Tribunal's Report insists that it is unfair to 'judge' audiovisual products without considering the context, intention and explicitness of acts of violence.[30]

Clearly, scientific knowledge in this area is not fixed. What Atkinson and Gourdeau demonstrate is that the political context is also important in determining which knowledge is selected out for use as possible explanations of social behaviour. In this process many assumptions are made which may be politically convenient. As they note, the LaMarsh inquiry was also asked to investigate the cause of violence in schools and took for granted a link between that phenomenon and media violence.[31] Such an explanation may usefully deflect concern away from poor resources or inadequate curriculum. These latter considerations would require a reallocation of budget expenditure or even increased taxes. In seeking the answer to school violence in television viewing the state may be able to avoid more difficult political situations.

The conclusions in earlier government inquiries were soon challenged by reviews of the literature which argued that the connection between television violence and aggressive behaviour was not so clear.[32] Certainly such writing would have had some influence on the less conclusive reports which followed in the 1980s. These later reports can be understood as providing a more flexible underpinning for industry self-regulation. Certainly, if the views of the LaMarsh report had prevailed, through time it would have been difficult to justify self-regulation by an industry which was perceived to be more concerned with profit than the public interest concerns of media violence.

The latter reports also present the typical 'balance of considerations' approach. On the one hand, they argue, there is the concern with media violence and the effect it may have on crime rates, but on the other hand there is the problem of lack of clarity about the actual causes and the difficulty of definition. This lends justification for minimal state intervention. Of course, this approach also sits well with concerns about over-regulation by the state of the media and interference with free speech and the free exchange of ideas. The less conclusive reports also provide politically useful distractions from other causes of antisocial behaviour such as poverty and inequality. They do so because they tend to suggest 'workable', but long-term, solutions to violence. They may present the answers as more 'difficult' and 'contested', but that can be turned to political advantage as it suggests that a fight against media violence can be institutionalized as a lengthy process which has appeal to politicians who may see it as providing a useful political distraction for a long period of time.

Of course, the protection of children is another constant in discussions of television violence which is rarely challenged. As Atkinson and Gourdeau put it, 'the public demands that special attention be accorded children'.[33] This may be a view that they too take for granted, as there is little evidence in their work that there is a concern with the right of children to view programmes that they wish to see. The idea that children must be protected from media violence is a curious assumption to make when it is otherwise acknowledged that the idea of violence is problematic and hard to define. If children are to be protected from violence, then just exactly what is it we must filter from their viewing?

There is, one suspects, deeper matters at work here. Although the protection of children from television violence is the catch cry, it is possible to understand this debate as being about protecting the community *from* children. The link between aggressive behaviour and television violence is ultimately about juvenile crime and the fear that children will learn how to harm others from such broadcast programmes. This is one reason why parental responsibility looms large in discussions about children and television. Once that notion is introduced into debates on the regulation of television then the state can feel justified in intruding into a whole array of domestic considerations. These connections are made in this context as a senior counsel for a United States Senate Communications subcommittee observed:

> I recently read in a South Carolina newspaper that court and juvenile justice officials have found South Carolina to be among the top three states in the nation for violent crimes committed by children. There is also an interesting statement by the police officers in the town where this newspaper is published. Only eleven per cent of juveniles incarcerated from 1991 to 1992 were living with both natural parents. Fifty-three per cent were in single parent households and thirteen per cent were living with other relatives. If you do not have parents at home to monitor what the children are watching and to screen out the programs, the information made available to parents is irrelevant and will not work. Even Senators on the Committee who are parents and who have very strong desires to control and monitor what their children see on television admit that kids go next door. Children will see programs at their friends' houses; they will see programs whenever they are out of the house. It is impossible for parents to sit there with the children every minute of the day to see what it is they are watching.[34]

The central argument presented by the author of this passage is that as parents cannot always supervise the viewing patterns of their children then legislative action to control violent programming on television through the passage of legislation such as the Children's Protection from Violent Programming Act 1993[35] is justified. But other messages come through here. There is the connection made between the incarceration rate of young people from single parent households and television viewing. The suggestion in the passage is that such homes cannot provide the required level of parental supervision of television viewing and thus control their children's exposure to television violence. This results in a greater propensity to commit violent crime. This may appear to be a rather neatly packaged way to explain juvenile crime but it relies on the view that single parent families are not 'normal' in that they find difficulty in properly supporting their children. That explanation fits well with an ideology that celebrates the nuclear family. It also follows from the passage that parental supervision is the ideal and that as usually one parent works, one should stay at home to look after the children. Such views lead easily to an expectation that mothers should remain in the home looking after the children.

It has been argued that police perceptions of the likelihood of a young person being disciplined within the home affect the decision to prosecute when a young person is apprehended for an offence. Thus children with only a mother at home are more likely to be charged and taken to court when compared with a young person from a two parent family as the police perception is that the father will impose the necessary discipline. The consequence is that children from single parent (most often a single mother) families will be over-represented in conviction statistics.[36] What is evident here is not a greater propensity of some young people to offend or the inability of certain families to supervise their children but instead the role of police discretion in the process.

The above passage also indicates how the determination of acceptable behaviour on the part of parents is defined in relation to the nuclear family by the dominant culture of the society. As Carrington observes in relation to the likelihood of Aboriginal children being removed from their parents under child protection legislation:

> Because dysfunction is often defined in relation to what is regarded as the normal nuclear family, cultural differences in family can be equated with family dysfunction and hence constitute seemingly legitimate reasons for removing Aboriginal children from their families.[37]

Thus the observation that the Senators on the subcommittee find it difficult to supervise their children reinforces the correctness of this approach to children and television. They may fail on their own admission, but they fail in attempting to do the 'right' thing. Parents who do not supervise their children because they have a different view of such matters become part of the problem. Carrington suggests that in this way the juvenile justice system comes to 'regard the family as both the source and saviour of juvenile delinquency'.[38] In her view, state intervention in the family utilizes the notion of the 'bad' or 'incompetent' parent to justify 'punitive child protection policies' against poor and indigenous families.[39] What we have to consider here is whether in linking juvenile offending with television violence and thence parental guidance/ responsibility we are recreating the circumstances whereby the state can legitimate intervention in the family which is destructive and counter-productive to the creation of a diverse and tolerant society.

REGULATING VIOLENCE

It follows from the above that the regulatory framework for the control of television violence is bound to be replete with tensions and contradictions. At the core of the regulatory mechanisms in Australia, the United States, Canada and the United Kingdom is the imposition of 'community standards'. This is clearly politically safe ground for the state to occupy as it is likely to appease the majority of the population who are likely to have their standards applied. But it does suggest that the application of those standards has as much to with political expediency as it has to do with scientific understandings of violence in television programming.

In Australian commercial television, it is the 'frequency and intensity' which will be central in determining how a programme will be classified.[40] Thus for a G classified programme violence must be depicted as follows:

Visual depiction of physical and psychological violence must be very restrained. The use of weapons, threatening language, sounds or special effects must have a very low sense of threat or menace, must be strictly limited to the storyline or programme context, must be infrequent and must not show violent behaviour to be acceptable or desirable.[41]

For a PG classification violence must accord with the following criteria:

Visual depiction of violence must be inexplicit, restrained, and justified by the storyline or programme context. More leeway is permitted when the depiction is stylized rather than realistic, but all violence shown must be mild in impact, taking into account also the language, sounds and special effects used.[42]

There is clearly a fine line between these two classifications. In the G category violence must be 'very restrained,' while in the PG classification it must be 'inexplicit, restrained and justified by storyline or programme content'. The hierarchy of classifications would suggest that 'more' must be permitted in the PG classification than would be allowed under the G banner, but the precise boundary line between the two classifications is always going to be subject to matters of individual judgement. This difficulty is compounded further upon consideration of the M, MA and AV classifications. For an M classification violence:

[m]ay be realistically shown only if it is not frequent or of high impact, and is justified by the storyline or programme context. Violence should not be presented as desirable in its own right. Any visual depiction of or verbal reference to violence occurring in a sexual context must be infrequent and restrained, and strictly justified by the storyline or programme context.[43]

The MA criteria for violence is the same as for the M classification. In effect the MA classification is differentiated from the M classification only by way of sexual depictions, coarse language, adult themes and drug use rather than violence. However, the AV classification specifies in relation to violence:

Realistic depictions may contain some detail, but should not be prolonged and should not be unduly bloody or horrific. Such depictions must be justified by the story. Violence occurring in a sexual context must not be detailed, and must be brief and infrequent, justified by the storyline and not exploitative.[44]

gain, the differences seem marginal yet unclear. In the M zone violence
ould be 'not frequent or of high impact' while in the AV period it is to
e depicted in a manner that 'should not be prolonged and should not be
nduly bloody or horrific'. Such criteria are bound to present problems of
assification from time to time. Indeed, conventional wisdom is that any
rstem of classification built around community standards must accept that
rhat falls within a classification will ebb and flow as community standards
nange. But who owns this wisdom? There is no one community but
lany communities. In this process of classification just whose wisdom is
) be applied?

It could be said that the classification system is based upon the myth of
ommunity' and that the standards give effect to the belief in a causal
onnection between television violence and juvenile crime because this
ipports the idea that there is a 'consensus' and therefore a 'community'
om which that springs. It could also be said that it is designed to
erpetuate another myth, that structural factors such as poverty,
nadequate housing and poorly resourced schools are not the real causes
f juvenile offending and aggression. One then must add to this equation
ne lack of definition of violence in such classification systems. Thus at the
ase of the various possible myths lies the problem that a clear definition of
ne harm which children must be protected against cannot be adequately
rovided. In this sense the whole system of classification relies on a simple
otion of 'common sense'.

In the United States and Canada, V-chip technology, as mentioned in
Chapter 3, has necessitated a classification system be implemented in order
) allow programmes to be encoded so that a blocking system can be
tilized. The system in place in the United States grades violence that may
e included for each classification as follows: TV-Y7 (children over 7) –
lay include 'mild fantasy or comedic violence'; TV-G (general audience,
uitable for all ages) – 'little or no violence'; TV-PG (parental guidance
uggested) – 'moderate violence'; TV-14 (may be unsuitable for children
nder 14) – 'intense violence'; TV-MA (may be unsuitable for children
nder 17) – 'graphic violence'. There may be different standards at work
1 the United States from Australia which might explain why 'intense
iolence' is permitted for TV-14 in the former country while no
Australian classification appears to permit prolonged violence. Of course,
t may be that the word 'intense' carries different meanings and so does not
ermit 'prolonged' violence in the United States. It is at this point that we
an once again refer to King and Piper's argument. Although the
bjectives in Australia and the United States with respect to television
iolence are couched in similar terms, the different legal cultures give

effect to those objectives in a manner consistent with local legal discourse. Thus either system can become stuck in legal argument over the meaning of a word, be it 'prolonged' or 'intense'. In both cases such words carry inside them the concerns of both systems – that the legal regulatory response should be balanced and measured as reflected in the language used. For if one considers the language used it is clear that there is no attempt to remove violence completely. The classification system attempts to draw a line at a particular point for each level of classification. The impossible task is to convert the general term into a meaningful test of where that line lies. It is also possible that in either system the meaning given to the word will alter due to idiosyncratic readings by individual classifiers or judges. This only serves to further obscure the boundaries of the criteria.

The Canadian classification system possesses similar characteristics to the United States system. As noted in Chapter 3, the AGVOT classification system also grades the level of violence according to the level of classification. The C classification permits violence which 'might contain occasional comedic, unrealistic depictions', the C8+ classification allows for 'infrequent, discreet, low intensity realistic depictions of violence' but 'violence portrayed must be within the context of the storyline or character development'. The C8+ classification 'might include mild physical violence, comedic violence, comic horror, special effects; fantasy, supernatural or animated violence'. The G classifications may contain 'minimal' and 'infrequent' violence, comedic and unrealistic depictions of violence, and cannot contain any 'frightening special effects not required by the storyline'. The PG rating may contain depictions of violence which are 'limited and moderate' and might include 'physical, fantasy, or supernatural violence'. The violence cannot be 'pervasive' and must be justified by the 'theme, storyline or character development'. The 14+ classification permits violence as a dominant theme but it must be 'integral to the development of plot or character'. This classification can also include 'intense scenes of violence'. The 18+ category 'might contain depictions of violence, which while integral to the development of plot, character or themes, are intended for adult viewing, and thus not suitable for audiences under 18 years of age'.[45]

This last classification seems to determine that an 'adult' programme is so classified because it is intended to be an adult programme. This is the almost absurd result one can obtain with a classification system based around vague terms. Of course, this vagueness may serve various purposes. As noted in the previous chapter, the recourse to 'fantasy violence' may have more to do with the concerns of that part of industry which relies on much of its income generated by sales from merchandizing connected with cartoon characters than it has to do with a desire to provide for the needs of children. Many cartoons have elements of violence. To categorize such violence as 'fantasy violence' removes it from the apparently more concerning 'realistic' depictions which might presumably lead to imitative behaviour amongst the young. Yet is there any logic in the notion that the *type* of screen violence may or may not lead to aggressive behaviour? Are animated programmes really less likely to lead to antisocial behaviour when compared with 'real' characters? Is the removal of cartoon violence from the focus of concern simply instead pandering to the market interests of some producers? If so, then what does this say about the manner in which violence is constructed as a social problem on television?

FANTASY VIOLENCE OR SATANIC HARM?

Mighty Morphin Power Rangers and State Regulation

Cartoon and fantasy violence has in fact been a target of concern for some groups concerned with television violence for many years. The experience of complaints about such programmes says much about the meaning of violence and the nature of classification systems. The most celebrated example of a 'fantasy violence' programme which was castigated in many countries is *Mighty Morphin Power Rangers*. The background to this programme is explained by Phillips:

> The *Mighty Morphin Power Rangers* television program is produced by Saban Entertainment.
> Haim Saban began his career in Israel, but while working in Japan in the mid 1980s, he spotted a new breed of children's action show on Japanese TV that he thought would work in America. He thought the programs had the campy quality of the old *Batman* TV shows, with bloodless Pow! and Zap! kinds of violence, so he bought the rights to one program, titled *Che Je Yu Rangers*. He took the Japanese fight-scene footage – which featured six brightly-colored and helmeted figures – and added new scenes of young Americans playing high school students, and renamed the show *Mighty Morphin Power Rangers*. And with this revised product under his arm, he went calling on the networks.[46]

By September 1993 it was the number one show on Fox Children's Network and the programme played an important role in making that network the lead children's broadcaster. Eventually shown in 40 markets, Phillips claims that it was watched by 70 per cent of British child viewers and 75 per cent of French child viewers.[47]

Clearly the program was popular with children. The concern of many adults was the level of violence it depicted. Phillips is critical of the show but provides the basic storyline so parents 'know your enemy and why they are an enemy to your children'.[48]

The Power Rangers' origin is a classical mythical battle that supposedly occurred long ago in a faraway place.

The wizard, Zordon, led the forces of 'good' against the evil Rita Repulsa. The war ended in a tie, however, and Rita and Zordon made a deal to determine the victory with a coin toss. Zordon used magic coins to win the contest, but his victory was not complete. Zordon was trapped in another dimension – locked in a head-view-only column of green light at his Command Center; and Rita (who retained one of the magic coins) and her cohorts were not destroyed, but rather imprisoned on the tiny moon of a faraway planet. After ten thousand years of imprisonment, Rita was freed by space travellers, moved to the earth's moon, and targeted earth as the starting point for her renewed effort to take over the universe.

Hearing of Rita's escape, Zordon called Alpha 5, the robot he placed in charge of operating earth, and ordered him to teleport five of the 'wildest, most wilful humans in the area' to the Command Center. Alpha teleports five teenagers to the Command Center where Zordon informs them that they have been chosen to battle Rita Repulsa, and are responsible for saving the planet.

Zordon gives each teen one of the magic coins – also called a Power Morpher. He tells the teens that if they are ever in danger, all they need to say is, 'It's Morphin time,' then raise their Power Morpher to the sky, call out the name of their designated power source, and they will be 'morphed' into a mighty fighter – a Power Ranger! To morph means to 'transform into,' probably short for metamorphosis, although that is never stated.[49]

Phillips continues to explain the three rules Zordon sets down for the Power Rangers:
1. Never use your powers for selfish reasons or personal gain.
2. Never make a fight worse – unless Rita forces you to do so.
3. Always keep your Power Ranger identity secret.[50]

The *Mighty Morphin Power Rangers* was a very successful programme both in terms of audience share and in merchandizing related products.[5] The storyline appears to be one in which children would be interested, a they were, and the three rules mentioned above appear to be the type o values that many members of society would be comfortable with. But thi programme was the target of a campaign aimed at its content. Phillips, a part of that attack explains:

Mighty Morphin Power Rangers and *VR Troopers* are two of the most violent programs ever to be aired to children.

The Violence Factor, or V Factor is not the only major concern about these programs, but it is perhaps the most obvious to the casual viewer. Children who watch these programs are being fed a *concentrated* dose of violent images underscored with driving, 'power' music.[52]

Phillips then proceeds to outline the negative effects of television violence on children. These include the interesting assertion that '[a] study is yet to be conducted that proves there is no relationship between television violence and real-life acts of aggression' and that 'more than 50 studies concluded that the more violence a child watches, the more aggression a child displays'.[53] To support this latter claim he writes that:

Since 1982, TV violence has increased 780 percent. During that same period, teachers report a near 800-percent increase in aggressive acts in the playgrounds. Scientists are reluctant to say that the two sets of behaviors are related, but common sense concludes, 'There's obviously a connection.'[54]

The statistics look questionable. An appeal to 'common sense' appears simplistic. Yet the protests against this programme led to formal complaints being lodged and inquiries into whether the show breached content standards. But this cannot be explained nor understood as simply a matter of breaches of programme classification guidelines. Phillips' critique of the *Mighty Morphin Power Rangers* goes well beyond the violent content of the programme. He is concerned with the manner in which the programme portrays 'gang' behaviour. This concern is really about the lack of 'family' in the show:

The nuclear family doesn't exist in either of the *Mighty Morphin Power Rangers* or *VR Troopers* programs. That's true for most children's programming ...
    In cases of impending tragedy, parents are never consulted on programs such as *Mighty Morphin Power Rangers* or *VR Troopers*. The teens must defend themselves, their schools, families, neighbor-hoods, and nation. And in the case of two of these programs, the planet. The child-as-savior is a troublesome concept. Yet this theme is reinforced by many cartoons and movies.[55]

Thus the idea of the child portrayed in this programme is 'troublesome' as it depicts an independent child not reliant on parental advice or guidance. In other words, the programme does not support the 'family values' of Phillips through its lack of any role for parental authority.

Phillips' criticism of *Mighty Morphin Power Rangers* is fuelled by his particular Christian beliefs. He writes widely on the 'satanic and occult' symbolism of many toys which tie in with television programmes.[56] In relation to *Mighty Morphin Power Rangers* Phillips acknowledges that the characters in the programme are 'politically correct' in that the cast composition is multicultural and includes females and males.[57] But Phillips then asks whether cultural diversity is good for a young child. He replies:

> I certainly am not opposed to cultural diversity. We are living in a shrinking world, one in which communication technology is more readily available than ever before, and the *need* to communicate has never been greater.
>
> One thing we must openly recognize is that culture can be defined in various ways. It can be narrowly presented to focus on differences in: customs, food, clothing, architectural styles, language, methods of schooling, transportation, and commerce. When more broadly defined, however, culture includes religion. And holidays and traditions in many cultures are inextricably tied to religion.
>
> Is it a good thing for Christian parents to expose their young children to other religions? I don't believe it is.[58]

Phillips then embarks on a critique of the Japanese origins of the programme. This is of deep concern according to him because the philosophy which underpins the show is from the East and not Christianity:

> Children who watch *Mighty Morphin Power Rangers* know the 'liturgy' of the program. They know to stand and hold out their Power Morphin coins and say, 'It's morphin time.' They know next to call out the name of their power-source dinosaur or other creature. They know next to start doing karate moves, reach for their magic weapons, and call greater powers until they are fully empowered to defeat their enemies. When certain music begins to play, specifically, 'Go, go. Power Rangers' or 'We are VR,' they know the time has come for fighting.
>
> A ritualistic pattern was established, one not rooted in Christian values, but in Eastern philosophy, particularly the rituals of Japanese secularism and communal ritual. In other words, the 'religion' of modern Japan.[59]

He then sums up Japanese religion as having two aspects: 'be part of the group' and 'use power for your group's advantage'.[60] Phillips then comments on the Japanese:

> The Japanese are intent on winning and controlling. They do not share power or markets readily. Many Japanese openly advocate world domination by their culture.
>
> Japanese cartoons are nearly always focused on saving the world –

not a neighborhood, city, area, or particular people. The Japanese think globally, and when they do, they think of themselves as being in charge and the world running according to Japanese principles, methods, and protocol. When Japanese cartoon and live action TV programs are adapted to an American children's audience, the programs may feature American-looking and American-sounding heroes, but the methods and ideology are still very Japanese: be part of a group, and make sure your group wins.[61]

The philosophy which underpins the *Mighty Morphin Power Rangers* is then connected with the occult:

Programs such as *Mighty Morphin Power Rangers* and *VR Troopers* are rooted in a 'catechism' that promotes Eastern religions ...

Eastern religions and occult practices recognize that power resides outside the individual. But that power is always regarded as a neutral force. Therefore, it is something 'good' into which a person should tap.[62]

The challenge that Eastern religion poses for Phillips is that it derives from 'spiritism' which 'claims that there is a god in everything and an amorphous universal god spirit that can pervade any substance. It stands in opposition to the Judeo-Christian concept of One True and Living God.'[63] He then identifies the *Mighty Morphin Power Rangers* as being 'rooted and steeped in Eastern religion' and ideintifies '[a] number of very specific spiritism practices and symbols'[64] employed in the programme, including the use of half-human, half-animal figures, masks which 'are believed to be a direct link to the spirit world and a means to channel supernatural forces',[65] rainbow colours, seeing into the future, magic wands and astral projection, familiars (animals with demonic spirit powers), incantations, and possession (taking on a more powerful identity).[66] Phillips regards all this as dangerous for a child:

It is equally impossible for a child to differentiate between what is sacred and what is not. Your child does not know he is watching occult practices. He doesn't know that he's being entertained by programs grounded in spiritism and new brands of Hinduism. From his perspective he's watching a slice of life.[67]

Phillips quite literally demonizes *Mighty Morphin Power Rangers*. It seems that the violence is of lesser importance than the associations the programme has with the occult, according to Phillips. Of course, the critique which Phillips constructs may itself be critiqued as, despite his claims, showing a lack of commitment to diversity of culture and belief. Quite simply, one suspects Phillips would be supportive of 'community standards' in broadcasting provided they reflect his worldview.

What this tells us about violence in television programming is that it overlaps with many other agendas. Certainly, Phillips connects it with rising rates of 'aggression' by young people. He readily connects that phenomenon with television programmes such as *Mighty Morphin Power Rangers* not just because they teach children to be aggressive but also because they contribute to the loss of 'family values' and presumably respect for authority which this entails. It is important to note how Phillips complains about the absence of family in the programme and the concern he expresses that parents must protect their children from such programmes – the book is, after all, ostensibly written to parents. One might ask again, who will be at home with the children to provide that protection? It might be expected that this will fall to the mother, thus reinforcing the traditional roles of the nuclear family. But even if this is the implicit message to parents, the penultimate passage in Phillips' book on the *Mighty Morphin Power Rangers* sends an even stronger message about both how the child is to be regarded and how one might measure appropriate parenting:

> Above all, preserve your child's innocence and purity. Don't let your child become a dumpster for the world's garbage.[68]

Assessing *Mighty Morphin Power Rangers* as a Legal Problem

It is against this backdrop that complaints about *Mighty Morphin Power Rangers* were assessed by various regulatory authorities in Australia, Canada and New Zealand during 1994. In September 1994 the New Zealand Broadcasting Standards Authority decided that the programme breached various broadcasting standards. In concluding that the programme breached a standard which required broadcasters 'to ensure that any violence shown is justifiable'[69] the Authority concluded that it:

> did not consider that the fantasy aspect of the series mitigated the effects of the violence, because the realism, including the realism of some of the weaponry, the fast pace and the music were appealing to children. In addition, the predictable formula and theme reinforced that appeal, especially the use in each programme of identical sequences, accompanied by special effects and music ... The Authority supported TVNZ's decision to cut out some of the violent incidents in the later episodes, but it still believed that the overwhelming impression left by each of the episodes was that there was a relentless recurrence of violent acts. It also disagreed with TVNZ's assertion that the weapons were not realistic, noting the use of rocks, bows and arrows, swords and guns, which are all weapons familiar to children.[70]

It is of interest that what might be regarded as a programme based on 'fantasy violence' in this decision was condemned for its 'realistic' portrayals of violence. This immediately calls into question distinctions in types of violence that many ratings and classifications systems rely upon.

The kindergarten complainant had submitted to the Authority that the programme portrayed violence 'as the acceptable way of resolving conflict' and that it 'believed that was harmful to children'. In their submission 'there were many ways to portray teamwork and ... it was unfortunate that the Power Rangers were rewarded for their acts of violence.'[71] Children's Media Watch submitted that 'there was very little storyline or dialogue and that the programme appeared to provide an opportunity for every kind of fighting.'[72] The programme in their view 'contained excessive violence and was unsuitable for showing in children's viewing time'.[73]

The Authority accepted these submissions. It also found that the programme breached standards which required programmes to 'avoid giving an impression of excessive violence',[74] not to glamorize antisocial behaviour,[75] and that broadcasters should be 'mindful of the effect any programme may have on children during their normally accepted viewing times'.[76] On this latter standard the Authority openly acknowledged the role that public opinion played in reaching their conclusion:

> the Authority believed that the evidence of the harmful influence of the series, presented by the teachers and parents of younger children, was compelling, and it did not consider that TVNZ's initiatives [to cut certain violent scenes from some episodes] were sufficiently effective to counter the detrimental effects observed in children's behaviour. The Authority notes that it has taken into account the large number of informal complaints and telephone calls it has received which support its view that the series has had a significant effect on children.[77]

This provides a remarkable insight into the nature of decision–making in such a matter. The notion of 'community standards' which underpins the codes allows for such matters as 'public opinion' to intrude into the process. Yet there is no evident consideration here by the Authority as to *who* was complaining informally, and on what basis. Certainly, the programme contained 'violence', but what else underpins the complaints? Is the concern with violence concealing other concerns about the portrayal of family life? It is interesting that the Authority did not consider when violence might be justified. At the end of the day, it seems, it was just deemed to be 'unsuitable for children'. But once again, how can even that statement make any sense without a definition of childhood?

The Canadian Broadcast Standards Council (CBSC) also considered complaints against the *Mighty Morphin Power Rangers* programme.[78] The CBSC is responsible for overseeing the observance of the Voluntary Code regarding Violence in Television Programming. The Code itself can be regarded as the creation of public opinion. In the Power Ranger case the CBSC outlined that history as this was the first decision under the Code. In 1990 a petition with 157,000 signatures was presented by 'a group of youngsters representing ten Quebec socio-cultural organizations' to the Federal Minister of Communications asking the government 'to eliminate violent and war programming for children on television'. Then in 1992 a Quebec teenager, Virginie Larivière, presented a petition with 1.3 million signatures to the Prime Minister after her eleven-year-old sister had been the victim of robbery, sexual assault and murder. This petition called for governmental action to reduce violent programming on television. In 1993 a code of practice was developed by an industry action group and approved by the Canadian Radio-television and Telecommunications Commission (CRTC). In 1994 the Voluntary Code came into effect.[79]

Thus the Code itself was a legal and regulatory response to popular pressure and the perception that violent programming led to aggressive behaviour. The CRTC, in announcing its approval of the Code, stated that it was 'pleased that the Code establishes clear guidelines for the depiction of violence in children's programming that take into account the particular vulnerability of young viewers'.[80] It also made special note of the Code's reference to 'realistic scenes of violence':

> while most animated fairy tales, fables, and cartoons of slapstick humour do not contain realistic scenes of violence, a number of action cartoons *do* portray such scenes. Studies indicate that such scenes may alter the emotional reactions of some children to violence, and could result in such effects as desensitization and increased tendencies towards aggressive behaviour.[81]

As previously discussed, the causal connection between television violence and aggressive behaviour is difficult, in scientific terms, to establish. But the CTRC notice translates the public concern with violent programming into a legal and regulatory proposition. Whatever the doubts may be about the scientific evidence, and the lack of definition of violence wherever it is used, this CRTC notice can be referred to as official 'proof' of the link between television violence and aggression and so support state intervention and regulatory processes which seek to act against violence. In many ways, it all seems not too far from the 'common sense' approach of Phillips above.

The Voluntary Code regarding Violence in Television Programming which the CBSC had to apply in the *Mighty Morphin Power Rangers* case contains the following clauses in relation to children's programming:

> 2.1 As provided below, programming for children [defined as under twelve years of age] requires particular caution in the depiction of

violence; very little violence, either physical, verbal or emotional shall be portrayed in children's programming.

2.2 In children's programming portrayed by real-life characters, violence shall only be portrayed when it is essential to the development of character and plot.

2.3 Animated programming for children, while accepted as a stylized form of storytelling which can contain non-realistic violence, shall not have violence as its central theme, and shall not invite dangerous imitation.

2.4 Programming for children shall deal carefully with themes which could threaten their sense of security, when portraying, for example; domestic conflict, the death of parents or close relatives, or the death or injury of their pets, street crime or the use of drugs.

2.5 Programming for children shall deal carefully with themes which could invite children to imitate acts which they see on screen, such as the use of plastic bags as toys, use of matches, the use of dangerous household products as playthings, or dangerous physical acts such as climbing apartment balconies or rooftops.

2.6 Programming for children shall not contain realistic scenes of violence which create the impression that violence is the preferred way, or the only method to resolve conflict between individuals.

2.7 Programming for children shall not contain realistic scenes of violence which minimize or gloss over the effects of violent acts. Any realistic depictions of violence shall portray, in human terms, the consequences of that violence to its victims and its perpetrators.

2.8 Programming for children shall not contain frightening or otherwise excessive special effects not required by the storyline.[82]

The CBSC found that *Mighty Morphin Power Rangers* breached articles 2.1, 2.2, 2.5, 2.6 and 2.7 of the Code. In relation to article 2.1 the CBSC said:

> While the Council understood clearly that each programme attempted to convey a didactic or moral message to its viewers, whether relating to family values, the need for pollution control and recycling, or other matters, it was the view of the Council that these valuable messages were overwhelmed by the quantity of violence surrounding their transmittal. Far from containing *very little violence*, the series appeared to convey *considerable* violent physical activity.[83]

The CBSC decided that a breach of article 2.2 of the Code had been committed based upon similar reasoning to that of the New Zealand authority. Under article 2.2 the plot may justify depictions of violence, but the CBSC held that the violence 'overwhelmed' the message that the programme was attempting to convey.[84] A breach of article 2.6 was sustained because '[n]ot once in any of the episodes was there depicted *any* attempt to resolve conflict by any technique other than fighting.'[85] Article 2.5 is concerned with children imitating acts they view on screen. The CBSC found that the depictions of violence did not indicate any physical consequences of martial arts punching and kicking. This encouraged 'the seemingly risk-free imitation of the physical acts of aggression by children who have not reached the age of discernment, namely, the very audience for this program'. Thus article 2.5 was breached.[86] Article 2.7 is also concerned with the non-realistic portrayal of violence which glosses over the consequences of that violence. The Council commented:

> Those who view this absence of physical damage as a positive rather than a negative consideration lose sight of the importance of understanding the *consequences* of their acts. In real life, punching and kicking *do* have physical results in almost *every* instance. Further-more, the logic of this concern is enshrined in Article 2.7 of the Code which forbids programming which *minimizes or glosses over* the effects of violent acts.[87]

Although the Canadian Code provides some examples of acts which might encourage children to imitate behaviour which is dangerous, the Code does not attempt to define 'violent programming'. What constitutes 'television violence' is assumed rather than made explicit in the Code. It is also too simple to describe the Code as being about protecting children *from* 'violent programming', however that concept is to be defined. The concern that the Code expresses about children learning how to behave aggressively and seeing violence as a means of resolving conflict clearly has more to do with protecting the community *from* such children than it has to do with protecting those children. Even the CBSC referred to anecdotal evidence of a child kicking a teacher when imitating the high kicks of the *Power Rangers* programme. The process clearly has to do with how we wish to see children. It also has to do with ideas abut violence in society and who is to wield it. To complain that violent programming teaches children to regard violence as a means to resolve conflict and that that is a bad thing may well have some merit. But when violence is seen by many in society, including political leaders, as one way to resolve conflict or impose control, such incantations as appear in the Code wear thin.

This process is also about the manner in which law incorporates social science into its discourse. The CBSC refer to the logic enshrined in the Code when discussing the consequences of violence. Such language is how law converts what is presented as a scientific problem into a legal proposition. The social science thus legitimates the legal statement and as a consequence the law gains validity. But perhaps actions and consequences are moral not legal problems. The shift from moral to scientific to legal proposition is subtle. For example, once violent programming is presented as harmful to children then it is difficult to accept that any parent would be regarded as acting appropriately if they permitted their children to view such programming. This is despite the idea that 'parental choice' is the principle that is said to apply when it comes to determining what children should view. The state should not, it is contended by some, intrude into the privacy of the family and direct what they should view. But the way in which the problem of violent programming is constructed changes all that. The Canadian Code underscores this shift by the way in which the problem of violent programming is discussed. Although there is a 'balance' which is sought to be struck between creative freedom and the need to protect children, the underlying message has more to do with constraint and control:

> Through their programming, production and scheduling practices, the development of a program classification system, and the use of viewer advisories, Canada's private broadcasters undertake to play their part to protect our children and to use discretion in addressing the sensitivities of their viewers. In return, viewers, using the programming information provided to them, accept responsibility for their viewing behaviour and for that of their children.[88]

Once stated, this becomes the benchmark against which programming is measured. The moral and scientific analyses and debates fade away and are replaced by the undertakings given by broadcasters in the Code and the assumptions upon which they are made.

The Australian Broadcasting Authority reported on *Mighty Morphin Power Rangers* on 7 November 1995, having received a complaint in August 1994.[89] The question the Authority had to decide was whether, given the amount of violence in the programme, the G classification it had been given was appropriate. The Commercial Television Industry Code of Practice specified at the time that depictions of violence in a G classified programme had to conform to the following:

> **Violence**: Depictions of physical and psychological violence and the use of threatening language, weapons, special effects must not be likely to cause alarm or distress to children, must be strictly limited to the context or storyline of the programme and must not show violent behaviour to be acceptable or desirable.[90]

It was also required, as it still is, that a G classified programme 'must not contain any matter likely to be unsuitable for children to watch without the supervision of a parent'.[91] In determining whether there was any matter in the programme that was unsuitable for children, the Authority took a particularly legalistic approach to the task. It said that the word 'unsuitable' was well understood and the ordinary meaning could be used. The test was an objective one and the 'children' to be considered consisted of the 'ordinary and reasonable child' under fourteen, although because the programme appealed to a wide range of children the audience composition had to be considered, which included children as young as five.[92]

In assessing whether the violence in the programme was unsuitable the Authority also had to consider then paragraph 2.10.1 of the Code. The test to be applied in that paragraph was:

> where a programme contains depictions of physical and psychological violence, threatening language, weapons or special effects that are likely to frighten or cause anxiety to children, or not strictly related to the plot or surrounding facts and circumstances of the episode, or showed violent behaviour to be acceptable or desirable then that would constitute non-compliance with section 2.10.1 of the Code.[93]

This did not mean that 'violence cannot be depicted as acceptable or desirable in any context', according to the Authority, as 'the depiction of violence may be acceptable or desirable in a situation where one acts in self defence.'[94] Unlike the Canadian body and the New Zealand authority which investigated a series of episodes of the programme, the Australian Broadcasting Authority was limited to inquiring into two specific episodes of the programme. In relation to one episode the conclusion was that while the programme contained material which did not portray realistically the consequences of violence, this could have been explained to a child by a parent. However, as a G classification cannot contain any material which is unsuitable for a child to watch unsupervised then it was not properly classified and breached the Code.[95] In the second episode it was in issue of whether the storyline justified the violence. The Authority concluded:

> 8.10 The sequence depicts a very human-like and frightened Patroller, showing individual human characteristics, being obliterated by a monster because he can not reach the required standard. This is likely to cause anxiety to a child as it portrays the 'dispensability' of those who do not reach required standards. The ABA considers that it is likely that this sequence would cause alarm or distress to children or cause anxiety to children.

> 8.11 The ABA considers that this material does not strictly relate to the plot and the facts and circumstances of the episode 'Mighty Morphin Power Mutants'. That is, the obliteration of the human-

like Putty Patroller due to the fact that he shows awkward and uncoordinated actions does not relate strictly to the Power Rangers' attempts to save the planet from destruction by the evil sorceress Rita Repulser.[96]

This led to the conclusion that the programme breached the Code. But the Australian Broadcasting Authority acknowledged that the episode did not portray violence as acceptable in any context. The Power Rangers used violence when under attack and so acted in self-defence.[97] It was the obliteration of the creature with human-like traits which took the episode outside the Code.

What is also of interest in the Australian decision is that the programme had been classified as a G programme. That this occurred itself indicates the discretionary and subjective nature of the application of the criteria in any particular case. The original classifier clearly came to a different conclusion than the Authority in this case. While the original rating would have been in the hands of the broadcaster, self-interest may have determined the classification. But it must nevertheless be justified on the basis of the criteria. On any view, the classification criteria are subject to differing views on their interpretation.

SEARCHING FOR THE 'CHILD'

The small differences between the codes or classification systems in different countries can lead to slightly different emphases or outcomes from country to country. In the case of the *Mighty Morphin Power Rangers* the outcomes were remarkably similar – the programmes were held to have breached the standards or codes on violent programming. Yet there were differences. Particularly in the Australian decision, there seemed to be some acknowledgement of the redeeming values in the programme which were more readily regarded as being overwhelmed by the violent content in other jurisdictions. It is also the case that the Australian decision appeared to be more legalistic, seeking to find the meaning of each word in the Code, including coming to a view of the 'ordinary and reasonable child', while in Canada there was considerable influence placed on the weight of concern in the community about the programme.

It is true that in all countries there is a search for the 'child' against which to measure the suitability of the programming. The 'ordinary and reasonable child' constructed by the Australian Broadcasting Authority is particularly problematic as it is the view that children lack sufficient reason to understand violent programming which lies behind the need for such codes of practice or classification systems in the first place. Thus the child usually found in such searches is the innocent child in need of protection from harmful material, although it may be that the child which has greater influence on how the critieria are understood is the 'feared child' who may acquire knowledge which will make him or her dangerous to others. The case of *Mighty Morphin Power Rangers* illustrates well that fear, which is particularly evident in the Canadian decision with its reference to imitative behaviour. In the New Zealand decision the recourse to informal complaints and telephone calls which supported its view that the series 'had a significant effect on children' as a means to justify its decision shows well how when the problem is reconstructed as a legal test of 'community standards' or what is 'unsuitable for children' the process makes legitimate the use of material which in scientific discourse would be regarded as 'unscientific'.

UNITED KINGDOM CODES OF PRACTICE

The approach in the United Kingdom has been, as remarked in the previous chapter, to shun classification systems and to instead rely on more expansive discussions of what is suitable with respect to programme standards. The Broadcasting Standards Commission Standards Code begins with a broad statement about 'violence':

> Violence takes many forms. War. The outrages committed by terrorists. Human conflict in daily life and popular fiction. The antics of cartoon characters. Body contact sports. The ravages of natural disaster. They are facts of life. So long as it exists in society, television and radio programmes will reflect it, portray it and report it. Broadcasters have a duty to show real life in a violent world where natural disasters and human actions wreak havoc. To seek to prevent broadcasters from telling and retelling hard truths about the world would be a substantial disservice both to democracy and to our understanding of the human condition. The portrayal of violence has played a major part in popular storytelling throughout human history, and continues to have a place in the civilizing process of which broadcasting is a part.[98]

The British Code then refers to the concern that prolonged exposure to violence may desensitize audiences. Once again, this 'scientific' assumption finds its way into a 'legal' form and becomes the wisdom on the matter:

> There are some significant concerns about the portrayal of violence which broadcasters need to take into consideration. These include the fear that repeated exposure to violence desensitizes audiences, making them apathetic towards increases in actual violence or indifferent to the plight of victims or the copycat effect – outbreaks of violence similar to those shown on the screen – which could be a consequence of showing it in detail. Viewers might identify screen

violence with the reality of their own lives and become unreasonably fearful, for instance, being scared to go out at night alone. It could also encourage the view that violence is acceptable as the means of resolving disputes.[99]

Assertions as to the propensity to commit violence after watching television violence or the fears that broadcast violence can create in the minds of people are presented as scientific 'facts' here. The claim that broadcast violence may encourage viewers to consider violence as an acceptable conflict resolution tool also gains the respectable cloak of science. Yet this has nothing to do with a person's propensity to do something as a matter of scientific inquiry. This is a moral stance that violence is unacceptable and therefore one on which there may well be differences of opinion. As the Australian Broadcasting Authority stated in the *Mighty Morphin Power Rangers* case, violence in self defence may well be acceptable. So too resistance to brutal and oppressive regimes may justify civil disobedience. Is the 'violence' to which the Code refers to be read so narrowly?

The Code also calls for care in the reporting of violence in news programmes. In particular this is stated to be of concern when children are watching:

News bulletins are now part of the day-long output of many broadcast services. At some times of the day large numbers of children are viewing or listening, so broadcasters must continue to practise discretion over what is transmitted at different times and provide appropriate warnings.[100]

It is, as always, a matter of 'balance':

A balance needs to be struck between the demands of truth and the danger of desensitizing people. Where scenes of violence are included in television news bulletins, the fact that violence has bloody consequences should not be glossed over. There is also a danger of sanitizing violence. However:
- the dead should be treated with respect and not shown in close-up unless there are compelling reasons for doing so;
- close-ups of the injuries suffered by victims should generally be avoided;
- care should be taken not to linger unduly on the physical consequences of violence.[101]

The Independent Television Commission Programme Code reflects, as required, the concerns of the Broadcasting Standards Commission Code. In particular it refers to the susceptibility of young people:

There is portrayed violence which is potentially so disturbing that it might be psychologically harmful, particularly for young or emotionally insecure viewers. Research evidence shows that the socially or emotionally insecure individual, particularly if adolescent, is especially vulnerable. The susceptibilities of this minority must be balanced against the rights of the more robust majority. Responsible scheduling and appropriate content advice to viewers are both particularly relevant here.[102]

It is through the invoking of scientific 'research' that the codes claim thei legitimacy. But here there is a problem. The suggestion that adolescent are particularly vulnerable to portrayed violence appears to contradict th age based classification systems prevalent elsewhere which assum increasing age in a child, especially at around fourteen or fifteen, mean they will be able to view more violent images. The implication here is tha a child of that age may require special care to be taken. This may be ai oblique reference to the problem of youth suicide, but it also may be ai example of the contradictions which seem to permeate the whole world o television and children.

The British Broadcasting Corporation's *Producers' Guidelines* also addres children and violence. While the main 'buffer' between children an violent programming is the 9 p.m. Watershed, the guidelines also draw attention to the particular vulnerability of children:

> There is evidence that violence in circumstances resembling real life is more upsetting than violence in a fantasy setting. Children may feel particularly distressed when violence occurs in a familiar setting or between familiar figures. For instance, violence in the home between characters resembling their parents, or towards characters or pets, with which the child can sympathize, should be avoided. Children can also be particularly distressed by violence involving animals.

> The dangers of imitation are particularly real among children. Extra care should be taken, for example, over karate chops or the use of weapons that are easily accessible such as ropes or knives or bottles. Criminal acts, if shown, should not become lessons in 'how to do it'. It is also important not to conceal the consequences of real-life violence.[103]

Although the child is constructed as vulnerable, there is also here the chil as threat. This is the point to which the codes and other regulatory approaches seem to return constantly. The child as angel and as devil.

INCREASING STATE CONTROL AND VIOLENT PROGRAMMING

The rules and practices which regulate the relationship between childre and violent programming on television place into stark relief an importan theme of this book. The concern with television violence is not a simple one about the need to protect the easily upset child. This area of television regulation links with issues of juvenile crime, the role of parents and family and broader notions of authority and the use of force in society. As Collins and Kearns relate regarding the infamous case where two children killed a younger child:

> A range of social trends was implicated in the killing of Jamie Bulger, including the influence of television and movies on young people, the breakdown of the nuclear family, and the purported inability of adults to 'properly discipline' youth. Such themes are common in discussions about youth crime, a topic which is seldom far from the political agenda in Western nations.[104]

The same connections are made in discussions of violent programming. The 'panic' about television violence is part of the same debate which has demonized young people and denied them basic rights. It is no small accident that the consequence of linking television violence and juvenile crime is to place restrictions on what children may view on television, whether by way of self-censorship amongst broadcasters or parental control. This is nothing less than the denial to young people of the freedoms which adults enjoy. Nobody can argue with the role of parents to counsel and advise their children on the desirability of watching particular television programmes. But this process is not about that. The system of classification and regulation is about state control of what is appropriate for children and the manner in which it controls young people through the construction of what is deemed to be the 'appropriate' child. Those who fall outside that ideal risk being demonized.

It has also led to the demonization of parents too. There is a discernible shift away from regarding television viewing as a matter of family choice involving parental guidance towards the notion of parental responsibility. Again, this mirrors wider debates to do with the social control of young people of which parental responsibility laws form an important part. Thus one now observes National Society for the Prevention of Cruelty to Children pamphlets warning parents of the dangers to their children from violent programming:

> Take the issue of screen violence seriously. You know your children better than anyone, so it's your responsibility to protect them from images that may be harmful or disturbing.[105]

Parents, however, are not infallible. Part of the response to television violence has been the use of technology. The V-chip blocking device promises to remove the problem created by the absent parent who cannot be present to guide their child's viewing. Resort to this device also suggests that children cannot always be trusted to follow parental

guidelines. The idea of the child – here the disobedient child - intrudes
into the process at every turn. But the V-chip itself still requires someone
to switch it on, and more importantly, people who are able to classify the
programmes to be encoded. The classification criteria used to rate
programmes for such devices as the V-chip are fraught with difficulties.

There is first of all the problem of defining violence. In fact there is little
attempt in any code, law or inquiry to state a precise definition of
violence.[106] The approach instead tends to be one of 'common concern' or
'common sense'. As Atkinson and Gourdeau's summary concludes:

> Recent public inquiries into television violence seem to favour a
> more pragmatic approach to the problem by seeking to identify those
> types of violence to which the public seem particularly sensitive.
> While it should be noted that there is no unanimity as to the kinds of
> acts that are considered violent and undesirable, nevertheless, the
> inquiries reveal that the general public share a sufficient number of
> concerns about certain violent acts to justify that measures be taken
> to minimize and control the presentation of such violence.[107]

This public concern and shared understanding is just as likely to be the
result of the discourse on violence itself as to do with any rational
knowledge on the subject. The influence of Virginie Larivière on the
Canadian experience is a case in point. Official documents now proclaim
that her action had a 'profound impact' in the shaping of broadcast policy
on television. Yet it is rarely questioned what lay behind her 'crusade'. Her
stance was straightforward:

> Convinced that the influence of violent programming had been a
> factor in the rape and murder of her young sister, Ms Larivière
> demanded legislation banning all violence on TV.[108]

Her conviction that violent programming lay behind the death of her sister
might also be understood as a need to find an explanation for a crime for
which she needed an explanation. In the same way the judge who presided
at the trial of the two children who killed James Bulger in Liverpool stated
in his sentencing remarks that there was a possible link between their
actions and violent videos,[109] even though this had not been raised as an
issue at the trial. The need to explain 'irrational' acts can easily lead to
blame being ascribed for far from rational reasons. In this context, a
'violent' programme will tend to look like those acts which we fear. Yet
who is to say that the interviewee who espouses racist, sexist or
homophobic viewpoints is not more likely to encourage violence? It is
common sense which leads us to assume that screen violence looks like
real-life violence. But that is not the concern that most people share. For
them the issue is what might influence people to harm others. When
looked at in this way the concern of the V-chip rating system could

logically shift from the stylized dramatic portrayal of a violent event to the 'violence' contained within programmes which may appear docile.

Of course, this will not happen because it sounds like political censorship. The point is that the regulation of violence on television has little to do with the protection of children and a lot to do with state control of the definition and appropriate use of violence. What we learn from laws which seek to control violent programming is a particular definition of violence which distracts our attention from other more insidious forms of violence, such as state sponsored violence towards marginalized people, the violence of poverty and its causes and violence inflicted on women and children by the people who television law would lead us to believe will provide protective guidance.

Attempts to incorporate into law the 'science' of television violence illustrate how contradictory and confused such endeavours become. In January 2003 the Children's Protection from Violent Programming Bill was introduced into the United States Senate. Clause 2(5) and (6) provide:

(5) There is empirical evidence that children exposed to violent video programming have a greater tendency to assume that acts of violence are acceptable behavior and therefore to imitate such behavior.

(6) There is empirical evidence that children exposed to violent video programming have an increased fear of violence, resulting in increased self-protective behaviors and increased mistrust of others.

This is the child as angel and devil. Perpetrator and victim. Both are appropriate targets of state control as both must be protected from harmful material which will lead them, perhaps unwittingly, to hurt others or harm themselves. The popular representation of this Bill is that it is designed to close loopholes in the way in which blocking technology operates through more comprehensive rating systems. Opponents claim that this will create more effective censorship through the combination of technology and ratings systems. But it is through the manner in which such laws construct the child that state control is really asserted.

CHAPTER 5

The Sexualized World of Television and Children

In the final analysis the responsibility rests with directors, script writers and programmers to ensure that where sexuality appears in programming it does not portray a distorted view of human relations but reveals a range of behaviour and emotions which more accurately reflect these relations. We believe that good quality and absorbing programmes can be produced which avoid the gratuitous portrayal of sexuality without stifling artistic creativity or intellectual freedom.
(Senate Standing Committee on Education and the Arts Children and Television (Canberra, Australian Government Publishing Service, 1978), p. 43.)

... constitutional interpretation has consistently recognized that the parents' claim to authority in their own household to direct the rearing of their children is basic in the structure of our society...

The State also has an independent interest in the well-being of its youth.
(Ginsberg v New York 390 US 629 (1968))

The issues surrounding the portrayal of sexual behaviour on television and how it affects children have been some of the most keenly contested matters in broadcasting. It is no surprise then that the law and regulatory mechanisms have often been called upon to strike a 'balance' between often deeply entrenched and opposing views about the nature of childhood, the role of television as a moral educator and artistic and editorial freedom. In this regard the issues and approaches are similar with respect to sexual matters on television as we have seen with violence. However, in recent times much more attention has been directed towards violence as a problem on television and there has been less concern with sexual content.

There may be a number of reasons for this. Attitudes to sexual content in programming may be changing. Research undertaken in 1998 for the British Broadcasting Standards Commission found that there had been some marked shifts in attitudes towards sexual content since an earlier study in 1992.[1] It found that a more liberal attitude to sexual matters on television was more evident.[2] Even as early as 1978 in Australia the Senate Committee which inquired into Children and Television found that 'the portrayal of sex in television programmes did not emerge as a significant issue' although there were some complaints to the Committee that programming tended to concentrate 'on the physical side of sex as opposed to sex as an integral part of human relations'.[3] When in 1981 the Australian Senate returned to review its 1978 Report, sex in programmes barely rated a mention.[4] The Victorian Parliamentary Committee's inquiry into the effects of television on children and families did not even devote a separate chapter on sexual content. It did, however, discuss sexually aggressive behaviour as a part of television and multimedia violence,[5] although it has to be acknowledged that debates on pornography include the question whether all pornography is by definition 'violent' on the basis it demeans particularly women and contributes to negative attitudes towards them by men.[6] This raises again the issue of the definition of violence and blurs the distinction between violence as a separate area of inquiry and sexual content on television. But such concerns probably have more relevance for other forms of media apart from television, such as video recordings and the internet where there is what is regarded as more 'sexually explicit' material available.

Another possible reason for a decline in concern about sexual content on television is that, as the above suggests, television has been surpassed by other media forms as a focus of concern.[7] Prior to video recorders and home computers, it was relatively easy to control the viewing of children. A combination of 'adults only' viewing periods, parental supervision and responsible broadcasting could work to limit most children's access to 'unsuitable' programmes. The major concern was the child who watched unsupervised or whose parents failed to apply appropriate guidance. The video recorder changed all that. Children could access taped programmes at any hour of the day and so eliminate the barrier of the watershed. Parents busy at work could not then assume their children were protected from unsuitable programmes because of the time of the day. The video recorder also offered the possibility of freezing the image or rewinding the film. Thus scenes could be taken out of context and replayed. The 'wicked' child could circumvent the classification of films that might justify sexual content in the context of the storyline by removing the context altogether.

If the video recorder deflected some attention away from television, then the internet has of course been an even larger distraction. Technologically astute children able to operate computers and access sexual content on the internet pose even greater fears for many adults than their competence with the humble video recorder ever did. Of course, at the base of this concern about the new forms of media is still the problem of how children are to be viewed and constructed. The new technology simply alters the manner in which that debate is conducted, as Potter and Potter remark:

The clear message is that parents need to monitor their children's activities and react to them when they see their children heading in an objectionable direction. The equally clear signal is that children are growing up faster than they did in 'our' day and we need to stay one step ahead of them in order to control them. In a sense, the message remains the same, only the technology changes. New technology brings uncertainty and danger if parents do not police its employment in the home.[8]

Thus, the concern about children and their access to sexual material has not disappeared, although the focus of that concern may have moved away from television and to the internet and other new media. A recent Australian study on youth and pornography reported high numbers of young people, mainly boys aged sixteen and seventeen, had watched X-rated videos and accessed internet sex sites.[9] Such statistics can be used to create a moral panic and may not take into account children reporting that they have accessed such material as a means of achieving social status amongst their peers.[10] But whether or not such material is being viewed by children, the fact that adults are concerned enough to research the area indicates some continuing concern in some quarters about the access of children to sexual content in the media. The Victorian Parliamentary Committee thus noted that 'there is little doubt that young people are accessing such material for their own titillation or being shown such material in an attempt to seduce them to engage in similar activity.'[11] Once again here is the dual image of the child. The little devil who seeks titillation and who must be controlled together with the innocent child seduced no doubt by preying adults from whom he or she must be protected.

SEXUAL CONTENT AND CHILDHOOD INNOCENCE

Clearly, there is a continuing concern about the access of children to depictions of sexual activity on television and through other forms of media. The question is whether the censorship of sexual imagery on television, done in the name of protecting children, in fact disguises the fears and insecurities of adults. The desire to perpetuate 'childhood innocence' rather than any well thought out theory of child development has been used to explain the censorial motivations of adults. Thus Hendershot writes:

> Adults both produce and censor TV for children, and they speak to and for children through such activities. By examining that process, we can see how adults use television to reinforce their own ideas about what constitutes childhood innocence and how that innocence is (according to reformers, censors, and some parents)

or is not (according to TV producers, free market advocates, and some parents) imperilled.[12]

Such work is in the tradition of Phillipe Ariés and his contribution to the history of childhood, and in particular the idea that 'childhood' is a changing concept through time which each epoch constructs in a manner appropriate for that time.[13] On matters of sexuality Ariés makes the point that our attitudes today with respect to the mixing of sexuality and children were not always so:

> One of the unwritten laws of contemporary morality, the strictest and best respected of all, requires adults to avoid any reference, above all any humorous reference, to sexual matters in the presence of children. This notion was entirely foreign to the society of old. The modern reader of the diary in which Henry IV's physician, Heroard, recorded the details of the young Louis XIII's life is astonished by the liberties which people took with children, by the coarseness of the jokes they made, and by the indecency of gestures made in public which shocked nobody and which were regarded as perfectly natural.[14]

Ariés proceeds to describe various interactions between adult carer and child focusing on the child's genitals which as Ariés acknowledges would raise concern, if not a child protection inquiry, if practised today. As he comments:

> The lack of reserve with regard to children surprises us: we raise our eyebrows at the outspoken talk but even more at the bold gestures, the physical contacts, about which it is easy to imagine what a modern psycho-analyst would say. The psycho-analyst would be wrong. The attitude to sex, and doubtless sex itself, varies according to environment, and consequently according to period and mentality. Nowadays the physical contacts described by Heroard would strike us as bordering on sexual perversion and nobody would dare to indulge in them publicly. This was not the case at the beginning of the seventeenth century.[15]

Richard Sennett describes how Ancient Greeks also approached sexuality in a manner which would be regarded as abhorrent today. For those who lived in ancient Athens the introduction to sexuality was an aspect of preparation for full citizenship:

> Unlike modern moralists, the Athenians thought sexuality to be a positive element of citizenship. This was more than a matter of observing sexual prohibitions, like the belief that masturbation was fit only for slaves, with whom no one else would want to make love; more than a matter of imposing laws such as those forbidding slaves

to go to the gymnasia, 'being in love with a boy of free status, or following him.' [Aiskhines, *Prosecution of Timarkhus*, 138ff; quoted in Kenneth Dover, *Greek Homsexuality* (Cambridge, MA: Harvard University Press, 1989)] In the gymnasium a boy learned how [to] use his body so that he could desire and be desired honourably.

As a Greek male passed through the life cycle, he would be loved by older men, then feel love for boys as he aged; he would also feel erotic love for women . . .'[16]

The idea that childhood sexuality exists at all appears confronting to many in contemporary society. Current concerns surrounding paedophilia also fuel criticism of anyone who appears to advocate the sexualization of childhood. But the problem in the regulation of television is that it is a sexualized form of entertainment. Television often focuses on body image and appearance. Sexuality is an important part of life and will feature in film and other dramas. Sex sells and advertising too uses sexual imagery to market products. While it is more often teenage children who become part of this sexualized media, even the reporting of child sexual abuse 'sexualizes' children: for while such coverage is the serious business of news, at another level it serves to bring to our attention that a certain number of people exist who seek sexual gratification from children.[17]

THE DISCOURSES OF CHILDREN, SEXUALITY AND TELEVISION

To understand the legal response to calls for the regulation of children's exposure to sex on television it is first necessary to appreciate the various discourses which operate in this area. As suggested above, the discourses are centred on one of two views of childhood. The first regards childhood as an age of innocence where the vulnerable child must be protected from harm or the corrupting influences of sexual imagery on television. In this view, such children have no real interest in sexual content, but can be deprived of their childhood by those adults who would exploit their vulnerability through exposing them to sexual imagery. A related view of the child is that he or she is an inquisitive creature that will seek out sexual information on television and unwarily be seduced by the messages encountered. The other view upon which discourse in this context is based is that the child is a 'little devil' that will actively search for sexual content on television with at least some understanding of its potential 'wickedness'. Such children, it is said, must be tamed and controlled.

The discourses which operate here give rise to competing under-standings of the need for censorship with respect to sexual content on television. One view which arises from the idea of the 'innocent child' is that children are not particularly interested in sex and as a consequence regulation of sexual content serves little purpose. This view has most resonance in the case of young children who are not yet old enough to understand the nature of what they are viewing. But as Heins notes, the debate about sexual content on television really centres on children over seven and teenagers, that is those children old enough to understand the nature of what they are viewing, and in the case of teenagers those children who represent the group most in need of being tamed.[18] In the case of the 'untamed' child the need for censorship and control is akin to that which justifies control of violent programming. The child is feared, and in this case the concern is as much to do with the harm such a child may do to others as it is to do with any self harm they may commit. Clearly, the conceptions of childhood present here are competing and contradictory. It is to the regulatory mechanism in television we now turn to see how it attempts to reconcile these images of the child.

REGULATING SEX ON TELEVISION: THE USE OF AMBIGUITY

The various codes of practice which operate in Australia, Canada and the United Kingdom address the broadcasting of sexual content. As with the area of violent programming, these sections of the codes raise similar approaches and problems. For example, the Australian Broadcasting Corporation's Code of Practice refers to the broadcasting of 'sex and sexuality':

Provided it is handled with integrity, any of the following treatments of sex and sexuality may be appropriate and necessary to a programme:

– it can be discussed and reported in the context of news, information or documentary programmes;
– it can be referred to in drama, comedy, lyrics or fictional programmes; and
– it can be depicted, implicitly or explicitly.[19]

The proviso that such matter be 'handled with integrity' is certainly vague. Such a test for the appropriateness of the programme provides little clarity about what might be acceptable. This may not be surprising, as whether sexual material is handled properly or not is clearly subject to the particular views of the producer, artist and individuals in the audience. There is unlikely to be a consensus on such matters. Indeed, one of the purposes of such programming will be to inform, shock or challenge people's views and the very notion that attitudes to sexual content on television is said to be changing owes much to programming which has 'pushed the boundaries' in the past.

The danger in such guidelines is that in order not to offend, broadcasters will impose self censorship so as to appeal to the broadest possible audience.[20] This is consistent, of course, with achieving the aim of maximizing exposure of programmes so as to increase revenue from advertising. Another view is that commercial pressures operate as a force which encourages the use of sexual content to attract larger audiences. There is no doubt that many groups in the community exploit this perception to challenge the nature of programme content in commercial television. Such considerations are probably not as much to the fore in non-commercial television and so the state run Australian Broadcasting Corporation can afford to impose guidelines which appear more flexible around appropriate programme content. Nevertheless, it would be difficult for even a state owned network to screen programmes with a substantially higher 'extreme' sexual content that is clearly at odds with standards being applied in the commercial sector. There is also the pressure that is brought to bear by those in the community concerned with the 'morality' of broadcast programmes, regardless of their source.

The Australian Commercial Television Code of Practice links the nature of sexual content to the particular classifications in use in that country. Thus for the G classification the treatment of sex and nudity must comply with the following criteria:

> Visual depiction of, and verbal references to, sexual behaviour must be brief, infrequent, contain little or no detail and be strictly limited to the storyline or programme context. Restrained, brief and infrequent visual depiction of nudity only when absolutely necessary to the storyline or programme context.[21]

In addition it must be noted that all G classified material must not contain any material that could be unsuitable for a child to watch unsupervised. Such provisions take on the mantra of legislative provisions when applied to individual cases. Thus while the partial justification for the Code is the need to protect children from harmful material, this soon becomes lost in the legalistic interpretation of the section. For example, in one case the Australian Broadcasting Authority was asked to investigate a complaint under the Code with respect to nudity screened during a G classified programme. In the offending programme (a morning current affairs programme) a report contained a segment on the making of a commercial for a low fat food – 'Skinny Dip'. The commercial was to involve three men dancing naked but holding cards in front of them to represent lids of the product. The selection of the men required them to rehearse the dance routine and the programme segment used a camera angle whereby three shots of the men's buttocks was included. The interviewer also made sexually suggestive remarks about the 'averageness' (in relation to their genitalia) of the applicants.[22]

The network argued that the report was light-hearted, and that the nudity was justified by the programme context. It claimed that the nudity was discreet and was intended to be comical.[23] The broadcasting authority commented that it recognized that the segment was meant to be humorous and that the majority of the programme's audience would not have been offended. However, the Authority had 'to assess the programme in relation to the Code'.[24] This led the Authority to make two findings. First, in relation to the sexually suggestive remarks:

> the ABA considers that while they could be seen to be sexually suggestive and therefore regarded as inappropriate material for an immature audience, such as unsupervised children, the commentary in itself did not breach the criteria for 'G' classified programmes under the Code.[25]

It then proceeded to comment on the nudity:

> the ABA found that the broadcast of the bare buttocks shots was not a 'discreet' portrayal of nudity. The ABA also found that the depiction of bare buttocks was not absolutely necessary to the programme context. The ABA considers that the viewers of the *Today* programme would have guessed that the men were naked by the way they appeared before the seated judges, holding cards taken from lids of 'Skinny Dip' in front of their genitals, and that therefore it was not necessary to view their bare buttocks to be aware of their nakedness. The ABA notes that the actual broadcast of the 'Skinny Dip' commercial after the segment in question, did not show the men from behind and yet gave the same concept and humour.[26]

There is in this decision little mention of children even though they are the primary group for which the provision is designed to protect. The analysis becomes embedded in the interpretation of a word or phrase and seems removed from the apparent reasons for bringing the Code into existence. Such is the nature of the legal and regulatory process. There is thus the seeming inconsistency between the 'sexually suggestive' comments that might have been and the portrayal of nudity which was not 'discreet', although it is not clearly explained why that conclusion was reached. It is the lack of necessity with respect to the programme context which ultimately decides the matter, but then it could be complained that a segment of naked dancing is not the same thing if one removes the nudity. Reliance was also placed on the role of the Code in reflecting 'community standards'. This point was not lost on the network who attempted to justify the segment on the basis that:

> The segment was a light-hearted, comical report of the making of a commercial involving naked men. It could not, in Nine's view, have

offended any reasonable viewer. Further, there is no basis on which that material could be considered unsuitable for children to watch without the supervision of a parent.

The Code of Practice is intended to reflect community standards. In Nine's view, brief shots of three ordinary men from behind in a clearly comical context are clearly acceptable within the confines of both Clause 2.10.2 [the equivalent part of the Code at the time] and current community standards.[27]

This demonstrates the problem of articulating such amorphous concepts as 'community standards'. Indeed, the Authority did not necessarily disagree. The difficulty was that this missed the point, as the ABA explained:

the ABA accepts that most viewers of the programme would not have been offended and would have been aware of the reliance on visual humour. However, as the Code stands, 'G' classified programmes must satisfy the relevant criteria irrespective of the actual profile of the target audience. As such, the ABA finds that there was a breach of Clause 2.10.2 of the Code. If the Nine Network considers that the Code is 'at odds' with current community standards it is suggested that they raise this in the context of the next review of the Code.[28]

What is not clear is whether the network in referring to the 'reasonable viewer' or the ABA when it mentions 'most viewers' are including children within those terms. The fact that the Code requires an examination of what is 'unsuitable' for children to watch unsupervised would appear to suggest that some examination of community standards – at least around that point – is required. The ABA on the other hand adopted a bureaucratic approach in arguing that it must merely 'apply' the Code.

This case indicates once again the manner in which scientific concern about harm to children is translated into a legal problem and then becomes part of a different discourse. The focus of legal discourse is not simply about the original purpose for the particular provision. The process becomes concerned with the language of the law and how it now constructs the problem. The question of 'community standards' becomes sidelined by the words in the Code. In this case, the ABA can always resort to the defence of having to apply the law regardless of the apparent absurdity of imposing a protective provision which protects no one. But there is also the manner in which this whole process makes the child invisible. There is no consideration in the decision as to the likely impact on the child of such images. Such harm to children is assumed rather than proven. Once the child is invisible in the process it becomes difficult to shift from a protective view of the child to one which might consider their right to view such material on television.

The higher classification ratings in Australia possess similar problems of interpretation. The 'PG' classification requires that depictions of sexual behaviour must be 'restrained, mild in impact and justified by the storyline or programme context'.[29] The 'M' classification provides that 'visual depiction of intimate sexual behaviour may only be implied or simulated in a restrained way. It must be justified by the storyline or programme context. Verbal references to sexual activity should not be detailed.'[30] The highest rating, 'MA', states that sexual content is within the classification where there is 'visual depiction of intimate sexual behaviour (which may only be discreetly implied or discreetly simulated) or of nudity only where relevant to the storyline or programme' context.[31] But an MA classification cannot be granted to a programme 'where the subject matter serves largely or wholly as a vehicle for gratuitous, exploitative or demeaning portrayal of sexual behaviour or nudity. Exploitative or non-consenting sexual relations must not be depicted as desirable.'[32]

The Code of Ethics overseen by the Canadian Broadcast Standard Council contains a number of provisions which relate to sexual content in programming. Clause 10 includes in relation to scheduling that:

(a) Programming which contains sexually explicit material or coarse or offensive language intended for adult audiences shall not be telecast before the late viewing period, defined as 9 p.m. to 6 a.m. Broadcasters shall refer to the Voluntary Code Regarding Violence in Television Programming for provisions relating to the scheduling of programming containing depictions of violence.

(b) Recognizing that there are older children watching television after 9 p.m., broadcasters shall adhere to the provisions of Clause 11 below (viewer advisories), enabling viewers to make an informed decision as to the suitability of the programming for themselves and their family members.

. . .

(d) Broadcasters shall take special precautions to advise viewers of the content of programming intended for adult audiences, which is telecast before 9 p.m. in accordance with Clause 10(c).

(e) Promotional material which contains sexually explicit material or coarse or offensive language intended for adult audiences shall not be telecast before 9 p.m.

(f) Advertisements which contain sexually explicit material or coarse or offensive language intended for adult audiences, such as those for theatrically presented feature films, shall not be telecast before 9 p.m.[33]

Clause 11 of the Code also provides for the placing of viewer advisories at the beginning of programmes and after commercial breaks where the programme includes 'mature subject matter or scenes with nudity or sexually explicit material, coarse or offensive language or other material susceptible of offending viewers'.

The contrast in terms between Australia and Canada is stark. While in Australia sexual content even at the highest rating must be 'discreetly implied', in Canada it is 'sexually explicit material' that can only be screened after 9 p.m. This does not necessarily mean that the Canadian Code provides greater latitude in sexual content. But the different use of language between jurisdictions can confuse the issue of what is permissible to broadcast. After all, if 'community standards' are what the codes are designed to implement, then one might expect variation from community to community. But in an age of global television programming, one could ask, just where is the community located?

The United Kingdom Code on Standards is formulated by the Broadcasting Standards Commission. In relation to the portrayal of sexual conduct the Code first notes the current climate of opinion:

> Research shows that audiences in Britain have generally become more liberal and relaxed about the portrayal of sex, but broadcasters cannot assume a universal climate of tolerance towards sexually explicit material. Offence may be given by making public and explicit what many people regard as private and exclusive.[34]

It then continues to attempt to indicate the 'balance' that must be drawn when dealing with sexual content:

> 80 Radio and television have to meet the expectations of wide audiences which will encompass a spectrum of tolerance towards the portrayal of sexual relationships. However, even those unlikely to be offended themselves may be concerned about viewing some programmes in the company of others, and are likely to be mindful of the effects on children. Broadcasters have a duty to act responsibly and reflect the fact that relations within and between the sexes normally reflect moral choices. Audiences should not be reduced to voyeurs, nor the participants to objects. The youth and physical attractiveness of the participants are no justification for explicitness.

> 81 Sensitive scheduling, especially within the hour around the Watershed, is particularly important for items involving sexual matters. Broadcasters should provide straightforward labelling in clear language and sufficient warnings about programmes containing explicit material.

> 82 Encrypted subscription and Pay Per View services offering explicit sexual content cater to self selected adult audiences. But the

depiction of sex is bound by the law relating to hard–core pornography and obscenity.[35]

Although the Code requires broadcasters 'to act responsibly' and to ngage in 'sensitive scheduling', this does not provide clarity as to what ight offend the Code. Even the reference to the law of pornography and bscenity is not particularly helpful, as this is an area of the law with many rey areas. The Independent Television Commission in the United ingdom continues this tendency to generalize around the issue of sexual ontent. The language is florid but not clear as to the requirements:

Much great fiction and drama have been concerned with love and passion which can shock and disturb. Popular entertainment and comedy have always relied to some extent on sexual innuendo and suggestive behaviour but gratuitous offence should be avoided.

Careful consideration should be given to nudity before the Watershed but some nudity may be justifiable in a non-sexual and relevant context.

Representations of sexual intercourse should not occur before the Watershed unless there is a serious educational purpose. Any portrayal of sexual behaviour must be defensible in context. If included before the Watershed it must be appropriately limited and inexplicit.

Sex scenes of a more adult nature, which are more graphic and prolonged, should be limited to much later in the schedule.[36]

The Independent Television Commission Code also refers to the uropean Council's Television Without Frontiers Directive 1997 (Article 2.1) which requires broadcasters to take 'appropriate measures to ensure hat television broadcasts ... do not include any programmes which might eriously impair the physical, mental or moral development of minors, in articular programmes that involve pornography or gratuitous violence'. he Code also refers to the other requirements in the directive that varnings about content which might be 'likely to impair the physical, nental or moral development of minors' are to be broadcast prior to the ommencement of the programmes.[37] This exemplifies the problem of community standards' in the regulation of television. Can it be assumed hat what is regulated as harmful or beneficial to children will be the same n different countries?

Even within communities there must be difference. As the British Broadcasting Corporation's *Producers' Guidelines* indicate, the tolerance of he United Kingdom audience still requires 'sensitivity' in handling of exual content as not all members of an audience possess the same views:

The portrayal and depiction of sex will always be a part of both drama and factual programmes because of the important part it plays in most people's emotions and experience. In this, as in most areas of taste, public attitudes have shifted over time. Broadly, audiences in the United Kingdom have become more liberal in their acceptance of sexually explicit material while attitudes around the world are mixed. Even so programme-makers broadcasting to diverse audiences in their homes, are not as free as film-makers, theatre dramatists and novelists whose audiences are self-selected.

Adults who accept frank portrayal of sex and sexuality in other formats or on television in the later evening often demand different standards at other times. Those watching with children before 9 p.m. expect programme-makers to observe the Watershed by exercising appropriate restraint. Context, the intention of the production, the expectations of the audience, the Watershed and signposting are all vital.

When sexual subjects feature in news, documentaries and discussion programmes, programme-makers must observe the need for careful scheduling, labelling and signposting. Sensitive handling can help prevent the most delicate of subjects from causing widespread offence. Sensationalism should be avoided and extremes of sexual behaviour should not be presented as though they are the norm.[38]

Questions of definition arise once more. What is meant by 'extremes o sexual behaviour'? The Code appears to contain a host of unstate assumptions about normality with respect to sexual behaviour. It is as i 'common sense' is the required ingredient. But in an increasingly diverse community, how can one rely on that? What is clear is that children have no place in the portrayal of sexual matter, apart from perhaps 'se education'. The *Guidelines* stress the distinction between 'adult material and suitable programming for children. The *Guidelines* thus continue:

Some drama series, factual and discussion programmes have shown that they are able to deal with difficult material and adult storylines in a way that is acceptable to a pre-Watershed audience. However, sensationalism in choice of subject and explicitness in the treatment of sexual themes should be avoided.

We use the Watershed to try to ensure that adults view what is intended for adults. Sexual activity is linked to moral decisions, therefore its portrayal should not be separated from an acknowledgement of the moral process.

Drama and factual programmes have a part to play in illuminating the darker side of human nature. Sometimes themes and images are explored which may shock. The tests to apply are intention, (are we illuminating?), and judgement (does our portrayal demean or degrade?). We must draw the line well short of anything that might be labelled obscene or pornographic. For example, real, as opposed to simulated, sexual intercourse should not be shown.

We try to operate by certain basic rules that apply to all programmes that deal with sexual activity:

– programmes should be adequately and clearly signposted
– scenes should have a clear and legitimate editorial purpose and not be gratuitous
– sexually explicit material will not appear before the Watershed, nor at inappropriate times too close to the Watershed
– there are limits to explicit portrayal at any time
– material involving sexual violence or sadism will be treated with particular care and circumspection.

Sexual scenes that will disturb or shock should occur only for good dramatic reasons. In particular, viewers remain concerned about the depiction of sexual violence against women and sadistic sexual material. Such material demands careful consultation within departments and with Channel Controllers or, at their request, Chief Adviser Editorial Policy.[39]

The *Guidelines* then refer to the need to provide information about the content of programmes, that 'sexually explicit' programming should not be scheduled before the Watershed, that there are limits to explicit material at any time and that 'material involving sexual violence or sadism will be treated with particular care and circumspection'.[40] They also include reference to stereotyping and sexuality as issues to consider:

Care should also be taken not to reflect in an unthinking way stereotypes of either male or female behaviour or apply different standards to male or female nudity. Sexuality is a universal human attribute: depiction of sex should not be linked solely or inevitably to the physical attractiveness of the characters involved.

Attitudes to homosexuality differ both domestically and internationally. Research suggests that in Britain audiences are becoming more tolerant of the portrayal and discussion of homosexuality, and while some international audiences are more liberal, some are more conservative. Nevertheless programme-makers should be mindful that a significant part of the audience is critical of any depiction of homosexual acts.[41]

It is easy to be critical of such a guideline as it illustrates the recurring inconsistencies in the regulation of television generally. On the one hand there is an apparent recognition of the need to avoid stereotyping on the basis of gender. Such concern appears perfectly valid if a more diverse and tolerant society is the objective. What follows is in effect a caution about particular form of sexuality and a concern, not with 'communit standards', but with 'a significant part of the audience' who may b critical of homosexuality. If it was open to question whether 'communit standards' do in fact lie beneath the codes and guidelines which regulat broadcasting then here is an example of a guideline which appears to flou other laws of the land which prohibit discrimination on the grounds c sexual preference. It raises the question: whose standards do suc guidelines actually seek to enforce?

THE MISSING CHILD

What is clear from the rules and guidelines surrounding sexual content o television is the absence of the child. There is no ambiguity here. Childre are defined out of the discussion which takes place in relation t depictions of sexual behaviour. The Watershed is the main device whic achieves this in Australia, Canada and the United Kingdom and th manner in which its justification is articulated defines both the nature c sexual content and the place of children with respect to that matter. I 1995 the Canadian Broadcast Standards Council explained the Watershe when deciding on a complaint about the airing of an advertisement whic was said to offend good taste by way of sexual references. The complain in particular was concerned about the promotion for the programm which was broadcast during a movie which was popular with youn people. Two of the advertisements were aired in the half hour befor 9 p.m. and one was screened in the half hour after that time.

The Council came to the conclusion that no breach of the Cod occurred. In coming to that conclusion it commented on the Watershed

> Since this is the Council's first decision dealing in any significant way with the 'Watershed' hour, it is worth noting what it is and what purpose it serves. In its literal sense, it, of course, denotes the line separating waters flowing into different rivers or river basins. Popularly, the term has been applied to threshold issues but the literal meaning of the word gives the best visual sense of programming falling on one side or other of a defined line, in this case a time line. Programming seen as suitable for children and families falls on the early side of the line; programming targeted primarily for adults falls on the late side of the line. It should be noted that the definition of that time line varies from country to country, from 8.30 p.m. in New Zealand to 10.30 p.m. in France. (Great Britain, Finland, South Africa and Australia all share the Canadian choice of 9 p.m. as the Watershed.)

In Canada, the Watershed was developed as a principal

component of the 1993 Violence Code, establishing the hour *before which* no violent programming intended for adult audiences would be shown. Despite the establishment of the Watershed for *that* purpose, the Council has reason to believe that broadcasters regularly consider this hour as a rough threshold for *other* types of adult programming. There is, in fact, no formal restriction on the timing of broadcasting of slightly 'racy' material but the earliest of the promos under consideration here could not be said to have been run in a time slot which was *primarily* a *young* children's slot or even at a time when one would have expected significant numbers of young children to be watching television at all. The broadcaster's research showed 'that the audience for this show was overwhelmingly adult'. The Council did not agree with the complainant's contention that the programme audience could be expected to have ' "general" viewer appeal (age ten and up)'. Had the broadcaster desired or expected that result, the show would have been aired at an earlier hour.[42]

The analysis of the application of the Code appears to be legalistic. The decision is delivered in language which draws on the analytical approach of the law. Yet at every turn the concepts seem to be subject to the exercise of arbitrary judgements. When is an audience 'overwhelmingly adult'? Is not the composition of the audience relevant in determining whether a programme is suitable for screening? If any children are viewing does that affect what can be broadcast? These are the type of questions which any legal analysis of the codes will raise. How then does a broadcaster determine the meaning to give to the words in the codes of practice?

In practice, one might expect broadcasters to exercise a form of self-censorship. Hendershot attempts to explain the process of self-censorship which operates within United States networks to make the formal laws effectively irrelevant for the content standards of programmes. She explains:

Cartoon producers send their scripts, storyboards, and final cartoons to the Standards department of the network to which they are contracted. Producer and network exchange memos, haggle over details, and sometimes reach an equitable compromise. Standards criteria are constantly revised by individual networks; there is no single set of rules to which all networks adhere. Technically, only the networks (ABC, CBS, NBC and Fox) need Standards departments, the reasoning being that the networks use the publicly owned broadcast spectrum and their programming is available to all, whereas cable is paid for, does not use the spectrum, and is not required by law to operate in 'the public interest, convenience, and necessity.' In the name of public relations, however, cable venues that direct much of their programming to children, such as the Cartoon Network, do have their own internal Standards departments. Each Standards department upholds different criteria, and in fact, each person within each Standards department has a slightly different conception of how to regulate cartoons.[43]

She notes that the criteria which are imposed by the networks are 'malleable' and cannot be read using a legal model.[44] Her anlaysis is that such documents are manipulated and avoided by producers and industry self-regulators in order to achieve desired outcomes. An examination of standards, codes and guidelines will not reveal how self-censorship actually works, maintains Hendershot, as it is the unwritten communications and negotiations which would actually reveal how the system works.[45]

It may be that there is a little more transparency in Australia, Canada and the United Kingdom when compared with the United States as far as the availability of content standards and codes of practice goes. But the general point made by Hendershot seems to be just as applicable in those countries as it is in the United States. The codes of practice are in the first instance interpreted by the producers and networks. It is only in Australia where some pre-classification by the industry regulator occurs in the case of the Children's Television Standards. As has been seen, the language of the codes is often vague and general. In part, this is due to the nature of the material to which most concern is usually addressed. Sexual content is extremely difficult to handle without offending some part of the audience and the taboo nature of sexual matters for many in the community make even the writing of a workable code a vexed project. Ambiguous language is very useful in such circumstances as it may then please everyone as each reads into the code their own meaning of the words. Herein lies the problem of course, for it is at this point that producers, network executives, members of the public, and ultimately regulatory bodies are able to manipulate that language to justify or denigrate a particular programming choice as the case may be.

I do not agree entirely with Hendershot that the codes cannot be read with a 'legal model'. It is true that a positivist legal approach is unsatisfactory as a means of understanding the codes and content standards which operate in the regulation of television. But this is not the only legal model which exists. A more critical approach to the idea of law would regard the use of the ambiguity in the relevant documents, the reliance on amorphous concepts such as the 'ordinary reasonable child' and the behind the scenes negotiations which take place between producers and network executives as very much a part of the legal process.[46] There is according to this approach no such thing as a contradiction within the law, law *is* contradiction:

law operates with conflicting principles and contradictory effects at every level from High Court judgements to administrative law. As Hirst has pointed out, there is now considerable dispute as to what law is. Notwithstanding this, the collectivity to which the label law is applied presents us with the appearance of unity and singularity. Hence law contains a plurality of principles, knowledges, and events, yet it claims a unity through the common usage of the term 'law'.[47]

It should not then surprise that the Codes and standards utilize concepts which are difficult to define. Nor should it surprise that the type of behaviour thought to be inappropriate in one context is not so labelled in another. This is the manner in which legal rules permit other considerations to be given importance in some instances but not in others. It will not always be consistent or rational. It is not designed to be so.

In a visit to the Australian Film Censorship Board (as it was then called) a number of years ago I asked one member how he worked out what was suitable for children to view, as this was a core criteria of many classifications. He thought for a moment and referred to the fact that he had children and could use his observations of their reactions and understanding of the world to gauge what was suitable for children. I think he appreciated the point that the idea of what was suitable for a child to watch in a film was very subjective but I am not sure that he considered this part of his approach to be part of the legal process. When the 'law' sets down vague tests, one must often then go outside 'the law' to apply them. This would be the orthodox understanding of this process. This is not what happens. The law has built into itself concepts which are fluid to accommodate difference in the community. These concepts lead to subjective and at times arbitrary decision-making. In this, the value positions and assumptions of the decision-maker become central to the process. We need to understand this before we can address the 'fairness' of the law. It is only then that we can address the fundamental assumptions upon which decisions are based in order to achieve fairer outcomes. In this area various assumptions about children underpin decisions abut classification and therefore what children will be able to view. As I have argued, many of these assumptions are either ill-considered or lacking in completeness in their view of the child. Left to subjective interpretation, the rules also offer little effective protection for children from broadcasters pursuing their own interests, while at the same time failing to acknowledge the independent rights of the child.

But the law also has the ability to create the illusion of unity around these assumptions about the child. The idea of childhood to which most but by no means all of the law subscribes is one which constructs the child as vulnerable, immature and incompetent. This fits well with *a* view of childhood that many adults are content to nurture. Once internalized by adult lawmakers and transferred into the law it will surface as legal principle and become the benchmark for judging those matters to which that law applies. The regulation of sexual content on television is clearly one such area.

The rules which regulate this aspect of the relationship between children and television thus conspire to make the child 'invisible'. The import of the notion of the Watershed is that children will either simply not be there when sexual matter is being depicted, or if they are it will be because the material is being discussed in the most slight manner. The broad message is that children and sexual content do not mix. What happens, of course, is that complaints which are raised about the appropriateness of programming which appears to be 'sexually suggestive' or unsuitable for children due to sexual content then become an analysis of the meaning of 'sexual' and a discussion of the ability of the child to watch the material unsupervised, for example. The application of that 'law' cannot countenance any questioning of the internal assumptions which the law makes. Children's immaturity is the given, not as a matter of child development but as a matter of law.

The problem, naturally, is that this is not the only understanding of the child with respect to sexuality. The contradictions are obvious in terms of the manner in which children are portrayed in the media itself and in their actual behaviour. As Thomson points out there are many children in the United Kingdom, for example, who engage in sexual intercourse before they become sixteen, the legal age of consent.[48] As she states:

> The child is central to modern sexuality. Children and teenagers are sexualized by the way that youthfulness is sold to adult consumers and ultimately sold back to the young as they enter into market relations as consumers of make up, fashion, music and games ... Children are also sexualized by the attention that we pay to those who prey on them, with media coverage of paedophiles and abusers revealing a prurient fascination with the child as a passive yet sexual object, sexually innocent yet corruptible.[49]

The first inclination is to suggest that the law which regulates the relationship between children and television is out of step with the reality of childhood sexuality. It is clear, it might be argued, that many children handle sexual matters with more competence than they may be thought to possess. Codes and guidelines look odd when they perpetuate a view of the child which has for many children little semblance with their reality. But this approach, of explaining the dissonance between law and 'reality', would be wrong. For there is within legal discourse a construction of the child that does recognize its autonomy and capacity for independent action. It is the view of the child which forms the basis of the dissent in *Marion's Case* and *Irwin Toys*.[50] It is the philosophical underpinning of various articles in the United Nations Convention on the Rights of the Child. In juvenile justice statutes it is the rationale for providing young people with legal representation and punishing them so that they understand the consequences of their behaviour. In family law it is the reasoning behind the child's wishes being considered when making a decision as to where the child should live when parents separate.

The question is not therefore how television law should be rewritten to equate with other conceptions of the child. It is how television law can be recast to incorporate those legal approaches which emanate from a different understanding of the child. It is a matter of getting more 'law' into the field, and not the narrow and limited legal approach which we currently witness around the globe. This way into the problem of the content of television law as it affects children is most apparent in the case of the United States and the way in which First Amendment rights come into play when considering sexual content on television.

UNITED STATES BROADCASTERS AND THE FIRST AMENDMENT

The Federal Communications Commission has issued guidance with respect to the broadcasting of obscene or indecent matter on television.[51] The guidance notes that 'obscene' material does not attract the free speech protection of the First Amendment to the United States Constitution. 'Indecent' material does attract that protection, which means that to regulate indecent programming requires a compelling interest and the means adopted must be the least restrictive in order to so regulate it.[52] In this regard the Federal Communications Commission has adopted a definition of 'indecent' which defines it to be:

> language or material that, in context, depicts or describes, in terms patently offensive as measured by contemporary community standards for the broadcast medium, sexual or excretory activities or organs.[53]

In *Ginsberg v. State of New York*[54] the Supreme Court held that the protection of children was a compelling state interest as would justify restrictions being placed on indecent speech. In that case, a New York statute prohibited the sale to children under seventeen of obscene publications even if the matter was not regarded as obscene to adults.[55] In making its decision the Court noted that the state had greater authority over children when compared with its authority over adults. In effect the Court found a rationale for restricting the application of the Constitutional protection of free speech to children. It quoted with approval various statements which supported this approach to the child. For example, the Court referred to the view of Emerson:

Different factors come into play, also, where the interest at stake is the effect of erotic expression upon children. The world of children is not strictly part of the adult realm of free expression. The factor of immaturity, and perhaps other considerations, impose different rules. Without attempting here to formulate the principles relevant to freedom of expression for children, it suffices to say that regulations of communication addressed to them need not conform to the requirements of the first amendment in the same way as those applicable to adults.[56]

It is the construction of a different world for children which places them outside the Constitutional privileges which adults enjoy. The Court relied on 'the factor of immaturity' for the application of 'different rules'. This is the core of the decision, a statement borrowed from child development theories and converted into a legal proposition.

But the Court may have chosen a different rationale and a different legal proposition. Less than a year before *Ginsberg* the Supreme Court had decided *In re Gault*,[57] a landmark case in juvenile justice where the Court had decided that children were entitled to the same due process rights under the Constitution. In articulating the rationale for its decision in *Gault* the Court said of the paternal attitude underlying the juvenile court at the time:

> ... the highest motives and most enlightened impulses led to a peculiar system for juveniles, unknown to our law in any comparable context. The constitutional and theoretical basis for this peculiar system is − to say the least − debatable. And in practice, as we remarked in the Kent case, supra, the results have not been entirely satisfactory. Juvenile Court history has again demonstrated that unbridled discretion, however benevolently motivated, is frequently a poor substitute for principle and procedure. In 1937, Dean Pound wrote: 'The powers of the Star Chamber were a trifle in comparison with those of our juvenile courts ...' The absence of substantive standards has not necessarily meant that children receive careful, compassionate, individualized treatment. The absence of procedural rules based upon constitutional principle has not always produced fair, efficient, and effective procedures. Departures from established principles of due process have frequently resulted not in enlightened procedure, but in arbitrariness.[58]

This was not a different world for children, divorced from the rights accorded to adults. Justice Fortas wrote the opinion of the Court in *Gault*. He was one of the dissenting judges in *Ginsberg*. In his dissenting opinion in that latter case he demonstrated that the notion that children were in a different world was not the only way to understand their situation:

It begs the question to present this undefined, unlimited censorship as an aid to parents in the rearing of their children. This decision does not merely protect children from activities which all sensible parents would condemn. Rather, its undefined and unlimited approval of state censorship in this area denies to children free access to books and works of art to which many parents may wish their children to have uninhibited access. For denial of access to these magazines, without any standard or definition of their allegedly distinguishing characteristics, is also denial of access to great works of art and literature.[59]

This is not the child who merely requires protection from the harm of indecent magazines. Justice Fortas points out that what is also at stake is the right of the child to access information and ideas from other sources. Such arguments are advanced more generally when censorship of what adults wish to see or read is attempted. In other words, Fortas placed children in that world too, where the right to access information is defended even if it means that others may not like some of what is made available as a consequence.

As it stands, the regulation of broadcast decency in the United States has been an area subject to much debate and litigation since the late 1980s.[60] In a series of cases brought to challenge the Federal Communications Commission's regulation of broadcast indecency, the courts on the one hand have held that the harmful impact of indecent programming on children justified state regulation, while on the other hand strong dissenting judgments questioned the evidence that supported the view that such material was harmful to children.[61] The resulting situation is that the broadcasting of indecent programming has been confined to the hours of 10 p.m. to 6 a.m.[62]

The test of whether a programme is obscene has been explained by the Federal Communications Commission as follows:

the broadcast must be patently offensive as measured by contemporary community standards for the broadcast medium. In applying the 'community standards for the broadcast medium' criterion, the Commission has stated:

The determination as to whether certain programming is patently offensive is not a local one and does not encompass any particular geographic area. Rather, the standard is that of an average broadcast viewer or listener and not the sensibilities of any individual complainant.[63]

This appears as the main question in the United States, for once it has been decided that material is obscene such programming is not protected speech and is assumed to be harmful to children and thus a legitimate target of regulation. But the more difficult question which needs to be asked is, in determining whether indecent programming may harm children, to whose construction of the child does the community turn?

CHAPTER 6

Ads, Fads and Green Tomato Sauce: Advertising to the Child

Can it be said that the welfare of children is at risk because of advertising directed at them?

There was evidence that children are incapable of distinguishing fact from fiction in advertising. This is hardly surprising: many adults have the same problem. Children, however, do not remain children. They grow up and, while advertising directed at children may well be a source of irritation to parents, no case has been shown here that children suffer harm. Children live in a world of fiction, imagination and make believe. Children's literature is based upon these concepts. As they mature, they make adjustments and can be expected to pass beyond the range of any ill which might be caused by advertising.
(J. McIntyre, A-G of Quebec v Irwin Toys Ltd
58 DLR 4th 577 (1989))

The consumers of commercial television are not the viewers but those who buy time to advertise their products.[1] In this understanding of television, children who watch television represent a market which may be targeted by this advertising. This link, when made, strikes fear in those concerned with the quality of children's lives on the one hand, and excitement for those manufacturers and retailers who crave new markets on the other. It is no surprise then, that many of the laws and rules which regulate advertising directed at children operate from the premise that children must be protected from the dangers of those who would profit from their vulnerability. But as we have seen in the areas of violence and sexual content on television, there is an alternative legal discourse which places greater stress on the independent capacity of children to process information in their own right.

TELEVISION ADVERTISING IN CHILDREN'S LIVES: FROM INNOCENT CHILD TO CONSUMER CHILD

As Kline observes, the impact of television advertising on children is both complex and multifaceted. While television has been blamed for the decline of reading, street play and family meals, he notes that what has occurred in television advertising is the co-opting of the patterns of children's existence in order to bring the child into the world of consumption through the use of marketing that interacts with those patterns:

> one thing television didn't displace from children's culture was story telling. Nor did television completely banish those traditional literary themes from modern childhood. Indeed, one of contemporary television's singular achievements has been the rearticulation of those traditional patterns of fiction within a future mythic framework – a process in which the basic narrative forms have been refashioned to harmonize them with the task of gathering kids to the box and interesting them in the appropriate merchandise. Television similarly didn't eliminate the peer group or peer interaction either: rather, it discovered that the peer acceptance was a value that could be added to the motivation to purchase goods. Nor did television eliminate the traditional images of innocence and play; it simply made watching television a prerequisite for children's experience of that charmed realm. In short, it is not what television has displaced from children's lives that fuels the public's criticisms and discomfort with this medium, but the way it continues to promote particular patterns of social understanding, attitudes and self-expression.[2]

In other words, television advertising does not so much redefine the child as take the idea of childhood and develop it. The 'consumer child' is therefore not a break from the child of innocent play but an evolution from it. This analysis challenges more orthodox understandings of the effect of television advertising on the child. It does so by confronting the notion that marketers take away childhood, and suggests that they expand on it in various ways. As a consequence, the regulation of television advertising which appears to be for the protection of children may well be protecting them from childhood, or at least those patterns of childhood which marketers find useful for their campaigns.

Television is thus a powerful force in shaping our understanding of ourselves, whether through the use of dramatic portrayals of life,[3] or by way of advertising. In the case of marketing directed to children this has led to the use of shrewd marketing strategies which have co-opted children's culture and redefined it. Some seem to bemoan this phenomenon while recognizing the manner in which it shapes childhood:

> There's now an entire industry devoted to youth marketing. Children's media outlets like Nickelodeon in the US and YTV in Canada periodically run focus groups for pre-teen kids to try to find out about upcoming trends, then sell their findings to advertisers and marketing consultants. (Both broadcasters have come under criti-

cism for recruiting kids for their focus groups through the public school system.) One technique that's growing increasingly popular with youth marketers is 'buzz advertising'. In an effort to generate word-of-mouth buzz for its new hand-held video game POX, for example, toy giant Hasbro recently gave away free games to 1600 Chicago boys aged 8–13 who had been identified as 'trendsetters', acknowledged leaders in their peer groups ...

However, we shouldn't make the mistake of thinking that kids are just the brainwashed puppets of the youth marketer. They're responding to pressure from advertisers, but they're also clamouring to get into the marketplace themselves. Which shouldn't surprise us. Young people can be excused for concluding that, in our culture, the status of personhood is attained by becoming a consumer. They're surrounded on all sides by the message that the marketplace is where the action is: I buy, therefore I am.[4]

The conceptualization of the child which is presented here is one that paints the child as one who craves to be a person with full participation rights in the market-place. This may not be surprising given that such status is associated with having more power over one's life. There is an underlying sense that children are being robbed of their childhood, and that they are being turned into 'consumers' subjected to the manipulative ways of advertisers. What we find again are these conflicting ideas about how childhood is shaped in its relationship with television. It is important to question how this understanding of the processes translates into the legal regulatory framework and how that legal regulation itself constructs the culture of childhood which it seeks to regulate.

LEGAL CONSTRAINTS ON ADVERTISING TO CHILDREN: 'BALANCED' PROTECTION OR SELF-DETERMINATION?

In 1978 the United States Federal Trade Commission proposed a ban on all advertising to children. The basis of this ban was that such advertising when directed at children too young to understand the 'persuasive intent' of the advertising was 'unfair and deceptive'.[5] Intense lobbying by business opposed to the ban followed and eventually the jurisdiction of the Commission to regulate this area was removed by legislation.[6] However, such a ban does exist in the Canadian province of Quebec pursuant to the provisions of the Quebec Consumer Protection Act. Section 248 of that Act is straightforward in its effect in that it provides that 'no person may make use of commercial advertising directed at persons under thirteen years of age.'[7] Whether or not an advertisement is directed at a person under thirteen is to be determined by 'the context of its presentation' with particular reference to the nature and intended purpose of the goods advertised, the manner of presentation and the time and place the advertisement is shown.[8]

In 1989 this legislation was challenged by a toy manufacturer on the grounds that it offended the protection of freedom of expression contained in section 2(b) of the Canadian Charter of Rights and Freedoms.[9] The Canadian Supreme Court upheld the legislation in a 3:2 decision. The question the Court had to consider was whether this restriction on advertising to children was a reasonable restriction on freedom of expression which is permitted by the Charter.[10] This examination requires the Court to consider the purpose of the Act in order to determine whether the purpose of the Act is to restrict expression – which would offend the Charter – or whether it is to 'address some real or purported social need' – which would not offend the Charter.[11] The legal test to determine this has two parts. The first part 'involves asking whether the objective sought to be achieved by the impugned legislation relates to concerns which are pressing and substantial in a free and democratic society.'[12] In other words, the reason for limiting free expression in this context must be of such an order as would justify the limiting of this fundamental freedom.

According to the majority of the Court there was such a reason for limiting free expression – the protection of children:

> In our view, the Attorney-General of Quebec has demonstrated that the concern which prompted the enactment of the impugned legislation is pressing and substantial and that the purpose of the legislation is one of great importance. The concern is for the protection of a group which is particularly vulnerable to the techniques of seduction and manipulation abundant in advertising. In the words of the Attorney-General of Quebec (translation), 'Children experience most manifestly the kind of inequality and imbalance between producers and consumers which the legislature wanted to correct.' The material given in evidence before this court is indicative of a generalized concern in Western societies with the impact of the media, and particularly but not solely televised advertising, on the developmental needs and perceptions of young children ...
>
> Broadly speaking, the concerns which have motivated both legislative and voluntary regulation in this area are the particular susceptibility of young children to media manipulation, their inability to differentiate between reality and fiction and to grasp the persuasive intention behind the message, and the secondary effects of exterior influences on the family and parental authority. Responses to the perceived problems are as varied as the agencies and governments which have promulgated them. However, the consensus of concern is high.[13]

clearly, this is an approach which conceptualizes the child as vulnerable and in need of protection. The Court relied for its 'factual basis' on a United States Federal Trade Commission report which had concluded that young children between the ages of two and six 'cannot distinguish fact from fiction or programming from advertising and are completely credulous when presented with advertising messages'.[14] This allowed the majority in the Supreme Court of Canada to conclude on the basis of this report that there was 'a sound basis on which to conclude that television advertising directed at young children is *per se* manipulative. Such advertising aims to promote products by convincing those who will always believe.'[15]

The evidence which was presented to the Court on the effects of advertising on older children was less conclusive. But the validity of the legislation did not have to rely on *all* children being in need of protection from the harmful effects of advertising. It was only required that there be known that there was a vulnerable group for which protection was deemed to be reasonable. Where the line was to be drawn was properly a matter for the legislature:

> Where the legislature mediates between competing claims of different groups in the community, it will inevitably be called upon to draw a line marking where one set of claims legitimately begins and the other fades away without access to complete knowledge as to its precise location. If the legislature has made a reasonable assessment as to where the line is most properly drawn, especially if that assessment involves weighing conflicting scientific evidence and allocating scarce resources on this basis, it is not for the court to second guess. That would only be to substitute one estimate for another. In dealing with inherently heterogeneous groups defined in terms of age or a characteristic analogous to age, evidence showing that a clear majority of the group requires the protection which the government has identified can help to establish that the group was defined reasonably. Here, the legislature has mediated between the claims of advertisers and those seeking commercial information on the one hand, and the claims of children and parents on the other. There is sufficient evidence to warrant drawing a line at age 13, and we would not presume to re-draw the line.[16]

For the majority of the Court this law which sought to prohibit advertising directed towards children was akin to consumer protection legislation, that is laws which 'protect a group that is most vulnerable to commercial manipulation'.[17] This analogy is interesting for it posits the debate in terms of a battle between conflicting interests. The case, in other words, turned on the question of how a balance was to be struck between the free speech of advertisers (which presumably carried with it the

possibility of the exploitation of children's vulnerabilities) and th
protection of children from harm. Cast in these terms it is easy to se
why the Court ultimately concluded that the legislation was a reasonabl
limitation on free speech. But as we have seen before in the area (
violence and sexual imagery on television, to construct the matter in tern
of a 'balance' is to merely provide a smokescreen under which the interes
of children can be easily compromised. There is no 'balance' betwee
these considerations. What does occur in the name of such a balance is th
serious erosion of the possibility that the child will have his or he
independent right to self-determination recognized.

The minority in the Canadian Supreme Court of Canada in *Irwr
Toys* chose to articulate a quite different understanding of the child an
its need for protection. J. McIntyre, (with whom J. Beetz, concurrec
when faced with the issue of whether the ban on advertising to childre
was a reasonable limitation on free speech in order to protect childrer
wrote:

> It is settled that to override a constitutional guarantee a government
> supporting a limitation imposed by law must show a purpose or
> objective of pressing and substantial importance. Certainly, the
> promotion of the welfare of children is an objective of pressing and
> substantial concern for any government.

> Can it be said that the welfare of children is at risk because of
> advertising directed at them? I am not satisfied that any case has
> shown that it is. There was evidence that children are incapable of
> distinguishing fact from fiction in advertising. This is hardly
> surprising: many adults have the same problem. Children, however,
> do not remain children. They grow up and, while advertising
> directed at children may well be a source of irritation to parents, no
> case has been shown here that children suffer harm. Children live in
> a world of fiction, imagination and make believe. Children's
> literature is based upon these concepts. As they mature, they make
> adjustments and can be expected to pass beyond the range of any ill
> which might be caused by advertising. In my view, no case has been
> made that children are at risk. Furthermore, even if I could reach
> another conclusion, I would be of the view that the restriction fails
> on the issue of proportionality. A total prohibition of advertising
> aimed at children below an arbitrarily fixed age makes no attempt at
> the achievement of proportionality.[18]

From this perspective the view of the majority in the case can be cast a
one which attempts to preserve childhood as an age of innocence. Th
majority seem motivated by a desire to perpetuate the vulnerable child, bu
it might be asked of this approach: how do children develop into adul

itizens if they do not begin to acquire the skills of citizenship from an
arly age?

There is an alternative legal discourse which does not so readily accept
1e notion of the innocent and vulnerable child as has been argued in
arlier chapters. This alternative understanding of childhood, which has
een evolving in the law for some time, recognizes a decline in the power
f parents to control their children while at the same time granting more
>rmal recognition to the autonomy of the child. While this shift does not
eny the need to protect children where appropriate, just when such
rotection is 'appropriate' is the basis upon which this different
onception of the child is based.

It might be asked, in relation to advertising directed to children,
vhether it is in the best interests of a child that they are exposed to such
roadcasting. But as J. Brennan, observed in *Marion's Case*:

> Professor Kennedy[19] points out that, by transforming a 'complex
> moral and social question' into a question of fact, the best interests
> approach leaves the court in the hands of 'experts' who assemble a
> dossier of fact and opinion on matters which they deem relevant
> 'without reference to any check-list of legal requirements . . .'[20]

This seems to be particularly relevant in the context of television
.dvertising, as it is to the 'experts' that courts would often turn in such
ases, as they did in *Irwin Toys*. But this may miss the real question in such
case. The question of whether children have rights to access information
nd ideas is the issue in this case. If such rights do exist they come from a
onception of the child which is based on a moral and social stance with
espect to the proper place of children in society, and not from any expert
pinion. As J. Brennan observes (citing Kennedy), it is often the case that
noral and social questions are recast as questions of fact and opinion,
ressing the court into reliance on 'experts' who assess the 'evidence' for
he best outcome for the child. Thus in television advertising to children
he question is usually phrased in terms of whether such broadcasting
1arms children and may therefore be against their interests. The question
ould instead be cast as one which focuses on which rights children might
:laim in this area and whether restrictions on their access to advertising on
elevision so harms those rights that it may undermine their position as
:itizens or their ability to develop the skills of judgement and reason
which all citizens might claim as a fundamental need. It is then not a
cientific discussion at all – even though social science may well have
evidence of harms caused to children through broadcast advertising – but a
moral discussion about which rights shall be denied to children in the
name of some greater social objective.

The dissent of J. McIntyre, in *Irwin Toys* reflects a similar approach to
. Brennan, in *Marion's Case*. He also tends towards a construction of the

problem as one which stems from issues to do with the primacy of certai
fundamental principles rather than a simple consideration of the be
interests of the child. Thus he does not cast this matter in terms of a simp
battle between opposing sides, where one side has the objective (
manipulating the immaturity of the other. Rather, he sees it as a proce
whereby the protection of the free speech of advertisers may well lead t
the development of children – albeit by way of becoming more wary (
the guile of commercial interests through exposure of their practices. Tht
he concludes in a style reminiscent of J. Brennan in *Marion's case*:

> I would say that freedom of expression is too important to lightly
> cast aside or limited. It is ironic that most attempts to limit freedom
> of expression and hence freedom of knowledge and information are
> justified on the basis that the limitation is for the benefit of those
> whose rights will be limited. It was this proposition that motivated
> the early church in restricting access to information, even to
> prohibiting the promulgation and reading of the scriptures in a
> language understood by the people. The argument that freedom of
> expression was dangerous was used to oppose and restrict public
> education in earlier times. The education of women was greatly
> retarded on the basis that wider knowledge would only make them
> dissatisfied with their role in society. I do not suggest that the
> limitations imposed by ss. 248 and 249 are so earth shaking or that if
> sustained they will cause irremediable damage. I do say, however,
> that these limitations represent a small abandonment of a principle of
> vital importance in a free and democratic society and, therefore, even
> if it could be shown that some child or children have been adversely
> affected by advertising of the kind prohibited, I would still be of the
> opinion that the restriction should not be sustained. Our concern
> should be to recognize that in this century we have seen whole
> societies utterly corrupted by the suppression of free expression. We
> should not lightly take a step in that direction, even a small one.[21]

This dissenting opinion is grounded in a very different construction o
childhood to that which was espoused by the majority of the Court. It link
the notion of childhood, not with the special vulnerability of the child, bu
with the need to ensure that children grow up to participate in robus
democracies. It places the protection of fundamental freedoms ahead o
action designed to shield the 'innocent' from the truth. J. McIntyre is clearl
suspicious of the dangerous paternalism which often disguises a desire t(
perpetuate the status quo. Bertrand Russell described this process as on(
which invokes the notion of the 'superior virtue of the oppressed' – wher(
indigenous peoples, women and children have been kept from civic lif(
because to do so would blemish their sacred status. Of course, this is simply
a process of exclusion of those groups from power and influence.[22]

This judgment illustrates how different conceptions of childhood influence the manner in which arguments are framed by law around the issues raised by children, television and advertising. The majority in *Irwin Toys* adopted scientific explanations of the link between advertising and harm to children. But the minority operated within a different legal discourse within which there lies suspicion about the manner in which vulnerable people have been harmed under the guise of protection in the past. This discourse does not assume that laws which seek to protect children from the assumed perils of television advertising are any different to other laws which have sought to protect children from harm and which have been shown in time to disguise harsh treatment of children under the guise of articulating their best interests. As King and Piper would say, this is an example of law as a self-referential system, as there is no necessary scientific basis to the suspicion that this legal discourse may exhibit. Yet it also operates to remind us that in these areas what sometimes passes for a scientific issue is in fact a moral one.

THE CONTENT OF REGULATION

In Australia the regulation of advertising directed towards children is achieved by way of a combination of television standards prescribed by the Australian Broadcasting Authority and industry codes, which in the latter case must be approved by the authority. The Children's Television Standards set down various requirements with respect to advertising during C and P periods. Children's Television Standard 10 provides that:

> No programme, advertisement or other material broadcast during a C period or P period may:
>
> (a) demean any person or group on the basis of ethnicity, nationality, race, gender, sexual preference, religion, or mental or physical disability;
> (b) present images or events in a way which is unduly frightening or unduly distressing to children;
> (c) present images or events which depict unsafe uses of a product or unsafe situations which may encourage children to engage in activities dangerous to them;
> (d) advertise products or services which have been officially declared unsafe or dangerous by a Commonwealth authority or by an authority having jurisdiction within the licensee's service area.

Children's Television Standard 13 provides that only G classified advertisements may be broadcast during C periods provided that they also meet the further applicable standards discussed below. The standard prohibits any advertising during P periods. It should be noted that the licensee determines the precise times when C and P periods operate for the station. That is, these restrictions on advertising operate during the times the broadcaster has nominated as times when it will screen C and P programmes.[23]

The amount of advertising that may be screened during a C programme is limited to five minutes in a 30-minute period.[24] But this restriction does not apply to advertisements screened during Australian children's drama programmes broadcast between 6 p.m. and 8.30 p.m. when the permitted amount of advertising rises to thirteen minutes in an hour.[25] This allowance is presumably made to encourage the production of Australian children's drama through enabling broadcasters to recoup the costs of such productions through increased advertising. It also shows once again the tension between the idea of protecting children from the harmful effects of advertising on the one hand while also facilitating the creation of 'suitable' children's programmes by commercial producers.

But this form of regulation also implies something further about the child viewer. There would be little commercial sense to permit advertising during children's programmes unless it was thought that the child audience represented a market to which to direct such advertising. While most of the focus in the regulation of advertising to children rests on the manipulative conduct of advertisers and the harm caused to children as a result, another aspect which is not so comfortably confronted is that of the 'child consumer'. While it may not be as threatening as the issues raised by children and sexuality, it is an image which nevertheless challenges the notion of the innocent child. Clearly manufacturers have an interest in marketing goods to or through children. But how do children develop the skills of the market-place – which today is more and more conducted electronically – unless they are included in, and not protected from, that world?

The Children's Television Standards also require that during C periods advertisements and sponsorship announcements 'be clearly distinguishable as such to the child viewer'.[26] No advertisement may be broadcast more than twice in any 30 minutes of a C period[27] and 'no advertisement may mislead or deceive children'.[28] Such standards confirm the notion that children are easily manipulated by advertisers. Consistent with this is Children's Television Standard 18 which states:

> (1) A licensee may not broadcast any advertisements designed to put undue pressure on children to ask their parents or other people to purchase an advertised product or service.
> (2) No advertisements may state or imply:
>   (a) that a product or service makes children who own or enjoy it superior to their peers;
>   (b) that a person who buys an advertised product or service for a child is more generous than a person who does not.

The standards also require that advertisements clearly represent the product or service and that where children are depicted using the product it 'must fairly represent the performance which a child of the age depicted can obtain from these products'.[29] This also extends to clarity if accessories, such as batteries, are required to operate the product[30] and the price of the product, which cannot be qualified with words such as 'only' or 'just'.[31] Advertisements for food cannot misrepresent the nutritional value of the food.[32] The need for clarity also applies to disclaimers, premium offers and competitions.[33] In the latter case, any statements about the chance of winning a competition must be 'clear, fair and accurate'.[34]

Restrictions are also placed on the ability to manipulate children through using their favourite personalities to promote certain products and services. It is stated in Children's Television Standard 22(1) that:

> No material broadcast during C or P programmes or in the break immediately before or after a C or P programme may contain an endorsement, recommendation or promotion of a commercial product or service by a principal personality or character from a C or P programme.

This restriction does not apply if the programme featuring the personality is not currently being broadcast in the particular area and has not been in the preceding twelve months.[35] Finally, the standards also prohibit the advertising of alcoholic drinks during C programs.[36]

Of course, it has to be noted that the above restrictions on advertising only apply during C and P periods. They do not apply during other times that children are viewing. This may appear to be a significant limitation on the effectiveness of the standards from the viewpoint of those who seek to protect children from the harmful effects of advertising. This is particularly important if it is considered that the most watched programmes by children in Australia are programmes other than C and P programmes. However, it has to be added that producers of advertising might also be limited in their ability to use personalities, for example, if they cannot use their services at times when children are more likely to be viewing, given the effect of Children's Television Standard 22(1).

The Commercial Television Code of Practice sets down further requirements with respect to advertising. The aims of the provisions which relate to commercials include 'the need to limit the exposure of children to material intended for adult viewing.'[37] Children are defined to be those of or under primary school age.[38] Commercials must comply with the classification requirements of other parts of the Code.[39] The advertising of alcoholic drinks which is a 'direct advertisement for alcoholic drinks' can only be done during M, MA or AV classification periods or during the live broadcast of sporting events on weekends or public holidays.[40] This latter exception is clearly a concession to the sponsors of such sporting events. A direct advertisement for alcoholic drinks does not include programme sponsorship announcements where the sponsor is a producer of alcoholic drinks, advertising of licensed restaurants or advertisements for companies whose business includes 'the manufacture, distribution or sale of alcoholic drinks'.[41] Clearly, the Code is prepared to compromise the exposure of children to such advertising in certain circumstances for market driven reasons.

Advertising which relates to betting or gambling may not occur in a G classification period or on weekends between 6 a.m. and 8.30 a.m. or between 4 p.m. and 7.30 p.m.[42] This does not include advertising of 'Government lotteries, lotto, keno or contests',[43] or 'a commercial relating to entertainment or dining facilities at places where betting or gambling take place, or a tourism commercial which incidentally depicts betting or gambling, provided in each case that the contents do not draw attention to betting or gambling in a manner calculated to directly promote their use'.[44] Commercials for condoms may only be broadcast in PG, M, MA or AV time zones (unless they are broadcast for public health and safety reasons)[45] but feminine hygiene products may be broadcast in a G classification zone 'if it is unlikely to cause embarrassment or offence to a broad cross-section of viewers'.[46] However, advertising of such products can only occur in the PG, M, MA and AV times if the commercial 'highlights product design features or involves an absorbency demonstration'.[47] Commercials for telephone sex lines must be classified MA and may only be screened after 11 p.m. and before 5 a.m. and 'should not be placed within any religious programme or sports programme or in any drama programme with a religious theme'.[48] Commercials for films, videos, computer games and CD games must comply with rules relating to programme promotions, must display their Office of Film and Literature Classification and if the commercial is for an R rated film it can only be broadcast after 8.30 p.m.[49]

All commercials directed to children 'must exercise special care and judgement' and the Children's Television Standards 17 to 21 apply to such advertising.[50] The effect of this clause would appear to be that those Standards then apply to advertising to children outside the C and P classification time periods. The Code also places restrictions on the use of programme presenters to promote products directed to children during children's programmes and requires that programme promotions and sponsorship announcement be kept separate from the programme, and any reference to prizes for competitions be kept brief.[51] Advertising which encourages the use of premium phone services (higher rate calls often used for competitions) when directed to children must make clear the terms and conditions of the competition and the cost of the call in a form which children can understand, and must advise children to obtain parental permission before calling.[52]

It is evident in the patchwork of requirements under this Code that a view of children as impressionable and in need of protection from manipulative broadcasting prevails. The problem is once again not just one of whether there is a need for consumer protection laws which protect the audience from unfair and misleading advertising. All people should have that protection. The concern is that in promoting a particular view of the child as gullible in such provisions this also reinforces an image of the child which affects how we think about children more generally. This view of the child is becoming redundant as it perpetuates views which have made it easier in the past to act against children's interests and may well limit the opportunities available to children in a more sophisticated future. Yet one can find statements in the codes which regulate television advertising which continue to state a view of the child as immature and vulnerable.

For example, the Canadian Association of Broadcaster's Code of Ethics provides that broadcasters shall adhere to the Broadcast Code for Advertising to Children as administered by Advertising Standards Canada.[53] That Code begins with a discussion of the 'background' to the Code. It reads:

> Children, especially the very young, live in a world that is part imaginary, part real and sometimes do not distinguish clearly between the two. Children's advertising should respect and not abuse the power of the child's imagination . . .
>
> The foregoing does not imply a call for the elimination of fantasy in children's advertising. Many childhood possessions become particularly meaningful as they are incorporated into the child's fantasy world and it is natural and appropriate to communicate with this audience in their own terms. But such presentations should not stimulate unreasonable expectations of product or premium performance.[54]

It is noteworthy that 'children' under this Code refers to persons under twelve years of age.[55] It is the case that the age of criminal responsibility in Canada is twelve.[56] But it is also the law that a jury no longer must be warned about convicting on the uncorroborated evidence of a child.[57] This does not mean that a child must be believed. The difficulty arises when in determining whether or not to believe a child those judging credibility begins from a presumption that children live in a 'fantasy world'. This may be the case, but it may be equally true of an adult. The Code of Advertising perpetuates an understanding of the child which if adopted more widely would destroy the rationale for removing the rule against convicting an accused on the uncorroborated evidence of a child. The implications for the ability of child to call to account those who do harm to them are clearly serious if this occurred.

The content of the Canadian Code follows from the assumptions upon which it rests. It contains similar provisions as exist in Australia with respect to placing undue pressure on children to purchase a product,[58] the use of 'puppets, persons and characters' well known to children to promote products,[59] and suggesting that owning a particular product will make the child superior or without it 'open to ridicule or contempt'.[60] The Code also requires that advertising directed to children 'must not portray a range of values that are inconsistent with the moral, ethical or legal standards of contemporary Canadian society'.[61] Such a clause confirms the contradictory nature of the law when one considers the underlying assumptions of the Code and their inconsistency with those legal rules which promote a child's competence.

The United Kingdom Broadcasting Standards Commission Code of Standards is mainly concerned with the placement of advertising in programmes, but in a manner which clearly implies concern for children:

> Advertisements also appear without warning and have the power to surprise and shock an audience which cannot selectively screen them out. Broadcasters should be sensitive to commercials which are out of step with their surrounding programmes and might cause offence – especially programmes which appeal to children. They should ensure that the content and style of an advertisement is suitable for the time of its transmission and likely audience.[62]

In the United States the Children's Television Act 1990 prescribes that television advertising during programming for children under twelve shall be limited to 12 minutes per hour on weekdays and 10.5 minutes per hour on weekends.[63] Programme length commercials (a programme 'interwoven' with the sponsor's advertising) are also caught by these time constraints. Until 1982 the National Association of Broadcasters administered a voluntary set of guidelines for advertising to children. This was disbanded in 1982 and since then the networks have been responsible for formulating their own guidelines.[64] In addition the Children's Advertising Unit of the Council of Better Business Bureau is an advertising industry created body which promotes responsible children's advertising. It assesses advertising against its *Self-Regulatory Guidelines for Children's Advertising*. These guidelines contain similar provisions to those described above in relation to Australia and Canada with respect to undue pressure on children, promotions by programme characters and safety issues.[65] They also replicate the assumption made about a child's ability to distinguish reality from fantasy in the principles upon which the guidelines are established:

> Realizing that children are imaginative and that make-believe play constitutes an important part of the growing up process, advertisers

should exercise care not to exploit unfairly the imaginative quality of children.[66]

Stoltman regards the guidelines as raising the need to consider further the assumptions that they make about the child in this context. He notes that these guidelines:

[are] based on the premise that children lack the sophistication and maturity needed to deal appropriately with advertising. The implicit notion of a vulnerable child stands in contrast to the view of children as hardened realists. Research can make a significant contribution in this context, and we might expect an invigorated round of research on the capabilities of the child consumer.[67]

It might be asked how much this is a matter of 'research' and more a matter of what particular view of childhood one wishes to adopt. For example, a later principle in the same *Guidelines* recognizes the child's capacity to comprehend truthful information:

Recognizing that advertising may play an important part in educating the child, advertisers should communicate information in a truthful and accurate manner and in language understandable to young children with full recognition that the child may learn practices from advertising which can affect his or her health and well-being.[68]

The apparent inconsistent portrayal of children as being capable of having their imaginations exploited yet able to appreciate truthful and accurate material is not presented as problematic in the above guidelines. Yet it is this supposed inability to discern the difference between truth and reality which underlies much of the regulation of children's advertising. In 1991 the then Australian Broadcasting Tribunal inquired into the programme *Teenage Mutant Ninja Turtles* to determine whether it was a programme length commercial and therefore in breach of the television advertising conditions then in place.[69] The Tribunal found that the programme was not an advertisement and placed some reliance on the United States Federal Communications definition of a programme length commercial:

The primary test is whether the purportedly non-commercial segment is so interwoven with, and in essence auxiliary to, the sponsor's advertising ... to the point that the entire programme constitutes a single commercial.[70]

The Tribunal held that the programme could not be so described and pointed to their finding that the programme was not interwoven with the products so as to be a promotion of the products, that the programme did not include reference to the merchandise or where it could be purchased and that commercial breaks did not carry advertising for related products to the extent that the programme and the advertising became indistinguishable.[71] One can be critical of the conclusions of the Tribunal when it is considered that the merchandising of programme-related products is presumably an important consideration in the decision to produce certain programmes. But the issue here is not so much whether programmes connect with related goods as a matter of the ability of the child to understand the difference between the programme and the advertisement. The Tribunal in this inquiry received a high number of submissions from children and made use of this fact in its report. It was stressed that the children submitted that they understood the difference between the programme and advertisement and that there was 'no confusion for them between the cartoon and reality'.[72] The one child who did submit that the programme was an advertisement nevertheless displayed some maturity when she remarked that 'the programme encourages people to buy "things"'.[73]

The dilemma in such cases is that commercial programming relies on sponsorship and related merchandising to generate the revenue to continue to produce more programmes. To decide that programmes promote products and that this is the main purpose of programming – holding it in breach of standards as a result – might condemn commercial television to its demise. It is, as with so much of the regulation of television, a 'balance' which is sought to be struck. In the middle of this exercise is the problem of the child, so often the mechanism used to decide where to strike this balance. It is in this area that assumption and belief, rather than any scientific evaluation of a child's understanding of the world, operate to decide matters. It is on the rare occasions when the child is heard in the process that some of these assumptions can be successfully challenged.

'SELF' REGULATION: FAMILY FRIENDLY PROGRAMMING AND THE MARKET

An area which does demand further research is the influence of pressure groups on broadcasters to broadcast 'family friendly' programming. This approach is to use the 'market' to influence the content of television programmes. The Family Friendly Programming Forum states its mission to include the screening of 'more movies, series, documentaries and informational programs, aired between 8:00 and 10:00 p.m., that are relevant and interesting to a broad audience and that parents would enjoy viewing together with a child'.[74] Apart from lobbying the television industry, a smaller group of members of the Forum have funded a script development fund 'to finance new family friendly TV scripts'.[75] This smaller group is comprised of companies including The Anschutz Corporation, AT&T Corporation, FedEx Corporation, Ford Motor Company, General Motors Corporation, International Business Machines Corporation, Johnson & Johnson, The Kellogg Company, Lowe's Company Inc., McDonald's Corporation, Merck & Co., Nationwide, Pfizer Inc. (includes Pfizer Consumer Group), Procter & Gamble, Sears Roebuck and Co., Sprint Communications, Tyson Foods, Inc., Unilever United States, Inc., and Wendy's International, Inc.[76] Another part of their strategy is to fund scholarships for students interested in family friendly programming who are undertaking university television studies.[77]

This development raises many questions about the creative arts, the independence of broadcasters and the real motives of the corporations involved. But it also indicates the dangers inherent in understanding children as innocent and vulnerable. It is only because of this approach to children, which dominates so much of the discourse on children and television, that 'family friendly' can be construed in terms which seem consistent with the aims and objectives of major corporations. If the aim of television programming included the creation of wily and critical consumers who are well educated in the ways of the market-place then it might be less likely that family friendly programming would possess the same meaning as it does today. As it is, one suspects that 'family friendly programming' will lead to banal programming for mass audiences who are then delivered to advertisers. As the Forum itself indicates, '[a]s marketers, we are concerned about the dwindling availability of family friendly television programs during prime viewing hours – the environment in which we want to advertise.'[78]

For those who may be critical of such corporate attempts to take over the programming schedules of broadcasters in the name of children, the challenge will be to decide if the best protection for children is always a protective and paternalistic approach to the child, instead of promoting the child's competence and capacity to understand the market environment.

CHAPTER 7

The 'New' Legal Discourse: Children's Rights and Television in the Interactive Age

The record demonstrates that the growth of the Internet has been and continues to be phenomenal. As a matter of constitutional tradition, in the absence of evidence to the contrary, we presume that governmental regulation of the content of speech is more likely to interfere with the free exchange of ideas than to encourage it. The interest in encouraging freedom of expression in a democratic society outweighs any theoretical but unproven benefit of censorship.
(Reno v. American Civil Liberties Union *512 US 844 (1997))*

If one had to summarize the regulatory mechanisms surrounding television in Australia, Canada, the United States and the United Kingdom, then one would cast them as consistent on one matter – the need to protect children from 'harmful or inappropriate material'. Where those systems of regulation become confused and contradictory is the manner in which they come to terms with how that objective is to be achieved, for underlying this aim of child protection is the problem of how childhood is to be defined. While the protection paradigm and the conception of childhood as a stage of innocence or vulnerability remains dominant, there is another view of the child which stresses the child' capacity for independent thought and action. An additional tension within the regulation of television is provided by the pre-eminence of market forces as an influence on the production of television programming and advertising. It is important to note that the profit needs of commercial broadcasters and production houses do not just place constraints on the space allocated for programming directed to children. The need to create new markets also influences how childhood is constructed, as broadcaster and advertisers attempt to include children in the market-place and co-opt the patterns of childhood to further that aim.

Given these tensions and the contested meanings ascribed to childhood which they generate, it is little wonder that Cecilia Tichi has described debate about the relationship between children and television as one which is conducted as ritual rather than argument.[1] As she describes it:

No aspect of the acculturation of television has remained at once so vigorous and so static as the debate over the relation of children to television. The television child is precocious and sophisticated, according to the TV industry, and certain educators and child development experts cautiously agree. Yet that same child is otherwise profiled as a hostage to TV violence, as a child developmentally hastened into pseudomaturity, as a television 'wolf child' suckled by television and cut off from the 'real' world.[2]

The classification systems, ratings criteria, content standards and other guidelines which operate to regulate the relationship between children and television have the ostensible aim of protecting children from harm. But what are we really protecting them from? And *who* are we protecting? Is it that adults, afraid of the 'wolf child', attempt to 'rescue' the child – the child they think children should be – from such a fate? Are all these rules and codes more about adult fears than the welfare of children?

TELEVISION AND THE INFORMATION AGE

These questions become even more important as the nature of communications and information changes. The United Kingdom government has built its vision for communications policy around the importance of accessing information for citizens, as it explained in a recent White Paper:

> The explosion of information has fuelled a democratic revolution of knowledge and active citizenship. If information is power, power can now be within the grasp of everyone. No government can now rely on the ignorance of its population to sustain it. We are richer as citizens thanks to the expansion of modern media. This government wants to encourage this and give everyone access to all these riches as quickly as possible.[3]

These developments are apace in other countries too, of course, in this 'global village'. On the face of it such policy acknowledges the interconnectedness of citizenship and access to information. This change in communication and information technology is also occurring at a time of change in the notion of citizenship as it affects children. As has become apparent, the prevailing idea of childhood within legal discourse has been that of the vulnerable child in need of protection. But in recent times, an alternative legal discourse has begun to develop which depends on another way of seeing children. This discourse places much more emphasis on the autonomy of the child and the capacity of children to make their own decisions. As some describe it, the child can be regarded as the 'child citizen'.[4] The question is whether the child citizen can expect the same rights of access to the media as an adult.

RESTRICTING THE FREEDOMS OF ADULTS TO PROTECT MINORS

The issue which has until now dominated debate on the relationship between children and television has been about creating a 'balance' between permitting adults to view on television what they wish to see and the need to protect children from harmful content. This is the broad import of the various codes and content standards examined in earlier chapters. According to those documents the child's interest is in being protected from harmful material. The countervailing adult interest is in being able to freely express and receive information through the media. This debate is now also being repeated with respect to new forms of communications and media. European documents, for example, reflect this attempt to balance the 'competing interests' in addressing the issue of harmful content on the internet as a communication to the European Parliament states:

> The European Convention on Human Rights, signed by all Member States and part of the general principles of Community Law, contains relevant provisions affirming the right to freedom of expression. These rights can be subject to some conditions, are not absolute and are subject to important qualification ...
>
> The borderline between what is protected by free speech and what can be restricted may not be easy to draw by Member States ...
>
> One general conclusion is that any regulatory action intended to protect minors should not take the form of an unconditional prohibition of using the Internet to distribute certain content that is available freely in other media ...[5]

The document then proceeds to discuss parental control software as a means of 'empowering parents to protect minors'. This is the way in which the interests of children have been articulated for most of the last century. The role of the law, in this schema, is to balance between the needs of the child and the rights of adults. Parents have the responsibility to protect their children while at the same time as adults they may wish to see the material which their children should not. The broader community also wishes to protect children but not at the expense of the basic freedoms of adulthood. These are presented as competing interests and the role of the law is to strike the appropriate balance. This European communication refers to the United States Supreme Court decision in *Reno v The American Civil Liberties Union*[6] as an example of this balancing act. In that case the Court was asked to decide upon the constitutionality of the Communications Decency Act 1996 which sought to prohibit the transmission of obscene or indecent material over any telecommunications device nowing the recipient to be under eighteen or to use any interactive evice to send or display images or depictions of sexual activities. The issue for the Court was whether the legislation was consistent with 1e First Amendment guarantee of free speech. Although the decisions in *;insberg* and *Pacifica* had upheld the regulation of indecent speech where 1ere was a compelling state interest – such as the protection of children om harmful material – the Court found that the Communications)ecency Act was too broad in its scope and should be struck down as nconstitutional. Importantly, the nature of the internet was a significant ictor in its decision. The Supreme Court noted, as the District Court elow it had found, that unlike radio broadcasting 'the risk of ncountering indecent material by accident is remote because a series of ffirmative steps is required to access specific material'.[7] The Supreme :ourt also quoted the lower court's finding that 'communications over 1e Internet do not "invade" an individual's home or appear on one's omputer screen unbidden. Users seldom encounter content "by ccident".'[8] The Act was also vague in the manner in which it attempted) regulate 'indecent' speech and speech which was 'patently offensive as 1easured by contemporary community standards', on which the Court ommented:

> Given the absence of a definition of either term, this difference in language will provoke uncertainty among speakers about how the two standards relate to each other and just what they mean. Could a speaker confidently assume that a serious discussion about birth control practices, homosexuality, the *First Amendment* issues raised by the Appendix to the *Pacifica* opinion, or the consequences of prison rape would not violate the CDA? This uncertainty undermines the likelihood that the CDA has been carefully tailored to the congressional goal of protecting minors from potentially harmful materials.[9]

lthough the decision refers to regulation of the internet it raises broader mplications for the place of children in the regulation of television, where esort to 'community standards' also occurs. The Court recognized the agueness of such a test, the very foundation against which standards for elevision programming are often judged, particularly as they affect hildren. Clearly, the judges formed the view that such a notion is highly roblematic as there exist many views in the community about what hould be the applicable standards.

Yet the Court did not apply the same analytical reasoning to the roblem of 'harm to minors' which the legislation was ostensibly trying to revent. There was in relation to this concept no discussion of what that neant and whether such a notion was a value based idea or one grounded n scientific fact. This issue was reduced to the legal problem of whether the law had been drafted such that it achieved that objective without overreaching into adult freedoms. The case proceeded on the simple assumption that children needed protection from harmful material on the internet. The legal question was how this was to be done. Thus the notion of childhood upon which these assumptions rest has not been challenged and in 1998 the United States Congress enacted the Children's Online Privacy Protection Act.[10] This legislation continues this concern with the protection of children from commercial exploitation over the internet.

FEAR AND PANIC IN THE INTERACTIVE AGE

There is a need to protect children from exploitation on the internet, just as there is a need to do so in relation to certain forms of television advertising. Any person who is vulnerable, gullible or easily led by others may require the state to intervene to protect their interests. But the protection of children does not proceed on that basis. It is because children are *children* that they are deemed to be in need of protection. A simple conception of the child is developed which defines the child as vulnerable with the consequence that any capacity of the child to articulate his or her own interests or needs become submerged in that conception. This has significant implications for the lives of children as a consequence.

The first problem created by this narrow conception of the child as in need of protection is that it leads to the creation of 'moral panics' around issues of what children are viewing on television or seeing on the internet. The term 'moral panic' was popularized by Cohen.[11] As Green notes, new technology is often the subject of such a panic.[12] Thus, as with the introduction of television a half century ago, adults become fearful of the 'dangers' posed by the new technology to their children. One panic surrounding the internet is connected with the fear of adults that their children know more about the new technology and as a consequence will take power away from parents, according to Green:

> Panic reflects the fear of the powerful faced with the emerging competence of 'powerless others' in arenas where established social leaders feel threatened.[13]

Potter and Potter take a similar approach.[14] Their analysis attempts to debunk the mythology that children are readily exposed to harmful material such as cyberporn on the internet which they describe as a 'middle-class moral panic'.[15] The dangers of the internet, have transformed in recent times to the fear of children being 'cyberstalked' or lured into meetings with paedophiles through the latter posing as children in chat rooms. In the United Kingdom a current government campaign aims to raise awareness of this matter. These panics thus create the conditions within which increased control of children appears justified. This may take the form of the V-chip on television sets, filtering software on computers, as well as increased surveillance of the activities of the child. What needs to be considered here, however, is not just how this constructs the child for the purposes of their interaction with the media, but also how this constructs the child generally. We are rapidly creating the conditions which will destroy for many the idea of childhood they think they are saving: childhood as spontaneity, imagination and experimentation. If the new media is to be the pathway to new and more informed forms of citizenship, then what type of citizenry will be created if children grow up subject to constant monitoring and oversight of their activities?

Those who criticize the manner in which moral panics build up around the use of the new technology often fail to challenge the notion of the innocent and immature child. The lie is in the panic, according to those critics, not in the perception that children can be harmed by exposure to certain material on the internet. The United Kingdom Government's Communications White Paper also reflects this concern that many people hold about the internet and new technology:

> Some people worry that increased diversity may harm the quality of programming available and reduce standards of decency. The new communications media can transform crime as well as commerce, by helping criminals to operate globally. It is difficult to control the availability of material on the Internet – which may be located on a computer server in a country with little or no ability to enforce standards. And, with more and more broadcast channels available, many people are concerned about the amount of inappropriate or offensive material that may be seen by children at home.[16]

The challenge, it is said, is to construct a regulatory environment which ensures that the new media will enhance democratic and commercial objectives, but not at the cost of a loss of standards in taste and decency. Thus regulation must guarantee the continuance of 'quality programming' and the rights of 'citizens and consumers' must be protected:

> We must protect the interests of citizens and consumers who rely on the media for entertainment, education and information, and who depend upon accessible, high quality communications systems. We want to protect their economic interests to make sure they are not overcharged by dominant players. We want to protect their interests as citizens to make sure the right balance is struck between freedom of speech and basic standards of decency and privacy.[17]

The problem is that the major concern with standards of taste and decency is to do with the protection of children. This leads to the dilemma of how children are to grow to understand the importance of free speech when their own first encounters with the media are premised on

the basis that there are certain matters they should not see or hear. In a
age when information access is to become even more critical for civic life
this question becomes more central to the type of democracy we seek t
evolve. We should be concerned that our regulatory system for television
built on the need to protect children from harm, now provides th
rationale for even greater control of children's access to new forms c
television and new media. We are creating a generation who will come t
accept surveillance of their activities as a matter of course unless we begi
to shift the way in which we think about children's access to the media

The narrow conception of the child also creates problems c
programming content. As we have seen, the production of qualit
programming for children is often stated to be a goal of regulatory systems
but it tends to flounder as problems of definition and resources take hold
This is often seen to be a problem of formulating appropriate criteria to b
able to judge such programming,[18] yet this does not resolve the manner i
which how childhood is conceptualized determines what one considers t
be good programming for children. It may be that much of what childre
view on television at present fails to impart information or understanding
of the world which they may find useful. But is that a product of poorl
drafted regulatory criteria, or the result of a system which removes fron
children the chance to view the full diversity of life because it may d
them harm? And, having constructed the child in relation to television a
being in need of protection – or sometimes to be controlled lest the
discover how to harm others – it is difficult for the child to articulate his o
her own case for what he or she wishes to see on television.

The message from the new media is that this brings a greate
complexity to social life. Many of the fears which are generated by th
internet have a lot to do with fear of that diversity. One may understan
that access to more diverse and sophisticated material will threaten thos
with power in society. It is also threatening because by its nature it i
difficult to control. Yet that is also seen to be the value of this new form c
communication. As the United States District Court judges said in th
challenge to the Communications Decency Act, this is the very strength
of the internet, that it cannot be easily controlled. Their concludin
remarks were:

> True it is that many find some of the speech on the Internet to be
> offensive, and amid the din of cyberspace many hear discordant
> voices that they regard as indecent. The absence of governmental
> regulation of Internet content has unquestionably produced a kind of
> chaos, but as one of the plaintiff's experts put it with such resonance
> at the hearing:

> What achieved success was the very chaos that the Internet is.
> The strength of the Internet is that chaos.[19]

The chaos, diversity and difference is in many ways the essence of democracy. But there is a paradox here. The United Kingdom government on the one hand identifies the new communication technologies as holding out so much for the future of democratic life, but then regards the diversity which this creates as a cause for improved regulation. The White Paper laments the current regulatory framework which is fragmented across different bodies responsible for different forms of media. This framework lacks the ability to address the needs of a 'converging' industry. Thus:

> As technologies bring together television and the Internet, computers and telecommunications, so the type and range of content available to consumers depends on the competitive environment in this converging sector. At the same time, the type of content that broadcasters are carrying in turn affects the economics of the market itself. This means that economic regulation of the market and regulation of content need to go hand in hand and the regulatory framework needs more and more to bring together issues which are economic and social, both about content and the way that it is carried to people.[20]

What is meant by 'the economic regulation of the market and regulation of content need to go hand in hand'? It seems to lead to the creation of a single body to regulate telecommunications, television and radio.[21] The Broadcasting Standards Commission and Independent Television Commission would be replaced by the new regulatory authority.[22] There is also to be 'a new system combining better representation of consumers and citizens and a careful balance between law, formal regulation and self-regulation'.[23] The objectives of the regulator are proposed to be the protection of consumer interests, particularly through the promotion of competition; the maintenance of quality content, diversity in programming and 'plurality of public expression'; protecting citizens' interests 'by maintaining community standards in content, balancing freedom of speech against the need to protect against potentially harmful or offensive material', and the protection of fairness and privacy.[24] In pursuing these objectives the proposed new regulator is to 'give proper weight to the protection of children and vulnerable persons'.[25] It also has to give the same consideration to the prevention of crime and disorder, the special needs of people with disabilities, those on a low income, and rural dwellers, and the promotion of efficiency and innovation.[26] Where the regulator's objectives conflict then the regulator would be required to 'strike the right balance' between them.[27]

These proposed changes to the regulatory framework probably bring the United Kingdom to resemble the broad approach taken in the United

States, Canada and Australia to the extent that a single regulatory authority oversees the various parts of the system. In particular there is a remarkable similarity here with the objectives of the Australian Broadcasting Authority mentioned in the first chapter. There is also the attempts in the United States and Canada to regulate television content through the V-chip, and the attempts in the United States to control the content of the internet for children. All of these developments signal increasing state control of access to the media which, in the state's own words, means access to information and ideas.

But this control is made easier because of the continuing adherence to the view of childhood as vulnerable and in need of protection. Although the United Kingdom government has identified the need to regard the new forms of communications as integral to democracy and full participation in it, there is no sense that the child's place is in any effective sense that of citizen. The other countries examined indicate a similar approach in the manner in which children and television are debated. But why is it important that child should be conceptualized in ways other than little innocents, vulnerable to harm in the context of broadcasting policy?

A 'NEW' DISCOURSE: THE NEED FOR THE RIGHTS OF CHILDREN IN TELEVISION LAW

There will be little point in devising new forms of media or increasing the technological capacities of television if children are excluded from many of its benefits. The question then is – how are children to be included? The experience of regulatory bodies which must balance between 'public interest' considerations such as the protection of children or the provision of educational programming with the needs of the market-place is that this is not a balance easily struck. The conceptual problems with such notions as quality or educational programming and the vexed notion of 'community standards' in pursuing violence and sexual content have meant that an industry committed to pursuing ratings and profits has been able to skirt around much of what is called the regulatory system. One must question whether a 'balance' between the competing objectives of broadcasting policy is more political rhetoric than a substantive approach to the needs of the community as a whole.[28]

It is not sufficient to grant to children the promise of 'proper weight' to be given to their interests when a regulatory body looks at broadcasting. As with the notion of the 'best interests' of the child, the true interests of the child can easily be swept aside when it suits more powerful interests. The final ignominy, however, in such cases is that the decision to move against another's position can be legitimated by arguing that it is in their interests. In other words, vague standards of conduct can act as a smokescreen and justify the outcome one wishes to achieve. This is the lesson from the operation of the 'best interests' of the child standard in much of our history, where it was used to mete out harsh treatment of children, though supposedly 'in their interests'. Thus television broadcasters can be criticized for placing profit (or budgets) ahead of quality but one can then proceed to argue that if broadcasters do not make profits then the economic well-being of the nation may suffer and affect the lifestyle of all, including children. This, no doubt, is often the concern of activist groups who agitate for better children's programming, less violence and more 'family viewing' displaying positive role models. Their primary purpose is to save the child from 'bad' programming generated by the crude demands of profit. There will be times when there is much to recommend this position, at least inasmuch as it trains a critical eye on the true motivations of those who own and control broadcasting.

My concern is, however, to apply the criticism in another direction. The starting point is to consider the nature of rights. As Donnison claims, rights are valuable commodities. They empower the powerless and allow them to claim space.[29] Rights convert what might otherwise be disregarded by the powerful as a 'consideration' into something which can be used to *require* the powerful to act. Rights can shift power.

There is clearly within legal discourse a strand of thought which does not conceptualize the child as vulnerable and immature but as competent and capable of exercising choices. This has surfaced in many ways, some of which have been mentioned in earlier chapters. In particular it is a way of thinking about children which is articulated in those parts of the United Nations Convention on the Rights of the Child which speak to the autonomy of the child. The Convention, for example, makes the child's right to access information clear:

> The child shall have the right to freedom of expression; this right shall include freedom to seek, receive and impart information and ideas of all kinds, regardless of frontiers, either orally, in writing or in print, in the form of art, or through any other media of the child's choice.[30]

Yet there is an immediate problem. This right is subject to the proviso that restrictions may be placed on it to protect 'public health or morals'.[31] While this may lead to a serious erosion of the right that children have to seek and receive information, it is important to note that the proviso operates as a qualifier of the child's right. This is a subtle but important shift in thinking about the place of the child with respect to media access.

Article 12 of that Convention also gives children the right to express their views in matters affecting them, and Article 31 grants to children the right to 'engage in play and recreational activities appropriate to the age of the child and to participate freely in cultural life and the arts'. Article 17 of the Convention also provides:

> States Parties recognize the important function performed by the mass media and shall ensure that the child has access to information and material from a diversity of national and international sources, especially those aimed at the promotion of his or her social, spiritual and moral well-being and physical and mental health. To this end, States Parties shall:
> (a) Encourage the mass media to disseminate information and material of social and cultural benefit to the child and in accordance with the spirit of article 29;
> (b) Encourage international co-operation in the production, exchange and dissemination of such information and material from a diversity of cultural, national and international sources;
> (c) Encourage the production and dissemination of children's books;
> (d) Encourage the mass media to have particular regard to the linguistic needs of the child who belongs to a minority group or who is indigenous;
> (e) Encourage the development of appropriate guidelines for the protection of the child from information and material injurious to his or her well-being, bearing in mind the provisions of articles 13 and 18.

Article 29 directs itself to the education of the child and includes provisions that such education should promote respect for human rights as well as 'the development of the child's personality, talents and mental and physical abilities to their fullest potential' and the 'the preparation of the child for responsible life in a free society'. This suggests an important role for the mass media in the construction of the child as an active participant in society. The Convention has been ratified by Australia, Canada and the United Kingdom. While it has no legally binding effect at a domestic level it contains principles which demonstrate that the notion of the autonomous rights of the child can be articulated and so has some influence in arguments advanced to support the rights of the child. In particular, it is clear that the Convention conceptualizes the child in much more complex and sophisticated ways than current laws and codes which regulate television.

It is true that the extent of the child's right to autonomy is an open question as parents too have various duties towards the child under the Convention which might appear to conflict with the child's right to independence.[32] Toope claims, for example, that there is no clear answer to the question of whether a parent is 'entitled to censor the reading material or television viewing of a child in the home'.[33] To not restrict the child's viewing and expose the child to harm may be regarded as a failure of the parent to protect the child from harm as is also required by the Convention,[34] as well as domestic child protection laws. On the other hand, if viewed as a restriction on the child's right to receive information and ideas, then this might breach Article 13 of the Convention.[35] Other laws are also relevant in this regard, for example, the United Kingdom Human Rights Act 1998 which incorporates the European Convention on Human Rights into United Kingdom law provides for the right to freedom of expression and to receive and impart information and ideas.[36]

Certainly some of the apparent inconsistencies about how to treat children – as vulnerable or independent – can be resolved in the specifics of particular cases. Some children are not as mature as other children and need perhaps more protection. Other children will have developed further and so can be granted more autonomy. The Convention itself recognizes this developmental aspect in Article 5, which requires the rights and duties of parents (or others responsible for the child) 'to provide, in a manner consistent with the evolving capacities of the child, appropriate direction and guidance in the exercise by the child of the rights recognized in the present Convention'.[37] Significantly, it is the child who exercises the rights in the Convention, even where this support and guidance is required. This might suggest that the tenor of the Convention is a move towards regarding the child as the possessor of rights and a citizen. This is important because if the rights belong to the child, then they can be asserted by, or on behalf of, the child to claim resources, recognition or protection. In simple terms, it gives the child the right to be heard and requires others to listen and to act.

But even if children are recognized as having such rights, how would such rights operate in relation to television law? The child's interests in television law are substantial and go well beyond matters to do with protection from harm. If television is to be part of a new package of information technologies which will underpin democratic participation in the future, then children's inclusion in that world must occur if they too are to be regarded as citizens and grow into adults who are comfortable with the notion of civic participation. As mentioned above, children are guaranteed the right to participate in cultural life and the arts under the United Nations Convention[38] and so have a direct interest, if that right is to have meaning, in the form of television programming. This would also extend to the manner in which children are portrayed in television programmes. It has been argued that the harshness of juvenile justice policy at present reflects the negative manner in which children have been portrayed in the media.[39]

Children thus have an interest in the content of television programming. The provision to children of access to ideas and information in the media is of little meaning if the information then available is of limited relevance for their lives. Part of the problem with content no doubt arises from the tensions between the needs of industry, which sees children as a 'market' to exploit, and the needs of young people to receive information beyond current fashion trends in clothing and music. It is true that there are examples within the regulatory systems of concern with the content of 'children's programming' – particularly in Australia and the United States – but this regulation tends to reinforce a narrow conception of the child rather than broaden it. With some notable exceptions, provision for children is often made by way of cartoon channels or 'family viewing' which limits content rather than expands the scope of the material covered.

The tendency with respect to issues of content is, as we have seen, to construct the problem as one to do with 'harmful content'. This removes the focus away from the vexed issue of 'quality' and on to an area where some community consensus seems achievable. To suggest that children should have greater access to the media in this context is seen to be absurd and against 'common sense' as it increases the risk, it is said, to exposure to harmful content. It is also apparent that this operates to control the child once again. Television also has to grapple with vague criteria which make the handling of matters of content quality difficult. What is harmful is not clear and the corollary of that proposition is that we run the risk of keeping from children material that is not harmful and may in fact be very useful for them. Part of the difficulty is the idea of the child upon which the codes of practice, guidelines and classification systems rest and which lead to the 'common sense' conclusion that children will be harmed by various broadcast material. Essentially, unless children are perceived to have an interest in such matters which are otherwise seen to be 'adult' concerns it will be difficult to advance the view that children have a legitimate interest in viewing material which would be deemed unsuitable for the 'immature' child.

The recognition of the rights of the child in relation to television thus requires us to transcend a narrow understanding of the child and childhood and to embrace a view of the child which recognizes the child's independent interest in social affairs. Heins puts the case with eloquence:

> What then is wrong with censoring minors in the interests of socialization and morality? Most societies, after all, have an impulse to do so ... The ponderous, humorless overliteralism of so much censorship directed at youth not only takes the fun, ambiguity, cathartic function, and irony out of the world of imagination and creativity; it reduces the difficult, complicated, joyous, and some-times tortured experience of growing up to a sanitized combination of adult moralizing and intellectual closed doors.[40]

Censorship and control of what children can see or hear deprives them of the opportunity to 'confront and work through the messiness of life', according to Heins.[41] And it is likely to be children from the social margins who suffer most when censorship occurs, as their worlds often contain those matters which most preoccupy the community in broadcasting – sex, violence, drugs, and coarse language.[42] It has been recognized that a lack of access to the internet can disadvantage children at school and that it is children from deprived backgrounds who are more likely to have difficulty in this regard, given the costs of access.[43]

O'Neill argues against children's fundamental rights on the basis that children are not analogous to other social groups who experience oppression. They are not permanently powerless, she claims, and 'their main remedy is to grow up'.[44] But her analysis suffers from consideration of the role of television and media in shaping the individual. Children may well grow up, but if they have become used to control being imposed on the information they receive and the ideas they encounter, then they may simply grow up to be adults with little sense of what it means to be an active and informed citizen. For this reason, it is important that this debate avoids too great a concern with the age of children who should be actively involved in the processes of receiving and imparting information through various media. Certainly, some children will not be able to participate to any significant extent due to infancy. But if we conceptualize children as too young to receive and impart ideas then we will not attempt to construct processes which facilitate their involvement.[45]

What is needed is an office to oversee, in the area of broadcasting law and policy, that the principles contained therein reflect a concern, not just with the need to protect children from harm, but also that children can be autonomous persons with the capacity to participate in matters which affect them. In some jurisdictions there exists a Children's Commissioner or Children's Ombudsman. Generally, television law is not an area which has been considered to be relevant for their functions. But it is time to reconsider the manner in which that area of the law does have implications for the rights of the child. The advances in technology and communications do not only create dangers for children, which of course should be properly policed, but importantly information contained in new forms of media will have serious implications for how power is wielded in the future. If the rights of children to access information and ideas through that media are not guaranteed then even greater harm may be done to them.

The point of this book has been to demonstrate that the child is constructed in a manner which makes it difficult to regard it as having the maturity to make its own decisions about television viewing. The law and the various regulatory codes and guidelines in the regulation of television tend to adopt that view of the child and reinforce it. The form which state regulation of the relationship between children and television takes as a result also fits well with increased control of young people in the community and the imposition of parental responsibility to deal with families who do not conform to 'appropriate' standards of behaviour.

The case for greater autonomy for children in the context of the relationship between children and television can be made out as the information contained in the television and new media becomes more central for full participation in civic and economic life. Access to information will thus have a great bearing on the life chances of individuals in the future and it is important that from an early age individuals have rights to receive and impart ideas and information through that media. If such rights are to be extended to children, the law, of course, must be able to formulate principles to give effect to this aim. It has been argued that such a discourse does exist in the law where the independent rights of the child have been recognized. This discourse both demonstrates the inconsistencies in the approach to children of the dominant paradigm, which stresses the need to protect children, while at the same time demonstrating that there is an alternative legal discourse capable of constructing the child as autonomous and mature in certain circumstances. If the regulation of the relationship between children and television is going to pay due attention to the rights of children, then it is around this alternative legal approach that it will occur.

Notes

INTRODUCTION

1   National Inquiry into the Separation of Aboriginal and Torres Strait Islander Children from Their Families, *Bringing Them Home* (Human Rights and Equal Opportunity Commission, Commonwealth of Australia, 1997), p. 69.
2   P. Pierce, *The Country of Lost Children: An Australian Anxiety* (Cambridge, Cambridge University Press, 1999), p. 198.
3   Department of Health, *Referrals, Assessments and Children and Young People on Child Protection Registers Year Ending 31 March 2002* (http://www.doh.gov.uk/public/cpr2002.htm).
4   U.S. Department of Justice, Office of Justice Programs, Bureau of Justice Statistics, *Homicide Trends in the United States, Age Trends* (http://www.ojp.usdoj.gov/bjs/homicide/teens.htm).
5   J. Holt, *Escape From Childhood* (London, Pelican, 1974), p. 24.

CHAPTER 1

FORCES THAT SHAPE CHILDREN AND TELEVISION LAW: MARKET VERSUS REGULATION

1   M. Tracey, *The Decline and Fall of Public Service Broadcasting* (Oxford, Oxford University Press, 1998).
2   G. Grainger, 'Broadcasting, Co-Regulation and the Public Good', *1999 Spry Memorial Lecture* (Graham Spry Fund for Public Broadcasting) (28 October 1999), p. 13.
3   Ibid.
4   Ibid. (original emphasis) citing Tracey, op. cit.
5   Broadcasting Services Act 1992 (Cth), s.3.
6   Children's Television Act 1990 (US), Title 1, sec.101, cited in Federal Communications Commission, *Notice of Proposed Rule Making: In the Matter of Policies and Rules Concerning Children's Television* (MM Docket No. 93-48, April 1995), p. 2.
7   Ibid.
8   Ibid.
9   George Bush, *Statement on the Children's Television Act of 1990*, 17 October 1990 (http://bushlibrary.tamu.edu/papers/1990/90101700.html)
10 E. B. Hilty, 'From *Sesame Street* to *Barney and Friends*: Television as Teacher' in S. R. Steinberg and J. L. Kincheloe (eds) *Kinderculture: The Corporate Construction of Childhood* (Boulder and Oxford, Westview Press, 1997), p. 73.

11 Ibid., p. 75.
12 Ibid., p. 76.
13 C. Lasch, *The Minimal Self: psychic survival in troubled times* (London, Picador, 1984), p. 185.
14 Ibid.
15 Ibid., p. 186.
16 N. N. Minow and C. L. Lamay, *Abandoned in the Wasteland: children, television and the First Amendment* (New York, Hill and Wang, 1995), p. 19.
17 This is one reason why sport is a target for pay television owners wishing to attract large audiences. In particular, sports which can be sold around the world are even more attractive for the large audiences they can generate and the even larger advertising revenue which can then be garnered. See e.g. E. Cashmore, *Beckham* (Cambridge, Polity, 2002), p. 63ff. and esp. p. 71.
18 J. Ralston Saul, *The Unconscious Civilisation* (Ringwood, Penguin, 1997), pp. 66–7.
19 See e.g. 'Head Attacks Quiz Show Culture' (BBC News report, 18 January 2003), http://news.bbc.co.uk/1/hi/education/2668305.stm.
20 Ralston Saul, op. cit., p. 167.
21 C. Lasch, *The Revolt of the Elites and the Betrayal of Democracy* (New York and London, W. W. Norton and Co, 1994), p. 162.
22 Ibid., pp. 162–3.
23 Commonwealth of Australia, *Report of the Royal Commission on Television* (Canberra, Government Printing Office, 1954), p. 82.
24 Ibid., p. 83.
25 Ibid.
26 Ibid., p. 84.
27 Ibid.
28 Minow and Lamay, op. cit., p. 20.
29 Ibid.
30 Ibid., pp. 20–1.
31 Hilty, op. cit., p. 77.
32 Ibid.
33 See e.g. H. J. Uscinski, 'Deregulating Commercial Television: will the marketplace watch out for children?' (1984) 34 *American University Law Review* 141; B. Watkins 'Improving Educational and Informational Television For Children: when the marketplace fails', (1987) 5 *Yale Law and Policy Review* 322.
34 J. Holmes a'Court, 'Children's Television – A business. Is it? Should it be?' (Paper delivered on 11 March 1998 at the Second World Summit on Television for Children in London).
35 Ibid.
36 Commonwealth of Australia, *Report of the Royal Commission on Television*, p. 41.
37 Senate Standing Committee on Education and the Arts, *Children and Television* (Canberra, Australian Government Publishing Service, 1978), p. 23.
38 Ibid.
39 L. D. Eron and L. R. Huesmann, 'Television as a Source of Maltreatment of Children', (1987) 16, 2 *School Psychology Review*, 2, 195–202, at 195.
40 Ibid., p. 201.
41 J. M. Giovannoni and R. M. Becerra, *Defining Child Abuse* (New York, The Free Press, 1979), pp. 4–5.

42 P. Hanley (ed.), *Striking a Balance: the control of children's media consumption* (a Report undertaken for the British Broadcasting Corporation, Broadcasting Standards Commission, Independent Television Commission, September 2002), p. 2.
43 Ibid.
44 Ibid.
45 Ibid., p. 3.
46 United Kingdom Department of Trade and Industry and Department of Culture, Media and Sport, *A New Future for Communications* (*Communications* White Paper, 2001), para. 6.3.6.
47 Ibid., para. 6.3.3.
48 *Communications Bill* 2002 (UK), cl.3(3)(a) and (h).
49 See e.g. J. E. Tyler and T. W. Segady, 'Parental Liability Laws: Rationale, Theory, and Effectiveness', *Social Science Journal*, 2000, 37, (1), 79–96.
50 Ibid., p. 92.
51 Ibid.
52 Senate Standing Committee on Education and the Arts, *Children and Television* (Canberra, Australian Government Publishing Service, 1978), p. 24.
53 Ibid.
54 Ibid., p. 25.
55 Ibid., p. 27.
56 M. Winn, *The Plug in Drug* (New York, Bantam, 1978), p. 8.
57 Ibid.

CHAPTER 2

LEGAL DISCOURSE AND THE REGULATION OF THE RELATIONSHIP BETWEEN CHILDREN AND TELEVISION

1 H. Stipp, 'The Challenge to Improve Television for Children: a new perspective' in G. Berry and J. K. Asamen, *Children and Television: Images in a Changing Socio-Cultural World* (Newbury Park, Sage, 1993), p. 296.
2 D. Kunkel, 'Policy Battles over Defining Children's Educational Television' in *The Annals of the American Academy of Political and Social Science* (Thousand Oaks, CA, Sage, 1998).
3 See e.g. A. Synott, 'Little angels, little devils: a sociology of children' (1983) 20 *Canadian Review of Sociology and Anthropology* 79–95.
4 J. A. Lee, 'Three paradigms of childhood', (1982) 19 *Canadian Review of Sociology and Anthropology* 591–608.
5 For example, laws which require parents to ensure their children attend school on pain of the criminal prosecution of the parent.
6 See e.g. J. E. Tyler and T. W. Segady, 'Parental Liability Laws: Rationale, Theory, and Effectiveness', (2000) 37 (1), *Social Science Journal*, 79–96.
7 This has been developed in particular in the context of medical consent cases: see *Gillick v West Norfolk and Wisbech Area Health Authority* [1986] 1 AC 112.
8 V. A. Zelizer, *Pricing the Priceless Child* (New York, Basic Books, 1985).
9 Particularly in the case of child support.
10 Lee, op. cit.
11 Such as the House of Lords in *Gillick*, above. See also *Minister Of State For*

Immigration And Ethnic Affairs v. Ah Hin Teoh (1985) 183 *Commonwealth Law Reports* 273.

12 See e.g. D. C. A. Collins and R. A. Kearns, 'Under curfew and under siege? Local geographies of young people' (2001) 32 *Geoforum* 389–403.

13 M. King and C. Piper, *How the Law Thinks About Children* (Aldershot, Gower, 1990), p. 122.

14 Ibid.

15 Ibid., esp. chapter 3.

16 Ibid., p. 6.

17 *European Broadcasting Union's Guidelines for Programmes When Dealing With the Portrayal of Violence*, para. 2.

18 Canadian Radio-Telecommunications Commission, *Voluntary Code Regarding Violence in Television Programming* (Public Notice CRTC 1993-149) (Ottawa, 28 October 1993).

19 Ibid.

20 Broadcasting Standards Council, *A Code of Practice* (2nd edn) (London, Broadcasting Standards Council, February 1994), p. 9.

21 King and Piper, op. cit., p. 6.

22 Ibid., pp. 12–13.

23 Ibid., p. 11.

24 G. Teubner, 'How the Law Thinks: toward a constructivist epistemology of law' 1989, 23(5), *Law and Society Revue*, 727–56 at 745, cited in King and Piper, op. cit., p. 18.

25 King and Piper, op. cit., p. 37.

26 Ibid., pp. 37–8.

27 Ibid., p. 38.

28 Ibid., p. 39.

29 Ibid., p. 40.

30 Ibid.

31 Parliament of Australia *Report of the Joint Select Committee on Video Material*, Volume 2 (Canberra, AGPS, 1988), pp. 512–13.

32 Ibid., pp. 549–50. (original emphasis)

33 King and Piper, op. cit., p. 40.

34 Ibid., pp. 51–2.

35 Parliament of Victoria, Social Development Committee, *The effects of Television and Multimedia on Children and Families* (Report No.49, October 2000), p. 2.

36 M. Barker and J. Petley, 'Introduction' in M. Barker and J. Petley (eds), *Ill Effects: The media/violence debate* (London and New York, Routledge, 1997), p. 5.

37 A. Dorfman and A. Mattelart, *How to Read Donald Duck: Imperialist Ideology in the Disney comic* (New York, International General, 1972) cited in Barker and Petley, op. cit., p. 6. (original emphasis)

38 Ibid.

39 See e.g. A. Charlow, 'Awarding Custody: The Best Interests of the Child and Other Fictions', (1987) 5 *Yale Law and Policy Review* 267.

40 *Secretary, Department of Health and Community Services v JWB (Marion's Case)* (1992) 175 *Commonwealth Law Reports* 218 per Brennan, J.

41 Ibid.

42 J. Cantor, *'Mommy, I'm Scared' How TV Movies Frighten Children and What We Can Do To Protect Them* (New York, Harcourt Brace, 1988), pp. 159–68.

43 A. C. Huston and J. C. Wright, 'Television and the Informational and Educational Needs of Children' in *The Annals of the American Academiy of Social Science* (Thousand Oaks, CA, Sage, 1998), pp. 14–19.
44 Ibid.
45 M. Winn, *The Plug in Drug* (The Viking Press, 1977).
46 For example, with respect to the connection between television violence and aggression, see Chapter 4.
47 Huston and Wright, op. cit., pp. 20–1.
48 N. N. Minow and C. L. La May, *Abandoned in the Wasteland: Children, Television and the First Amendment* (New York, Hill and Wang, 1995), p. 4.
49 Ibid., pp. 20–1.
50 Ibid., p. 36.
51 N. Postman, *The Disappearance of Childhood* (London, W. H. Allen, 1982).
52 Minow and La May, op. cit., p. 37.
53 Ibid., pp. 36–7.
54 See e.g. Human Rights and Equal Opportunity Commission, *Bringing Them Home: Report of the National Inquiry into the separation of Aboriginal and Torres Strait Islander children from their families* (Commonwealth of Australia, 1997).
55 See e.g. A. Gill, *Orphans of the Empire: the shocking Story of child migration to Australia* (Sydney, Millenium Books, 1997); United Kingdom Parliament, Health Committee, *The Welfare of Former British Child Migrants* (Third Report, 30 July 1998) (HC 755). The point here is that the child migration schemes were partly justified by the need to save children from poverty and neglect: 'The motivation underlying child migration policy was mixed. On the one hand, there was a genuine philanthropic desire to rescue children from destitution and neglect in Britain and send them to a better life in the Colonies. This went hand in hand with a wish to protect children from "moral danger" arising from their home circumstances – for instance, if their mothers were prostitutes. In 1870, Thomas Barnardo wrote that "to behold young men and women crowded together in pestilential rookeries without the least provision for decency and in such conditions of abominable filth, atmospheric impurity and immoral associationship as to make the maintenance of virtue impossible, is almost enough to fill the bravest reformer with despair"': United Kingdom Parliament, Health Committee, *The Welfare of Former British Child Migrants*, para. 15. The consequences did not match this aim: 'These children were placed in large, often isolated, institutions and were often subjected to harsh, sometimes intentionally brutal, regimes of work and discipline, unmodified by any real nurturing or encouragement. The institutions were inadequately supervised, monitored and inspected.' (Ibid. para. 13).
56 M. Heins, *Not in Front of the Children: 'indecency', censorship and the innocence of youth* (New York, Hill and Wang, 2001), pp. 256–7.

CHAPTER 3

REGULATING THE RELATIONSHIP BETWEEN CHILDREN AND TELEVISION

1 Broadcasting Services Act 1992 (Cth), s.129(1).
2 Children's Television Standard 1(1).
3 Children's Television Standard 3(1).

4　Children's Television Standard 3(1)(c).
5　Children's Television Standards 1 and 3.
6　Australian Broadcasting Tribunal, *kidz tv: an inquiry into children's and preschool children's television standards*, Volume 1 (Sydney, 1991), p. 31.
7　Ibid., p. 32.
8　Children's Television Standards objective.
9　Children's Television Standard 2.
10　Australian Broadcasting Tribunal, *kidz tv: an inquiry into children's and preschool children's television standards*, Volume 1 (Sydney, 1991), p. 93.
11　Ibid.
12　Ibid., p. 94.
13　www.aba.gov.au/tv/content/childtv/assessment/index.htm, pp. 9–10.
14　Ibid., p. 11.
15　Ibid., p. 7.
16　Australian Broadcasting Tribunal, *kidz tv: an inquiry into children's and preschool children's television standards*, Volume 1 (Sydney, 1991), p. 94.
17　www.aba.gov.au/tv/content/childtv/assessment/index.htm, p. 11.
18　Ibid., p. 11; see also Australian Broadcasting Tribunal, *kidz tv: an inquiry into children's and preschool children's television standards*, Volume 1 (Sydney, 1991) p. 94.
19　www.aba.gov.au/tv/content/childtv/assessment/index.htm, p. 12.
20　Ibid., p. 12.
21　See in Australia: Children (Criminal Proceedings) Act 1987 (NSW), s.5 *Children and Young Persons Act 1989* (Vic), s.127, *Criminal Code Act 1899* (Qld), s.29, *Young Offenders Act* 1993 (SA), s.5, *Criminal Code* (WA), s.29.
22　See e.g. *Consent to Medical Treatment and Palliative Care Act* 1995 (South Australia), s.12; *Gillick v Norfolk and Wisbech Area Health Authority* (1985) 3 All ER 402.
23　Family Law Act 1975 (Cth), s.68F(2)(a).
24　Ibid.
25　See e.g. C. A. Wringe, Children's Rights: a philosophical study (London, Routledge and Kegan Paul, 1981); J. Fortin, *Children's Rights and the Developing Law* (London, Butterworth, 1998).
26　Children's Television Standard 10.
27　See Children's Television Standards 11 and 12; for definitions and the 32 hour first release and 8 hour repeat requirement also see Australian Content Standards 12 and 13.
28　Broadcasting Services Act 1992 (Cth), s.123(2).
29　Broadcasting Services Act 1992 (Cth), s.123(3).
30　Broadcasting Services Act 1992 (Cth), s.123(3A).
31　Broadcasting Services Act 1992 (Cth), s.123(3A)(c).
32　Broadcasting Services Act 1992 (Cth), s.123(3A)(d).
33　Broadcasting Services Act 1992 (Cth), s.123(4).
34　Broadcasting Services Act 1992 (Cth), s.125.
35　Broadcasting Services Act 1992 (Cth), s.128.
36　Commercial Television Code of Practice, para. 1.1.2
37　The Broadcasting Services Act 1992 (Cth), s.123(3A) requires the Office of Film and Literature Classification's classification system to be used for the classification of films on television. The result has been the use of that classification system for all programming.
38　Commercial Television Code of Practice, para. 2.1.
39　Commercial Television Code of Practice, para. 2.12.

40 Commercial Television Code of Practice, para. 2.14.
41 Commercial Television Code of Practice, para. 2.16.
42 Commercial Television Code of Practice, para. 2.18.
43 Commercial Television Code of Practice, para. 2.20.
44 Commercial Television Code of Practice, para. 2.11.
45 Commercial Television Code of Practice, para. 2.13.
46 Commercial Television Code of Practice, para. 2.15.
47 Commercial Television Code of Practice, para. 2.17.
48 Commercial Television Code of Practice, para. 2.26.1.
49 Australian Broadcasting Corporation Act 1983 (Cth), s.79.
50 This is stated on the Australian Broadcasting Authority's website at www.aba.gov.au/tv/content/codes/index.htm.
51 ABC Code of Practice, para. 3.1.
52 ABC Code of Practice, paras. 4.8–4.9.
53 ABC Code of Practice, para. 1.
54 Australian Broadcasting Corporation Act 1983, s.6(2)(a)(ii).
55 Australian Broadcasting Corporation Act 1983, s.6.
56 SBS Code of Practice, para. 2.1.
57 The Community Television Code of Practice also mentions age discrimination.
58 SBS Code of Practice, para. 2.4.4.
59 SBS Code of Practice, para. 3.2.
60 See this discussion at the Australian Broadcasting Authority website: www.aba.gov.au/tv/content/codes/payTV/paytv_code1.htm#intro.
61 Community Television Code of Practice, para. 2.4.
62 Community Television Code of Practice, code 2.
63 Pub.L. No.101-437, 104 Stat.996-1000, codified at 47 USC §§ 303a.
64 Federal Communications Commission, *In the Matter of Policies and Rules Concerning Children's Television Programming: Revision of Programming Policies for Television Broadcast Stations* MM Docket No.93–48, Report and Order, 8 August, 1996, p. 2 citing Children's Television Act 1990, 47 USC § 303b.
65 Huston and Wright, op. cit., p. 11.
66 D. Kunkel, 'Policy Battles over Defining Children's Educational Television' in *The Annals of the American Academy of Political and Social Science* (Thousand Oaks, CA, Sage, 1998), p. 41.
67 Ibid., pp. 40–1.
68 Ibid., p. 42–3.
69 Ibid., p. 43 citing Federal Communications Commission, *In the Matter of Policies and Rules Concerning Children's Television Programming: Report and Order*, 6 FCC Record 2111.
70 Ibid.
71 Ibid., pp. 44–5.
72 Ibid., p. 45 citing E. Andrews, 'Broadcasters, to Satisfy Law, Define Cartoons as Education', *New York Times*, 1992, 30 September.
73 Ibid., p. 45.
74 Ibid., see Federal Communications Commission, *Notice of Proposed Rule Making: In the Matter of Policies and Rules Concerning Children's Television*, MM Docket No.93–48, April 1995.
75 Ibid., pp. 3–4.
76 D. Kunkel, 'Policy and the Future of Children's Television' in G. L. Berry and J. K. Asamen, *Children and Television: images in a changing sociocultural world* (Newbury Park, Sage, 1993), pp. 274–5.

77 See e.g. R. B. Chong, *Remarks of Commissioner Rachelle B. Chong*, Wor Summit on Television and Children 'Regulation: Alternative Nation Models', Melbourne, Australia, 14 March 1995. See also D. A. Hayes, 'Tl Children's Hour Revisited: The Children's Television Act 1990', (1994) Federal Communications Law Journal 293 at 306: 'A New Orleans televisic station listed the following plot summary for the cartoon *Bucky O'Ha* "Good-doer Bucky fights off the evil toads from aboard his ship. Issues social consciousness and responsibility are central themes of the program.

78 See e.g. Centre for Media Educaiton: www.cme.org.

79 The reports are available from the FCC website: www.fcc.gov. The examples were from the report for the New York area, quarter ending : June 2002.

80 Pub. LA. No. 104–104, 110 Stat. 56 (1996).

81 Telecommunications Act 1996 (US), s.551(a).

82 Ibid., s.551(b) and (c). All sets 13 inches and larger made after 1 Januar 2000 must have the blocking technology: FCC Commissioner K. (Abernathy: http://ftp.fcc.gov/commissioners/abernathy/news/children.htm

83 Ibid.

84 J. Cantor, 'Ratings for Program Content: The Role of Research Finding in *The Annals of the American Academy of Social Science* (Thousand Oaks, C/ Sage, 1998), pp. 54–69.

85 Ibid., p. 67.

86 Ibid.

87 Ibid.

88 Ibid.

89 Broadcasting Act 1991 (Can), s.3(1)(d)(iii).

90 Ibid., s.5.

91 Canadian Radio-television and Telecommunications Commission, *Poli On Violence In Television Programming*, Public Notice CRTC 1996-3(Ottawa, 14 March 1996.

92 Canadian Radio-television and Telecommunications Commission, *199 Policy on Gender Portrayal*, Public Notice CRTC 1992-58, Ottawa, September 1992.

93 Canadian Radio-television and Telecommunications Commission, *Buildir On Success – A Policy Framework For Canadian Television*, CRTC 1999-9' Ottawa, 11 June 1999.

94 Under the policy Canadian broadcasters are required to broadcast an averag of eight hours per week of Canadian produced programmes in certai categories (priority programmes) in the 7 p.m. to 11.00 p.m. time period

95 Canadian Radio-television and Telecommunications Commission, *Buildir On Success – A Policy Framework For Canadian Television*, CRTC 1999-9' Ottawa, 11 June 1999, paras. 65–7.

96 Ibid., paras. 42–3.

97 Canadian Broadcast Standards Council, 'Self-Regulation in Canad; Building on a Uniquely Successful System', Submission of the Canadia Broadcast Standards Council to CRTC Notice of Public Hearing 1995-! 29 June 1995.

98 Canadian Association of Broadcasters, *Code of Ethics* (Revised June 2002)

99 Canadian Association of Broadcasters, *Voluntary Code Regarding Violence i Television Programming* (1994).

100 Canadian Association of Broadcasters, *Sex Role Portrayal Code for Televisio and Radio Programming* (26 October 1990).

101 Canadian Association of Broadcasters, *Code of Ethics* (Revised June 2002), clause 4.
102 Ibid., clause 10.
103 Ibid., Appendix A. The suggestions are:
'The following programme contains scenes of coarse language and is not suitable for younger children.'
'The following programme contains sexually explicit material intended for adult audiences. Viewer discretion is advised.'
'The following programme contains sexually explicit material. Viewer discretion is advised.'
'The following programme contains scenes of violence, coarse language and nudity intended for adult audiences. Viewer discretion is advised.'
'The following programme deals with mature subject matter and is intended for adult audiences. Viewer discretion is advised.'
'The following programme deals with mature subject matter and contains scenes of nudity and coarse language. Viewer discretion is advised.'
104 Canadian Radio-television and Telecommunications Commission, *Policy on Violence and Television Programming*, Public Notice CRTC 1996-36, Ottawa, 14 March 1996.
105 V-Chip Canada website: http://www.vchipcanada.ca/english/index.html.
106 The Action Group on Violence on Television membership includes broadcasters, producers, advertising and community organizations.
107 See further, Canadian Radio-television and Telecommunications Commission, *Policy on Violence and Television Programming*, Public Notice CRTC 1996-36, Ottawa, 14 March 1996, Part 3(d).
108 http://www.vchipcanada.ca/english/index.html.
109 Canadian Radio-television and Telecommunications Commission, *Policy on Violence and Television Programming*, Public Notice CRTC 1996-36, Ottawa, 14 March 1996, Part 1.
110 Broadcasting Act 1996 (UK), s.108(2).
111 Broadcasting Standards Commission, Code on Standards, para. 6.
112 Broadcasting Standards Commission, Code on Standards, para. 7.
113 Broadcasting Standards Commission, Code on Standards, para. 6.
114 Broadcasting Standards Commission, Code on Standards, para. 26.
115 Broadcasting Standards Commission, Code on Standards, para. 27.
116 Independent Television Commission, Programme Code, para. 1.2. The Code refers to 'children' as those 'aged 15 or under' and 'young persons' as those aged sixteen or seventeen and 'very young children' as those aged four or under: Ibid.
117 Independent Television Commission, Programme Code, para. 1.3(i).
118 British Broadcasting Corporation, *Producers Guidelines*, chapter 43.
119 British Broadcasting Corporation, *Producers Guidelines*, chapter 6.
120 British Broadcasting Corporation, *Producers Guidelines*, chapter 14.
121 Ibid., part 5.
122 See Criminal Justice Act 1988 (UK), s.34.
123 King and Piper, op. cit., p. 3.

CHAPTER 4

IMAGES THAT HARM? CHILDREN AND VIOLENCE IN TELEVISION

1 H. T. Edwards and M. N. Berman, 'Regulating Violence on Television' (1993) 89 *Northwestern University Law Review* 1487 at 1487 citing *Times Mirror* poll, 28 April 1993.
2 D. Atkinson and M. Gourdeau, *Summary and Analysis of Various Studies on Violence and Television* (Institut québécois de recherché sur la culture, June 1991), (Ottawa, Canadian Radio-television and Telecommunications Commission), p. 3.
3 Commonwealth of Australia, *Report of the Royal Commission on Television* (Canberra, 1954), p. 39.
4 'Battling a tidal wave of violence', *The Advertiser* (Adelaide), 1993, 16 November, p. 15.
5 Parliament of Victoria, Family and Community Development Committee, *The Effects of Television and Multimedia on Children and Families in Victoria* (Report No. 49, October 2000), p. 69, n.11.
6 Parliament of Victoria, Family and Community Development Committee, *The Effects of Television and Multimedia on Children and Families in Victoria* (Report No. 49, October 2000).
7 Cited at para. 3.3.
8 National Institute of Mental Health, *Television and Behaviour: ten years of scientific progress and implications for the eighties*, Volume 1, Summary Report, United States Government Printing Office, Washington, DC, 1982 cited at para. 3.3.
9 American Psychological Association, *Violence and Youth: psychology's Response*, Volume 1, Summary Report of the American Psychological Association Commission on Violence and Youth, American Psychological Association, Washington, DC, 1992 cited at para. 3.3.
10 Parliament of Victoria, Family and Community Development Committee, *The Effects of Television and Multimedia on Children and Families in Victoria*, para. 3.3.
11 Ibid, para. 3.4.
12 Ibid, para. 3.57.
13 Ibid.
14 Ibid, para. 3.11.
15 Ibid.
16 Ibid, para. 3.13.
17 Ibid, para. 3.12.
18 Ibid., paras. 3.14–15, citing J. Federman, *National Television Violence Study 1* (Thousand Oaks, CA, Sage, 1996).
19 B. Hodge and D. Tripp, *Children and Television: A Semiotic Approach* (Cambridge, Polity Press, 1986), pp. 200–1.
20 Ibid., p. 213.
21 A. Synott, 'Little angels, little devils: a sociology of children' (1983) 20 *Canadian Review of Anthropology* 79–95.
22 See e.g. M. Freeman, 'The James Bulger Tragedy: childish innocence and the construction of guilt' in A. McGilvray (ed.) *Governing Childhood* (Aldershot, Dartmouth, 1997).
23 Hodge and Tripp, op. cit., p. 217.
24 Ibid., p. 217.

25 R. Silverstone, *Television and Everyday Life* (London, Routledge, 1994), pp. 154–5.
26 Hodge and Tripp, op. cit., pp. 217–18.
27 Ontario, *Royal Commission on Violence in the Communications Industry* (LaMarsh Commission) (Toronto, Queen's Printer, 1976).
28 British Broadcasting Corporation, *Violence on Television: the Report of the Wyatt Committee* (London, British Broadcasting Corporation, 1987).
29 Australian Broadcasting Tribunal, *TV Violence in Australia: report to the Minister for Transport and Communications* (Sydney, Australian Broadcasting Tribunal, 1990).
30 Atkinson and Gourdeau, op. cit., pp. 4–5.
31 Ibid., p. 5.
32 See e.g. J. L. Freedman, 'Effect of Television Violence on Aggressiveness', (1984), 96(2), *Psychological Bulletin*, 227–46.
33 Ibid., p. 6.
34 J. Windhausen, 'Congressional Interest in the Problem of Television and Violence' (1994) 22 *Hofstra Law Review* 789–90 at 783.
35 Ibid., p. 790
36 L. Hancock, 'Police Discretion in Victoria: the police discretion to prosecute' (1978), 14, *Australian and New Zealand Journal of Criminology*, pp. 33–40; L. Hancock, 'Issues in juvenile justice and police' in F. Gale, N. Naffine and J. Wundersitz (eds) *Juvenile Justice: Debating the Issues* (Sydney, Allen and Unwin, 1993).
37 K. Carrington, 'Policing Families and Controlling the Young' in R. White and B. Wilson, *For Your Own Good: Young People and State Intervention in Australia* (Special issue of *Journal of Australian Studies*) (Bundoora, LaTrobe University Press, 1991), p. 115.
38 Ibid., p. 113.
39 Ibid., p. 117.
40 Commercial Television Code of Practice, para. 2.5.
41 Ibid., para. 2.11.1.
42 Ibid., para. 2.13.1.
43 Ibid., para. 2.15.1.
44 Ibid., para. 2.19.1.
45 AGVOT classification: http://www.vchipcanada.ca/english/index.html.
46 P. Phillips, *The Truth About the Power Rangers* (Lancaster, PA, Starburst Publishers, 1995), pp. 7–8.
47 Ibid., p. 8.
48 Ibid., p. 11.
49 Ibid., pp. 11–12.
50 Ibid., p. 13.
51 Ibid., pp. 33–40.
52 Ibid., p. 59. (original emphasis)
53 Ibid., p. 62.
54 Ibid.
55 Ibid., pp. 72–3.
56 See e.g. a review of his book *Turmoil in the Toy Box* at http://www.paleotimes.org/newsletter/narrowWayMar2001.htm.
57 Phillips, op. cit., p. 79.
58 Ibid., pp. 80–1. (original emphasis)
59 Ibid., pp. 81–2.
60 Ibid, pp. 82–3.

61 Ibid., p. 83.
62 Ibid., p. 84.
63 Ibid., p. 85.
64 Ibid.
65 Ibid., p. 86.
66 Ibid., pp. 86–9.
67 Ibid., p. 90.
68 Ibid., p. 107.
69 Television Code of Broadcasting Practice (NZ), Standard V1.
70 *In the Matter of the Broadcasting Act* 1989 and *In the Matter of Complaints by Bayfield Kindergarten, Carolyn Barr, Children's Media Watch: Broadcaster Television New Zealand Limited* (Broadcasting Standards Authority, Decisions Nos.81–84/94, 19 September 1994), p. 4.
71 Ibid., p. 3.
72 Ibid.
73 Ibid.
74 Television Code of Broadcasting Practice (NZ), Standard V10.
75 Television Code of Broadcasting Practice (NZ), Standard V11.
76 Television Code of Broadcasting Practice (NZ), Standard G12.
77 *In the Matter of the Broadcasting Act* 1989 and *In the Matter of complaints by Bayfield Kindergarten, Carolyn Barr, Children's Media Watch: Broadcaster Television New Zealand Limited* (Broadcasting Standards Authority, Decisions Nos.81–84/94, 19 September 1994), p. 6.
78 *CIII-TV (Global Television) re 'Mighty Morphin Power Rangers'* (CBSC Decisions 93/94-0270 and 93/94-0277), decided 24 October 1994.
79 Ibid., pp. 2–3.
80 Canadian Radio–television and Telecommunications Commission, *Voluntary Code Regarding Violence in Television Programming*, Public Notice CRTC 1993–149, Ottawa, 28 October 1993.
81 Ibid.
82 Canadian Association of Broadcasters, *Voluntary Code Regarding Violence in Television Programming*.
83 *CIII-TV (Global Television) re 'Mighty Morphin Power Rangers'* (CBSC Decisions 93/94-0270 and 93/94-0277), decided 24 October 1994, p. 6. (original emphasis)
84 Ibid.
85 Ibid. (original emphasis)
86 Ibid., p. 7.
87 Ibid. (original emphasis)
88 Canadian Association of Broadcasters, *Voluntary Code Regarding Violence in Television Programming*, Part 1.
89 Australian Broadcasting Authority Investigation Report Mighty Morphin Power Rangers/G Classification: A report on the Australian Broadcasting Authority's investigation into compliance by licensees of the Seven network with the commercial television code of practice, 7 November 1995.
90 FACTS Commercial Television Industry Code of Practice, para. 2.10.1. The current provision in the Code is in similar terms: '**2.11.1 Violence**: Visual depiction of physical and psychological violence must be very restrained. The use of weapons, threatening language, sounds or special effects must have a very low sense of threat or menace, must be strictly limited to the storyline or programme context, must be infrequent and must not show violent behaviour to be acceptable or desirable.'

91 FACTS Commercial Television Industry Code of Practice, para. 2.10. The current Code is in similar terms: '**2.11** Material classified G is not necessarily intended for children but it must be very mild in impact and must not contain any matter likely to be unsuitable for children to watch without supervision.'

92 Australian Broadcasting Authority Investigation Report Mighty Morphin Power Rangers/G Classification, paras. 6.14–6.19.

93 Australian Broadcasting Authority Investigation Report Mighty Morphin Power Rangers/G Classification, para. 6.55.

94 Ibid., para. 6.56.

95 Ibid., para. 8.6.

96 Ibid, paras. 8.10–8.11.

97 Ibid., paras. 8.12–8.13.

98 Broadcasting Standards Commission, *Code on Standards*, para. 48.

99 Ibid., para. 49.

100 Ibid., para. 53.

101 Ibid., para. 56.

102 Independent Television Commission, *Programme Code*, para. 1.7.

103 British Broadcasting Corporation, *Producers' Guidelines*, para. 3.3.

104 Collins and Kearns, op. cit., p. 391.

105 National Society for the Prevention of Cruelty to Children, *Screen Violence: What every parent should know* (London, NSPCC, 1997), p. 7.

106 See e.g. Atkinson and Gourdeau, op. cit., p. 9.

107 Ibid., p. 10.

108 Canadian Radio-television and Telecommunications Commission, *Respecting Children: a Canadian approach to helping families deal with violence* (Ottawa, 14 March 1996).

109 D. J. Smith, *The Sleep of Reason: the James Bulger Case* (London, Arrow, 1994), p. 227.

CHAPTER 5

THE SEXUALISED WORLD OF TELEVISION AND CHILDREN

1 A. M. Hargrave, *Sex and Sensibility* (London, Broadcasting Standard Commission, January 1999).

2 Ibid., p. 81.

3 Parliament of Australia, Senate Standing Committee on Education and the Arts, *Children and Television* (Canberra, Australian Government Publishing Service, 1978), paras. 5.56, 5.58.

4 Parliament of Australia, Senate Standing Committee on Education and the Arts, *Children and Television Revisited* (Canberra, Australian Government Publishing Service, 1981), p. 5.

5 Parliament of Victoria, Social Development Committee, *The Effect of Television or Multimedia on Children and Families* (Report No. 49, October 2000), pp. 81–3.

6 Ibid. See also J. B. McConahay, 'Pornography: the symbolic politics of fantasy' (1988) 51(1) *Law and Contemporary Problems* 31–69.

7 See McConahay, op. cit., p. 51.

8 R. H. Potter and L. A. Potter, 'The Internet, Cyberporn, and Sexual Exploitation of Children: media moral panics and urban myths for middle-class parents?', 2001, 5(3), *Sexuality and Culture*, 31–48 pp., at p. 45.

9 M. Flood and C. Hamilton, Youth and Pornography in Australia: Evidence on the extent of exposure and likely effects (The Australia Institute, Discussion Paper No. 52, February 2003).

10 See e.g. M. Barker (ed.) *The Video Nasties: freedom and censorship in the media* (London, Pluto Press, 1984).

11 Parliament of Victoria, Social Development Committee, *The Effect of Television or Multimedia on Children and Families* (Report No. 49, October 2000), p. 82.

12 H. Hendershot, *Saturday Morning Censors: television regulation before the V-chip* (Durham and London, Duke University Press, 1998), p. 7.

13 P. Ariés, *Centuries of Childhood* (first published 1960).

14 Ibid., (Penguin edition, 1973), p. 98.

15 Ibid., p. 101.

16 R. Sennett, *Flesh and Stone: the body and the city in western civilisation* (London and Boston, Faber and Faber, 1994), pp. 46–7. See also M. Heins, *Not in Front of the Children: 'indecency', censorship and the innocence of youth* (New York, Hill and Wang, 2001), p. 15.

17 R. Thomson, 'Legal, Protected and Timely: young people's perspectives on the heterosexual age of consent' in J. Bridgeman and D. Monk (eds) *Feminist Perspectives on Child Law* (London and Sydney, Cavendish, 2000), p. 170.

18 Heins, op. cit., pp. 258–9.

19 Australian Broadcasting Corporation Code of Practice, para. 2.3.

20 See generally Hendershot, op. cit.

21 Commercial Television Code of Practice, para. 2.11.2.

22 Australian Broadcasting Authority, *Report of Investigation: Nine Network Australia Pty Ltd – QTQ-9 Brisbane: The 'Today' Show – 8 October 1997* (File No. 97/0792, Complaint No. 10017, Investigation No. 511).

23 Ibid., p. 2.

24 Ibid., p. 4.

25 Ibid.

26 Ibid.

27 Nine Network's response to the preliminary investigation into the complaint: ibid., pp. 4–5.

28 Ibid., p. 5.

29 Commercial Television Code of Practice, para. 2.13.2.

30 Ibid., para. 2.15.2.

31 Ibid., para. 2.17.2.

32 Ibid.

33 Canadian Association of Broadcasters, *Code of Ethics*, clause 10.

34 Broadcasting Standards Commission, *Code on Standards*, paras. 79

35 Broadcasting Standards Commission, *Code on Standards*, paras. 80–2.

36 Independent Television Commission, *Programme Code*, section 1.6.

37 Ibid., section 1.3(i).

38 British Broadcasting Corporation, *Producers' Guidelines*, chapter 6, section 10.

39 Ibid.

40 Ibid.

41 Ibid.

42 Canadian Broadcast Standards Council, *City-TV re Ed the Sock* (CBSC Decision 94/95-0100), 23 August 1995, p. 4.

43 Hendershot, op. cit., pp. 24–5.

44 Ibid., p. 25 citing A. Kuhn, *Cinema, Censorship, and Sexuality, 1909–1925* (New York, Routledge, 1988).

45 Ibid., p. 26.
46 See e.g. D. Kairys (ed.), *A Critique of Law: a progressive critique* (New York, Basis Books, 1998); A. Hunt, 'The Critique of Law: what is 'critical' about critical legal theory', (1987) 14, *Journal of Law and Society*, pp. 5–19.
47 C. Smart, *Feminism and the Power of Law* (London and New York, Routledge, 1989), p. 4 citing P. Hirst, 'Law and Sexual Difference', 1986, 8(1 and 2), *Oxford Literary Review*, pp. 193–8.
48 Thomson, op. cit., p. 169.
49 Ibid., p. 170.
50 See Chapter 6 below.
51 Federal Communications Commission, *In the Matter of Industry Guidance On the Commission's Case Law Interpreting 18 U.S.C.§ 1464 and Enforcement Policies Regarding Broadcast Indecency*, File No. EB-00-IH-0089, 6 April 2001.
52 Ibid. citing *FCC v Pacifica Foundation* 438 US 726 (1978). For an analysis of the history of the regulation of broadcast indecency see K. A. Finch, 'Lights, Camera, and Action for Children's Television v FCC: the story of broadcast indecency, starring Howard Stern' (1995) 63 *University of Cincinnatti Law Review* 1275.
53 Ibid.
54 390 US 629 (1968).
55 See S. D. Rubens, 'First Amendment – Disconnecting Dial-A-Porn: Section 223(b)'s two pronged challenge to First Amendment rights' (1990) 80 (4) *Journal of Criminal Law and Criminology* 968–95, at p. 974.
56 Emerson, 'Toward a General Theory of the First Amendment' (1963) 72 *Yale Law Journal* 877, 938, 939 cited in *Ginsberg v State of New York* .
57 387 US 1 (1967).
58 Ibid.
59 *Ginsberg v State of New York*, per Fortas, J.
60 See e.g. W. B. Wilhelm, 'In the Interest of Children: action for children's television v FCC: improperly delineating the constitutional limits of broadcast indecency' (1992) 42 *Catholic University Law Review* 215; Heins, op. cit., pp. 109–36.
61 Heins, op. cit., p. 130.
62 Federal Communications Commission, *In the Matter of Industry Guidance On the Commission's Case Law Interpreting 18 U.S.C.§ 1464 and Enforcement Policies Regarding Broadcast Indecency*, File No. EB-00-IH-0089, 6 April 2001.
63 Ibid. citing WPBN/WTOM License Subsidiary, Inc., 15 FCC Rcd at 1841.15.

CHAPTER 6

ADS, FADS AND GREEN TOMATO SAUCE: ADVERTISING TO
THE CHILD

1   D. Kunkel, 'Policy and the Future of Children's Television' in G. L. Berry
    and J. K. Asamen *Children and Television: Images in a Changing Sociocultural
    World* (Newbury Park, Sage, 1993), pp. 274–5.
2   S. Kline, *Out of the Garden: Toys, TV, and Children's Culture in the Age of
    Marketing* (London and New York, Verso, 1993), pp. 316–17.
3   Ibid., p. 317.
4   K. McDonnell, 'The hurried child', (2002) 343, *New Internationalist*, p. 23.
5   D. Kunkel and D. Roberts, 'Young Minds and Marketplace Values: issues
    in children's television advertising' (1991) 47(1), *Journal of Social Issues*, pp.
    57–72, 65.
6   Ibid., p. 66.
7   *Consumer Protection Act*, SQ, c.9. s.248.
8   Ibid., s.249.
9   *Attorney-General of Quebec v Irwin Toys Ltd.* (1989) 58 *DLR* 4th 577
    (Supreme Court of Canada).
10 Section 1 of the *Canadian Charter of Rights and Freedoms* guarantees the rights
    in the *Charter* 'subject only to such reasonable limits prescribed by law as can
    be demonstrably justified in a free and democratic society'. See also sections
    9.1 of the Quebec *Charter of Human Rights and Freedoms*: 'In exercising his
    fundamental freedoms and rights, a person shall maintain a proper regard for
    democratic values, public order and the general well-being of citizens of
    Quebec.'
11 *Attorney-General of Quebec v Irwin Toys Ltd.* (1989) 58 *DLR* 4th 577.
12 Ibid., per Dickson, C. J., Lames and Wilson, J. J.
13 Ibid.
14 Ibid., citing Federal Trade Commission *Final Staff Report and Recommenda-
    tions: In the Matter of Children's Advertising* (c. 1981) pp. 34–5.
15 Ibid.
16 Ibid.
17 Ibid.
18 Ibid., per McIntyre J. and Beetz, J. J.
19 I. Kennedy, 'Patients, doctors and human rights' in R. Blackburn and
    J. Taylor (eds), *Human Rights for the 1990s* (London, Mansell, 1991).
20 *Secretary, Department of Health and Community Services v JWB (Marion's Case)*
    (1992) 175 *CLR* 218, per Brennan, J.
21 *Attorney-General of Quebec v Irwin Toys Ltd*, per McIntyre, J.
22 B. Russell, 'The Superior Virtue of the Oppressed' in B. Russell, *Unpopular
    Essays* (London, Allen and Unwin, 1950).
23 See Children's Television Standard 3(1)(e).
24 Children's Television Standard 14(1).
25 Children's Television Standard 14(2) and (3).
26 Children's Television Standard 15.
27 Children's Television Standard 16.
28 Children's Television Standard 17.
29 Children's Television Standard 19.
30 Children's Television Standard 19(4).
31 Children's Television Standard 19(5).

32 Children's Television Standard 19(6).
33 Children's Television Standards 20, 21.
34 Children's Television Standard 21.
35 Children's Television Standard 22(2).
36 Children's Television Standard 23.
37 Commercial Television Code of Practice, para. 6.1.1.
38 Ibid., para. 6.3.1.
39 Ibid., para. 6.4.
40 Ibid., para. 6.7.
41 Ibid., para. 6.9.
42 Ibid., para. 6.12.
43 Ibid., para. 6.13.1.
44 Ibid., para. 6.13.2.
45 Ibid., para. 6.14.
46 Ibid., para. 6.15.
47 Ibid., para. 6.15.1.
48 Ibid., para. 6.16.
49 Ibid., paras. 6.17–6.19.
50 Ibid., para. 6.20.
51 Ibid., para. 6.23.
52 Ibid., para. 6.24.
53 Canadian Association of Broadcasters, *Code of Ethics*, clause 13.
54 Advertising Standards Canada, *Broadcast Code for Advertising to Children*, Part I.
55 Ibid., Code, Part II, para. 1.
56 *Criminal Code* (Canada), s.13.
57 Ibid., s.659.
58 Advertising Standards Canada, *Broadcast Code for Advertising to Children*, Part II, para. 5.
59 Ibid., para. 7.
60 Ibid., para. 11(b).
61 Ibid., para. 11(a).
62 Broadcasting Standards Commission, *Code of Standards*, para. 13.
63 47 United States Code sec.303a.
64 See Toy Industry Association, Inc. website: www.toy-tma.com.
65 www.caru.org
66 Ibid. *Self-Regulatory Guidelines for Children's Advertising*, Principle 2.
67 J. J. Stoltman, 'The Context of Advertising and Children' in M. C. Macklin and L. Carlson (eds), *Advertising to Children: Concepts and Controversies* (Thousand Oaks, CA, Sage, 1999), p. 295.
68 CARU, *Self-Regulatory Guidelines for Children's Advertising.*, Principle 4.
69 Australian Broadcasting Tribunal, *Public Inquiry Report: Inquiry into the Program Teenage Mutant Ninja Turtles, Decision and Reasons*, IP/90/114, December, 1991.
70 Ibid., p. 11.
71 Ibid.
72 Ibid., p. 6.
73 Ibid.
74 www.familyprogramawards.com.
75 Ibid.
76 Ibid.
77 Ibid.
78 Ibid.

CHAPTER 7

THE 'NEW' LEGAL DISCOURSE: CHILDREN'S RIGHTS AND
TELEVISION IN THE INTERACTIVE AGE

1 C. Tichi, *Electronic Hearth: Creating an American Television Culture* (New York and Oxford, Oxford University Press, 1991), p. 191.
2 Ibid.
3 United Kingdom Department of Trade and Industry and Department of Culture, Media and Sport, *A New Future for Communications* (Communications White Paper, Command 5010, 12 December 2000), para. 1.1.15.
4 See e.g. K. Funder, *Citizen Child: Australian Law and Children's Rights* (Melbourne, Australian Institute of Family Studies, 1996).
5 Info 2000, *Illegal and Harmful Content on the Internet*, Communication to the European Parliament, the Council, the Economic and Social Committee, of the Regions (2000).
6 117 S.Ct.2329, 138 L.Ed. 2d 87 (1997).
7 Ibid.
8 Ibid., citing *ACLU v Reno* 929 F Supp at 844.
9 Ibid.
10 15 U.S.C. §§ 6501–6.
11 S. Cohen, *Folk Devils and Moral Panics: the creation of the Mods and Rockers* (Oxford, 1972).
12 L. Green, *Technoculture: from alphabet to cybersex* (Sydney, Allen and Unwin, 2002), pp. 148–9.
13 Ibid., p. 150.
14 Potter and Potter, op. cit.
15 Ibid., p. 15.
16 United Kingdom Department of Trade and Industry and Department of Culture, Media and Sport, op. cit., para. 1.1.22.
17 Ibid., para. 1.2.11.
18 A. Alexander, K. Hoerner and L. Duke, 'What is Quality Children's Television?' in *The Annals of the American Academiy of Social Science* (Thousand Oaks, CA, Sage, 1998), pp. 70–82.
19 *ACLU v Reno* (United States District Court) at 929 F. Supp. 824 (1996), per Dalzell, D. J.
20 United Kingdom Department of Trade and Industry and Department of Culture, Media and Sport, op. cit., para. 1.3.3.
21 Ibid., para. 1.3.6.
22 Ibid., para. 8.3.1.
23 Ibid., para. 1.3.6.
24 Ibid., para. 8.5.1.
25 Ibid., para. 8.5.2.
26 Ibid.
27 Ibid., para. 8.5.3.
28 See e.g. D. Salter, 'With mates like these . . .', (2002) 6, *Dissent*, pp. 24–6.
29 D. Donnison, 'Rethinking Rights Talk' in L. Orchard and R. Dore (eds) *Markets, Morals and Public Policy* (Sydney, The Federation Press, 1989), p. 226.
30 United Nations Convention on the Rights of the Child, Article 13(1).
31 Ibid., Article 13(2).
32 See e.g. S. J. Toope, 'The Convention on the Rights of the Child: implications for Canada' in M. Freeman (ed.), *Children's Rights: a comparative*

perspective (Aldershot, Dartmouth, 1996), p. 42. See further, J . C. Hall, 'The Waning of Parental Rights' (1972) 31(1) *Cambridge Law Journal* 248–65; J.Montgomery 'Children as Property?' (1988) 51 *Modern Law Review* 323– 42.

33 Ibid.
34 Article 19(1).
35 See above n.5.
36 European Convention on Human Rights, Article 10. On the connection between this Article and the child's right to receive information, see L. Campbell, 'Rights and disabled children' in B. Franklin (ed.), *The New Handbook of Children's Rights: Comparative Policy and Practice* (London, Routledge, 2002).
37 United Nations Convention on the Rights of the Child, Article 5.
38 Ibid., Article 31.
39 B. Franklin, 'Children's Rights and Media Wrongs: changing representations of children and the developing rights agenda' in B. Franklin, op. cit.
40 Heins, op. cit., p. 256.
41 Ibid.
42 Ibid., pp. 256–7.
43 Department of Trade and Industry (United Kingdom), *Closing the Digital Divide: Information and Communication Technologies in Deprived Areas*, a report by Policy Action Team 15 (February 2000), p. 15.
44 O. O'Neill, 'Children's Rights and Children's Lives' in R. E. Ladd (ed.), *Children's Rights Re-visioned: Philosophical Readings* (Belmont, Wadsworth, 1996), pp. 38–9.
45 See e.g. P. Alderson, *Young Children's Rights: Exploring Beliefs. Principles and Practice* (London, Jessica Kingsley, 2000), pp. 72–84.

Bibliography

Alderson, P., *Young Children's Rights: Exploring Beliefs. Principles and Practice* (London, Jessica Kingsley, 2000).

Alexander, A., Hoerner, K. and Duke, L., 'What is Quality Children's Television?' in *The Annals of the American Academiy of Social Science* (Thousand Oaks, Sage, 1998), pp. 70–82.

Ariés, P., *Centuries of Childhood* (first published in 1960).

Atkinson, D. and Gourdeau, M., *Summary and Analysis of Various Studies on Violence and Television* (Institut québécois de recherché sur la culture, June 1991) (Ottawa, Canadian Radio-television and Telecommunications Commission).

Australian Broadcasting Tribunal, *TV Violence in Australia: report to the Minister for Transport and Communications* (Sydney, Australian Broadcasting Tribunal, 1990).

Australian Broadcasting Tribunal, *kidz tv: An Inquiry into Children's and Preschool Children's Television Standards*, Volume 1 (Sydney, 1991).

Australian Broadcasting Tribunal, *Public Inquiry Report: Inquiry into the Programme Teenage Mutant Ninja Turtles, Decision and Reasons*, IP/90/114, December, 1991.

Barker, M. (ed.), *The Video Nasties: Freedom and Censorship in the Media* (London, Pluto Press, 1984).

Barker, M. and Petley, J. (eds), *Ill Effects: the media/violence debate* (London and New York, Routledge, 1997).

British Broadcasting Corporation. *Producers' Guidelines*.

British Broadcasting Corporation, *Violence on Television: the Report of the Wyatt Committee* (London, British Broadcasting Corporation, 1987).

Broadcasting Standards Commission, *Code on Standards* (June 1998) (London).

Broadcasting Standards Council, *A Code of Practice* (2nd edn) (London, Broadcasting Standards Council, February 1994).

Campbell, L., 'Rights and disabled children' in B. Franklin (ed.), *The New Handbook of Children's Rights: Comparative Policy and Practice* (London, Routledge, 2002).

Canadian Broadcast Standards Council, 'Self-Regulation in Canada: building on a uniquely successful system', Submission of the Canadian Broadcast Standards Council to CRTC Notice of Public Hearing 1995–5, 29 June 1995

Canadian Radio-television and Telecommunications Commission, *Policy on Gender Portrayal*, Public Notice CRTC 1992–58, Ottawa, 1 September 1992.

Canadian Radio-television and Telecommunications Commission, *Voluntary Code Regarding Violence in Television Programming*, Public Notice CRTC 1993–149, Ottawa, 28 October 1993.

Canadian Radio-television and Telecommunications Commission, *Policy On Violence In Television Programming*, Public Notice CRTC 1996–36, Ottawa, 14 March 1996.

anadian Radio-television and Telecommunications Commission, *Respecting Children: a Canadian Approach to Helping Families Deal With Violence* (Ottawa, 14 March 1996).

anadian Radio-television and Telecommunications Commission, *Building On Success – A Policy Framework For Canadian Television*, CRTC 1999–97, Ottawa, 11 June 1999.

antor, J., *'Mommy, I'm Scared' – How TV Movies Frighten Children and What We Can Do To Protect Them* (New York, Harcourt Brace, 1988).

antor, J., 'Ratings for Program Content: the role of research findings' in *The Annals of the American Academiy of Social Science* (Thousand Oaks, Sage, 1998), pp. 54–69.

ashmore, E., *Beckham* (Cambridge, Polity, 2002).

harlow, A., 'Awarding Custody: the best interests of the child and other fictions' (1987) 5 *Yale Law and Policy Review* 267.

hong, R. B., *Remarks of Commissioner Rachelle B. Chong*, World Summit on Television and Children, 'Regulation: Alternative National Models', Melbourne, Australia, 14 March 1995.

ohen, S., *Folk Devils and Moral Panics: the creation of the Mods and Rockers* (Oxford, 1972).

ollins, D. C. A. and Kearns, R. A., 'Under curfew and under siege? Local geographies of young people' (2001) 32 *Geoforum* 389–403.

ommercial Television Code of Practice (Australia).

ommonwealth of Australia, *Report of the Royal Commission on Television* (Canberra, Government Printing Office, 1954).

epartment of Trade and Industry (United Kingdom), *Closing the Digital Divide: Information and Communication Technologies in Deprived Areas*, a report by Policy Action Team 15 (February 2000).

orfman, A. and Mattelart, A., *How to Read Donald Duck: Imperialist Ideology in the Disney comic* (New York, International General, 1972).

onnison, D., 'Rethinking Rights Talk' in L. Orchard and R. Dore (eds) *Markets, Morals and Public Policy* (Sydney, The Federation Press, 1989).

dwards, H. T. and Berman, M. N., 'Regulating Violence on Television', (1993) 89 *Northwestern University Law Review* 1487.

ron, L. D. and Huesmann, L. R., 'Television as a Source of Maltreatment of Children', 1987, 16(2), *School Psychology Review*, 195–202.

uropean Broadcasting Union's Guidelines for Programmes When Dealing With the Portrayal of Violence.

ederal Communications Commission, *Notice of Proposed Rule Making: In the Matter of Policies and Rules Concerning Children's Television*, MM Docket No.93–48, April 1995.

ederal Communications Commission, *In the Matter of Policies and Rules Concerning Children's Television Programming: Revision of Programming Policies for Television Broadcast Stations* MM Docket No.93–48, Report and Order, 8 August 1996.

ederal Communications Commission, *In the Matter of Industry Guidance On the Commission's Case Law Interpreting 18 U.S.C.§ 1464 and Enforcement Policies Regarding Broadcast Indecency*, File No. EB-00-IH-0089, 6 April 2001.

inch, K. A., 'Lights, Camera, and Action for Children's Television v FCC: the story of broadcast indecency, starring Howard Stern', (1995) 63 *University of Cincinnatti Law Review* 1275.

lood, M. and Hamilton, C., *Youth and Pornography in Australia: evidence on the extent of exposure and likely effects* (The Australia Institute, Discussion Paper No. 52, February 2003).

Fortin, J., *Children's Rights and the Developing Law* (London, Butterworth, 1998)

Franklin, B., 'Children's rights and media wrongs: changing representations children and the developing rights agenda' in B. Franklin (ed.) *The Ne Handbook of Children's Rights: Comparative Policy and Practice* (Londo) Routledge, 2002).

Freedman, J. L., 'Effect of Television Violence on Aggressiveness', (1984) 96(2) *Psychological Bulletin*, 227–46

Freeman, M., 'The James Bulger Tragedy: Childish Innocence and th Construction of Guilt' in A. McGilvray (ed.) *Governing Childhood* (Alde) shot, Dartmouth, 1997).

Gill, A., *Orphans of the Empire: the shocking story of child migration to Austral* (Sydney, Millenium Books, 1997).

Giovannoni, J. M. and Becerra, R. M., *Defining Child Abuse* (New York, The Fre Press, 1979).

Grainger, G., 'Broadcasting, Co-Regulation and the Public Good', *1999 Sp Memorial Lecture* (Graham Spry Fund for Public Broadcasting) (28 Octob) 1999).

Hall, J. C., 'The Waning of Parental Rights' (1972) 31 (1) *Cambridge Law Journ* 248–65.

Hancock, L., 'Police Discretion in Victoria: the police discretion to prosecute' (1978) 14, *Australian and New Zealand Journal of Criminology*, 33–40.

Hancock, L., 'Issues in Juvenile Justice and Police' in F. Gale, N. Naffine an J. Wundersitz (eds) *Juvenile Justice: Debating the Issues* (Sydney, Allen an Unwin, 1993).

Hanley, P. (ed.), *Striking a Balance: the control of children's media consumption* Report undertaken for the British Broadcasting Corporation, Broadcastin Standards Commission, Independent Television Commission, Septembe 2002).

Hargrave, A. M., *Sex and Sensibility* (London, Broadcasting Standards Commis sion, January 1999).

Hayes, D. A., 'The Children's Hour Revisited: the Children's Television Ac 1990' (1994) 46 *Federal Communications Law Journal* 293.

Hendershot, H., *Saturday Morning Censors: Television Regulation before the V-Chi* (Durham and London, Duke University Press, 1998).

Heins, M., *Not in Front of the Children: 'Indecency', Censorship and the Innocence* Youth (New York, Hill and Wang, 2001).

Hilty, E. B., 'From *Sesame Street* to *Barney and Friends*: television as teacher' i S. R. Steinberg and J. L. Kincheloe (eds) *Kinderculture: The Corpora Construction of Childhood* (Boulder and Oxford, Westview Press, 1997).

Holt, J., *Escape from Childhood* (Pelican, 1974).

Holmes a'Court, J., 'Children's Television – A business. Is it? Should it be (Paper delivered on 11 March 1998 at the Second World Summit o Television for Children in London).

Human Rights and Equal Opportunity Commission, *Bringing them Home National Inquiry into the Separation of Aboriginal and Torres Strait Island Children from their families* (Commonwealth of Australia, 1997).

Hunt, A., 'The Critique of Law: what is 'critical' about critical legal theory (1987) 14, *Journal of Law and Society*, 5–19.

Huston, A. C. and Wright, J. C., 'Television and the Informational an Educational Needs of Children' in *The Annals of the American Academiy* Social Science (Thousand Oaks, Sage, 1998).

Independent Television Commission, *Programme Code*.

airys, D. (ed.), *A Critique of Law: a progressive critique* (New York, Basis Books, 1998).

ing, M. and Piper, C., *How the Law Thinks About Children* (Aldershot, Gower, 1990).

line, S., *Out of the Garden: toys, TV, and children's culture in the age of marketing* (London and New York, Verso, 1993).

unkel, D. and Roberts, D., 'Young Minds and Marketplace Values: issues in children's television advertising', (1991) 47(1), *Journal of Social Issues*, 57–72.

unkel, D., 'Policy Battles over Defining Children's Educational Television' in *The Annals of the American Academy of Political and Social Science* (Thousand Oaks, Sage, 1998).

asch, C., *The Minimal Self: psychic survival in troubled times* (London, Picador, 1984).

asch, C., *The Revolt of the Elites and the Betrayal of Democracy* (New York and London, W. W. Norton and Co, 1994).

ee, J. A., 'Three Paradigms of Childhood' (1982) 19 *Canadian Review of Sociology and Anthropology*, 591–608.

IcConahay, J. B. 'Pornography: the symbolic politics of fantasy' (1988) 51(1) *Law and Contemporary Problems* 31–69.

IcDonnell, K. 'The hurried child', (2002) 343, *New Internationalist*, March, 23.

Iinow, N. N. and La May, C. L., *Abandoned in the Wasteland: Children, Television and the First Amendment* (New York, Hill and Wang, 1995).

Iontgomery, J., 'Children as Property?' (1988) 51 *Modern Law Review* 323–42.

)'Neill, O., 'Children's Rights and Children's Lives' in R. E. Ladd (ed.) *Children's Rights Re-visioned: Philosophical Readings* (Belmont, Wadsworth, 1996).

)ntario Royal Commission on Violence in the Communications Industry (LaMarsh Commission) (Toronto, Queen's Printer, 1976).

arliament of Australia, *Report of the Joint Select Committee on Video Material,* Volume 2 (Canberra, AGPS, 1988).

arliament of Australia, Senate Standing Committee on Education and the Arts, *Children and Television* (Canberra, Australian Government Publishing Service, 1978).

arliament of Australia, Senate Standing Committee on Education and the Arts, *Children and Television Revisited* (Canberra, Australian Government Publishing Service, 1981.

arliament of Victoria, Social Development Committee, *The effects of Television and Multimedia on Children and Families* (Report No. 49, October 2000).

hillips, P., *The Truth About the Power Rangers* (Lancaster, Pennsylvania, Starburst Publishers, 1995).

ierce, P., *The Country of Lost Children: an Australian anxiety* (Cambridge, Cambridge University Press, 1999).

ostman, N., *The Disappearance of Childhood* (London, W. H. Allen, 1982).

otter, R. H. and Potter, L. A., 'The Internet, Cyberporn, and Sexual Exploitation of Children: media moral panics and urban myths for middle-class parents?', *Sexuality and Culture*, 2001, 5(3), 31–48.

ubens, S. D. 'First Amendment – Disconnecting Dial-A-Porn: Section 223(b)'s two pronged challenge to First Amendment Rights', (1990) 80 (4) *Journal of Criminal Law and Criminology* 968–95.

ussell, B., 'The Superior Virtue of the Oppressed' in B. Russell *Unpopular Essays* (London, Allen and Unwin, 1950).

Salter, D., 'With mates like these...', (2001) 6, *Dissent*, 24–6.

Saul, J. Ralston, *The Unconscious Civilisation* (Ringwood, Penguin, 1997).

Sennett, R., *Flesh and Stone: the body and the city in western civilisation* (London Boston, Faber and Faber, 1994).

Smith, D. J., *The Sleep of Reason: the James Bulger Case* (London, Arrow, 1994)

Stipp, H., 'The Challenge to Improve Television for Children: a new perspecti in G. Berry and J. K. Asamen, *Children and Television: images in a chang socio-cultural world* (Newbury Park, Sage, 1993).

Stoltman, J. J., 'The Context of Advertising and Children' in M. C. Macklin a L. Carlson (eds) *Advertising to Children: Concepts and Controversies* (Thousar Oaks, Sage, 1999).

Synott, A., 'Little Angels, Little Devils: a sociology of children' (1983) : *Canadian Review of Sociology and Anthropology* 79–95

Television Code of Broadcasting Practice (New Zealand).

Teubner, G., 'How the Law Thinks: toward a constructivist epistemology of lav (1989) 23(5), *Law and Society Revue*, 727–56.

Thomson, R., 'Legal, Protected and Timely: young people's persepctives on t heterosexual age of consent' in J. Bridgeman and D. Monk (eds) *Femin Perspectives on Child Law* (London and Sydney, Cavendish, 2000).

Tichi, C., *Electronic Hearth: creating an American television culture* (New York a Oxford, Oxford University Press, 1991).

Tracey, M., *The Decline and Fall of Public Service Broadcasting* (Oxford, Oxfo University Press, 1998).

Tyler, J. E. and Segady, T. W., 'Parental Liability Laws: rationale, theory, a effectiveness', (2000) 37(1), *Social Science Journal*, 79–96.

United Kingdom Department of Trade and Industry and Department of Cultur Media and Sport, *A New Future for Communications* (Communications Whi Paper, 2001).

Uscinski, H. J., 'Deregulating Commercial Television: will the marketpla watch out for children?' (1984) 34 *American University Law Review* 141.

Watkins, B., 'Improving Educational and Informational Television For Childre when the marketplace fails' (1987) 5 *Yale Law and Policy Review* 322.

Windhausen, J. 'Congressional Interest in the Problem of Television a Violence', (1994) 22 *Hofstra Law Review* 783.

Wilhelm, W. B., 'In the Interest of Children: action for children's television FCC: improperly delineating the constitutional limits of broadc indecency', (1992) 42 *Catholic University Law Review* 215.

Winn, M., *The Plug in Drug* (The Viking Press, 1977).

Wringe, C. A., *Children's Rights: A philosophical study* (London, Routledge a Kegan Paul, 1981).

Zelizer, V. A., *Pricing the Priceless Child* (New York, Basic Books, 1985).

Index